The Macmillan

# Book 1 Write to Left
## Introduction to Script and Pronunciation

T. Francis M. Frost

First published 1980
Reprinted 1985

Published by *Macmillan Publishers Ltd*
London and Basingstoke
*Associated companies and representatives in*
*Accra, Auckland, Delhi, Dublin, Gaborone, Hamburg, Harare, Hong Ko*
*Kuala Lumpur, Lagos, Manzini, Melbourne, Mexico City, Nairobi,*
*New York, Singapore, Tokyo*

ISBN 0 333 23089 2

Printed in Hong Kong

The authors and publishers wish to thank the following who have kindly given permission for the use of copyright material:
Centre for Applied Linguistics for an extract from *Arabic Language Handbook* by Mary C. Bateson, © 1965 by the publishers
Hodder & Stoughton Education for extracts from *Language Made Plain* by Anthony Burgess
Hutchinson Publishing Group Limited for extracts from *The Arabs in History* by Bernard Lewis, and *The Arabic Language Today* by A. F. L. Beeston
Penguin Books Limited for extracts from *The Arabs* by Edward Atiyah (Pelican, Revised edition 1958) © the Estate of Edward Atiyah 1955, 1958
Routledge & Kegan Paul Limited for extracts from *A History of Foreign Words in English* by Mary S. Serjeantson
Thames and Hudson Limited for extracts from *Forgotton Scripts* by Cyrus H. Gordon, *The Phoenicians* by D. Harden and *The Splendour of Islamic Calligraphy* by Abdelkebir Khatibi and Mohammed Sijelmassi
University of Minnesota Press for extracts from *The Arabic Language: Its Role in History* by Anwar G. Chejne
Professor Hermann Zapf for extracts from *About Alphabets:* Some Marginal Notes on Type Design, published by MIT Press, Cambridge, Mass.

# Contents

**Tapes**

A tape has been recorded to accompany this book and is available on C60 cassette or open reel. We strongly recommend that the book be used together with the tape, particularly by those studying without regular contact with a native speaker of Arabic.

# Preface

This book has developed out of materials used in the pre-service training of British and American volunteers and government personnel working on aid programmes in the Arab world. In their original form these materials were intended as a bare reference manual for students, while supplementary information and instructions were delivered orally in the classroom. We have included much of this supplementary information in the present revised version to make it suitable for 'teach yourself' purposes (in conjunction with the tape designed to accompany it) as well as for classroom use. The major aims of the book are to teach an ability to write Arabic in a simple but clear hand, to read a common typeset style, and to pronounce the sounds of the language in a manner clearly comprehensible to a native speaker.

In our view a sound knowledge of the script is a pre-requisite to a full appreciation of the language, and we are therefore confident that this book will prove useful to those who intend to go on to a study of the Arabic language proper, whether in the Middle East or at schools, colleges or universities in the West. It will also be of great practical advantage to anyone living in, or planning to visit, the Arab world. An ability to decipher the graphic symbols of the Arabic language helps overcome the feeling of extra strangeness people commonly experience when living in countries where advertisements, street signs, car number plates, and public notices are written in an unfamiliar script. It can be reassuring to recognise even a familiar brand name in an otherwise exotic environment.

We have also borne in mind the interests of those living in the West whose curiosity has been tickled by growing exposure to a foreign and exotic culture, and who may have no further ambition than to gain some insight into an increasingly familiar visual aspect of that culture – the script. The notion of 'second script literacy' – an ability to read, write and pronounce the graphic symbols of a foreign language, without necessarily speaking it or studying its grammatical structure, is by no means new:

'Whether or not we wish to learn the languages that these (Cyrillic, Greek and Arabic) alphabets enshrine, sheer human curiosity should drive us to find out at least what the letters stand for . . .' (Anthony Burgess, *Language made plain*, page 85)

In the case of Arabic, this statement is even more appropriate today than it was when Anthony Burgess wrote it. In Western capitals we have recently seen the advent of Arabic television commercials, business signs and graffiti, not to mention a wider availability of Arabic newsprint no longer restricted, as it once was, to a handful of specialist outlets. In short, a living workshop for those in whom curiosity has developed into an active desire to learn.

We hope, therefore, that this book will provide encouragement to the curious, as well as a valuable introduction for the more seriously committed student.

# Introduction

'. . . to handle the Arabic alphabet is to be led into a little world of exquisite sensation.'
(Anthony Burgess, *Language made plain*, page 85)

For most people, even accomplished speakers of several foreign languages, this book will represent a first excursion into the unfamiliar territory of a new script. The Latin alphabet, with which we write English, is the most extensively used in the world, and in the normal run of affairs we, as Latin alphabet users learning a foreign language, are not faced by the obstacle of a foreign script. We do not need to learn how to read and write all over again, merely to modify our ideas on pronunciation.

The common exceptions are Greek, Russian and Arabic, each having its own alphabet and thus denying the Latin alphabet user the privilege of automatic literacy. In the case of the first two the obstacle does not seem too daunting – there is something familiar about the new letters, they clearly possess a common origin with those of the Latin alphabet. Greek, furthermore, has lent us several letters used in scientific notation; names of other letters have become everyday words in English – 'river *delta*', for example, and '*gamma* ray'; and the phrase 'from *alpha* to *omega*' is a familiar metaphor of completeness. The very word '*alphabet*' is, of course, nothing other than the names of the first two letters of the Greek alphabet.

The Arabic alphabet, on the other hand, though it too shares a common origin with the Latin, the Russian and the Greek, looks like none of them, effectively disguising its alphabetic identity in a literal Arabesque of elegant but totally unfamiliar lines. Popular misconceptions about the difficulty of the Arabic script, based primarily on its strangeness to the European eye, have deterred many people from learning to use either it or the languages whose sounds it represents. The major aim of this book is to dispel such myths and misconceptions.

Traditional approaches to the question of Arabic script acquisition, as evidenced by most available teaching materials, have unfortunately provided little encouragement to the eager, but naturally anxious first time learner. The predominant attitude, and one that has survived until the present day in some of our universities, is that learners should be able to teach themselves to read and write Arabic with the aid of little more than an alphabet table and an abundance of enthusiastic determination. This situation has been complicated by attempting to teach the language through 'transliteration', whereby the sounds of Arabic are represented by letters of our own alphabet. The problems associated with the exclusive use of transliteration are too numerous for discussion in this brief introduction, but reverse the situation and picture a class of Arab school children learning to write the English language in their own script, and the absurdity of the notion becomes clear. Why wrestle with the problems of recording a language in a foreign script when it has its own alphabet a few hours well-directed learning away?

**In what ways is the Arabic alphabet similar to our own, and in what respects does it differ?** In replying to this question, we will begin with the surprising contention that it is in our view a simpler task for a Latin alphabet user to learn to use the Arabic alphabet than for an Arabic alphabet user to learn to master the full range of the printed and handwritten forms of the Latin script.

We regard our own writing system as the norm because it is the only one we know, and we tend to think that anything which is different must be more complex. We are barely aware of the quirks of our own script, or the difficulties it poses children and foreign students learning it for the first time, and which it once posed us in the distant days of our early schooling. Let us attempt to gain a little perspective on the task of learning a second alphabet by first reviewing briefly some of the peculiarities of our own script which cause problems for learners.

Consider the various ways we can typeset and write our alphabet:

**Typeset**

| | | |
|---|---|---|
| 1 | capitals | ALPHABET |
| 2 | small letters | alphabet |

**Handwriting**

| | | |
|---|---|---|
| 1 | 'printed' in capitals | ALPHABET |
| 2 | 'printed' in small letters | alphabet |
| 3 | written cursively (all letters joined) | alphabet |

In addition to having to learn the modifications necessary for joining one letter to another, the differences between some typeset and handwritten small letter forms, and the existence of both capitals and small letters add significantly to the learner's task. As adults we are so used to these variations that we rarely give them a thought, though parents who have tried to teach their pre-school children how to read and write will be familiar with some of the problems they can cause. It is a significant feature of teaching English to Arab and Iranian students that they often experience difficulty in using the Latin alphabet, and in particular fail to develop a full appreciation of the distinctions in usage between capital and small letters.

As a Latin alphabet user learning to read and write Arabic you are faced by a considerably less daunting task. First of all *there are no capital letters in Arabic:*

'Arabic, we may note, has never had the tradition of small letters and capitals; the International Phonetic Alphabet gets on well enough with just lower case symbols. The original Roman alphabet was all capitals; small letters are a later development associated with a running or 'current' script, for capitals cannot easily be joined to each other. We would probably save much time and money if we followed the Arabic tradition of using small, or lower case, letters only. German insists on a capital initial for every noun; we all insist on capital letters for proper names, the beginning of a sentence, and abbreviations like UNO, NATO, USSR and the rest. Also, in English, we have the egomania of a capital for the first personal pronoun. Archy, the cockroach that wrote poems on Don Marquis's typewriter, could not use capitals and still became a best seller; the American poet e. e. cummings, though able to use the shift key, still preferred lower case letters all the time.' (Anthony Burgess, *Language made plain*, page 83).

Nor in Arabic handwriting is there the potentially confusing alternative of either 'printing' or writing cursively. The Arabic script is *always* cursive – of the twenty-eight letters in the alphabet, twenty-two always join to both the preceding and following letters within any one word, even when typeset. The remaining six always join to a preceding letter, but never to a following letter. True, the shapes of the letters themselves are strange at first sight, but certainly no stranger than the letters of the Latin alphabet to an Arabic alphabet user. Once you have learned to recognise and reproduce the basic shapes of the letters you will have little difficulty in mastering the modifications necessary for joining letter to letter.

Furthermore, the study of Arabic is not beset by difficulties of spelling, such as abound in English. The inconsistencies and apparent illogicalities of English spelling are stumbling blocks for both foreign learner and native speaker alike.

'Why is it that no foreigner can say with any confidence, seeing a new English word in print, what the pronunciation is likely to be? Why is the story of the Frenchman who drowned himself after reading 'Agatha Christie's Mousetrap pronounced success' not really funny? How has it come about that we can spell 'fish' quite logically as 'ghoti' (the 'gh' in 'laugh', the 'o' in 'women', the 'ti' in 'ration')?

. . . If only English would say that 'xgyjpth' stands for /i/ and 'zfrkhtgg' stands for /u/ and be absolutely consistent about it, then there would be no problem for anyone – native or foreigner. It is the total lack of logic that is so infuriating.' (Anthony Burgess, *Language made plain*, page 83)

In some languages the bogey of 'spelling' simply does not exist, and Arabic is one of them. Once you have mastered the skills of recognising, forming and pronouncing the letters in a word, you will be able to make a fairly confident guess at how it is pronounced. Conversely, a word heard can be accurately spelt so long as it is heard correctly.

The individual shapes of the letters apart, the major exotic feature of the Arabic script is that it is written from right to left across the page. Thus you read a page of Arabic starting at the top righthand corner and finishing in the bottom lefthand corner, and an Arabic book begins on what would be the last page of an English book. It is important to realise that this feature of Arabic is exotic only when seen from the biased perspective of a left to right script user. So used are we to uniform rows of letters marching straight as Roman roads left right, left right inexorably across the page all our reading lives, that to suddenly re-route the conscript legions in mid-step with a right (to left) about turn seems tantamount to countermanding some divine decree. The Greeks who adopted the old Phœnician alphabet, which was written from right to left, were initially in two minds as to which way they should write. They experimented with a system, theoretically the most equitable, though unfortunately not the most practical, of writing from right to left *and* left to right, changing direction from line to line alternately. There is no right way, merely convenience and convention.

'Our own left-right habit is not based on any law of nature, any more than traffic rules are. When it comes to painting a name on a factory chimney, we are as ready as the Chinese or Japanese to start at the top and move down . . . When I first learned to use Arabic script I feared I would get ink on my sleeve; it soon seemed to me the most natural and the cleanest – as well as the most sensuously satisfying – way of writing imaginable.' (Anthony Burgess, *Language made plain*, pages 80-1)

## Writing and alphabets

'We use letters of our alphabet every day with the utmost of ease and unconcern, taking them almost as much for granted as the air we breathe. We do not realise that each of these letters is at our service only as the result of a long and laboriously slow process of evolution in the age old art of writing.' (Douglas C. McMurtie quoted by Herman Zapf *About alphabets* pages 104-5)

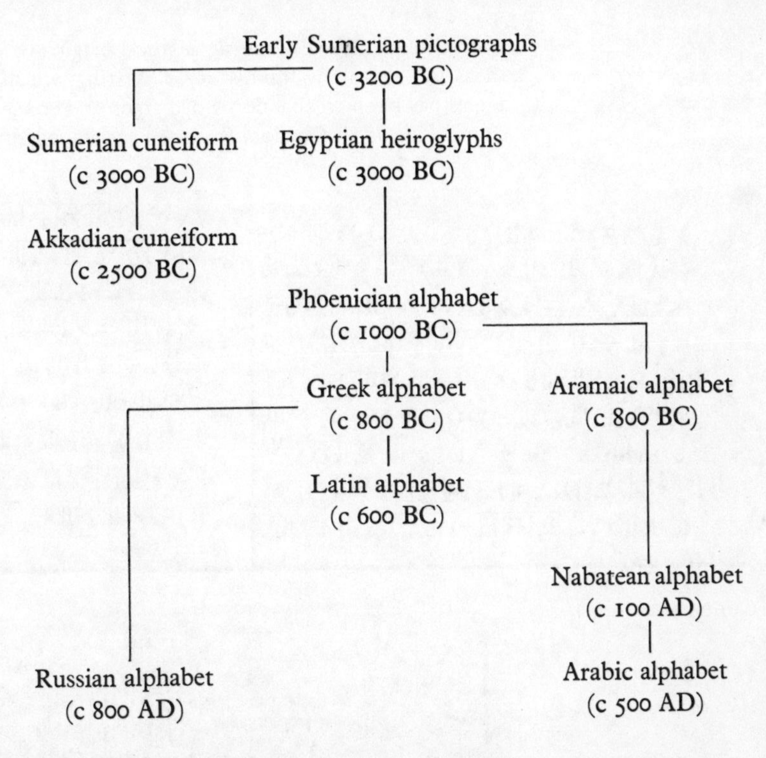


'Sometime around 3000 BC writing was invented and developed in the Near East. There is reason to believe that it first became established in Mesopotamia, but the idea soon spread to Egypt. The cuneiform of Mesopotamia has little obvious resemblance with the heiroglyphs of Egypt, and yet their principles are so similar that there must be a connection, through stimulus-diffusion; i.e. the Egyptians did not copy the actual signs of Mesopotamian writing but only applied the same basic idea. First, they established a large, but none the less limited repetoire of pictographic signs. For example, they had not only a general sign for 'man' but a number of other pictographs of men doing various things or in various states. Thus there might be a man eating, but there would not be different signs for a man engaged in the various aspects of eating such as biting, chewing or swallowing. If we draw each specific object or act, we are not writing but engaging in representational art. To be useful, any system of writing must limit its number of symbols.

The next principle (in both cuneiform and heiroglyphics) is that the pictograph can stand for the sound of what is drawn, without reference to its meaning. To take some simulated English examples by way of illustration: the 'man' pictograph could stand not only for 'man' but the syllable 'man'; even as the picture of a date could refer not only to 'a date' but to the syllable 'date'. Thus the two pictographs *man-date* could be pronounced 'man-date' and mean 'a mandate'. This is the most important and basic aspect of cuneiform and heiroglyphic writing: they are essentially phonetic systems even though as a rule the signs stood originally for words and ideas. As we follow the history of writing, we shall observe that the trend has been to abandon word signs and concentrate on sound signs.' (Cyrus H. Gordon, *Forgotten scripts*, pages 31-2)

Cuneiform

Heiroglyphics

'It is doubtful if the alphabet is much more than 3,000 years old, whereas speech is nearly as old as man. Thus the dawning of the principle of representing a spoken sound by a written letter has come very late in our history, and it still has not come to a large proportion of mankind – the Chinese for example. The alphabet is the last and most efficient device for giving symbolic permanence to the spoken word. Unlike fire and agriculture, it did not come at various times to various races – widely separated in space but undergoing parallel developments. It came once and once only to a race of semites trading in the Mediterranean lands . . . we believe that the Phœnician traders . . . were the first to take over the simplified Egyptian symbols and use them to represent consonants. They created a betagam: a BCD, not an ABC. They were not interested in finding vowel letters, because vowel letters were not necessary to the writing of Phoenician – a semitic language. This meant that they were able to make do with twenty odd symbols – a tremendous and epoch-making economy . . . the Phœnicians had the concept of free consonants. What urged them to create this system of easily learned and handled letters? Not literature, not religion, but trade. They presumably needed to make out their bills and enter their books with some speed: a few quick strokes, and there was the memo or delivery note or an invoice. Not for them the leisure of heiroglyphics . . . an Egyptian eye or head, bird or running water must become mere abstract lines or circles – as with letters of our own alphabet, which ultimately have the same derivation.' (Anthony Burgess, *Language made plain*, pages 70, 79-80)

Phœnician script

*Two examples of Phœnician script from the tenth century BC*

'Unlike some of the related languages (Egyptian attested by heiroglyphic from 3000 BC, and Akkadian first attested in 2400 BC), the earliest clearly Arabic inscriptions are dated AD 512 and 568, and there is no abundance of written records until well into the Islamic period (the 7th century AD). The peoples of Arabia had first contacted writing as it was used in the Mediterranean empires, primarily for Aramaic. Speakers of Arabic began to use the Aramaic alphabet as early as the beginning of the Christian era . . . This usage developed in two Arab kingdoms which had brief periods of power, the Nabatean kingdom at Petra, which was conquered by Rome in AD 106, and Palmyra conquered in AD 273. Over the years, more and more Arabic forms from the spoken language filtered into writing, and a number of ligatures began to appear between the slowly simplified forms of the letters. The modern Arabic script is descended from this Nabatean script, which was subjected to a number of modifications to suit the phonology of Arabic.' (Catherine Mary Bateson, *Arabic language handbook*, pages 53-4)

# The Arabic alphabet

The Arabic alphabet has 28 letters. This table shows them in their traditional order.

| No. | Letter | No. | Letter |
|---|---|---|---|
| 1 | ا | 16 | ط |
| 2 | ب | 17 | ظ |
| 3 | ت | 18 | ع |
| 4 | ث | 19 | غ |
| 5 | ج | 20 | ف |
| 6 | ح | 21 | ق |
| 7 | خ | 22 | ك |
| 8 | د | 23 | ل |
| 9 | ذ | 24 | م |
| 10 | ر | 25 | ن |
| 11 | ز | 26 | ه |
| 12 | س | 27 | و |
| 13 | ش | 28 | ي |
| 14 | ص | | |
| 15 | ض | | |

Do not attempt to write anything at this stage. Notice:

1 the resemblance between the shapes of some of the letters
2 the number and arrangements of the dots

1 **Shapes** Many groups of letters in the Arabic alphabet share the same basic shape:

OBSERVE

| letters sharing shape | | | basic shape |
|---|---|---|---|
| ث | ت | ب | ٮ |
| خ | ج | ح | ح |
| | ذ | د | د |
| | ز | ر | ر |
| | ش | س | س |
| | ض | ص | ص |
| | ظ | ط | ط |
| | غ | ع | ع |

Notice also the similarity in these two pairs of letters:

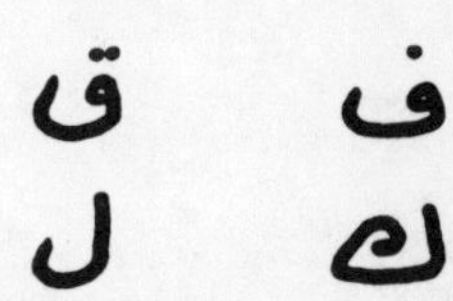

2 **Dots** The individual letters in the groups above are distinguished from one another only by the number of dots, if any, above or below the basic shape.
Dots occur singly, either above or below the basic shape:

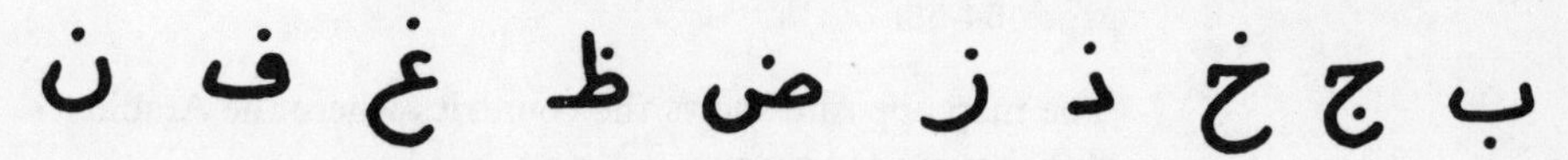

in pairs, either above or below the basic shape:

ت ق ي

or in threes, above the basic shape only:

ث ش

some letters have no dots at all:

ل م و ح

For convenience in handwriting
two dots / •• / are written as a horizontal stroke / – /
three dots / ∴ / are written as a small, inverted 'v' / ^ /
OBSERVE
Letters with two dots:

ت ق ي

Letters with three dots:

ث ش

'The Nabatean alphabet fell short of meeting the needs of Arabic in a number of ways . . . the simplification of the letter forms and the introduction of ligatures to form a cursive script had resulted in the loss of a number of distinctions which had existed previously . . . For some positions in the word the Arabic alphabet had only fifteen letter shapes to represent twenty-eight consonant phonemes. This made reading extremely difficult, and various solutions were experimented with even before the rise of Islam in the seventh century AD. The oldest written records in Islam – coins from the middle of the seventh century, inscriptions on tombs and milestones soon after, and papyruses by the end of that century – show that dots were already beginning to be placed above or below the letters in groups of one, two, or three, to distinguish identically written consonants. The system was not completely worked out for another 100 years: dots were used sporadically and inconsistently and some of the conventions used at the time were later changed. From about the middle of the eighth century on, however, the use of dots as necessary and regular parts of the letters was stabilized and the undotted script was only used for decorative inscriptions.' (M. C. Bateson, *Arabic Language Handbook*, pages 54-55)

**The map opposite shows the countries where the Arabic alphabet is used today.**

'The Arab conquests and the spread of Islam caused the spread of Arabic and the Arabic alphabet. Almost all Muslim peoples have used the alphabet at some time or other; in addition to Arabic, it has been used for Persian (and other Iranian languages), Osmanli, the Turkish of Turkey (and other Turkic languages, including Uighur and Kazakh), Urdu and Malay. In Africa it has been used for Berber (except by the Tuaregs), Swahili, Hausa, dialects in the area

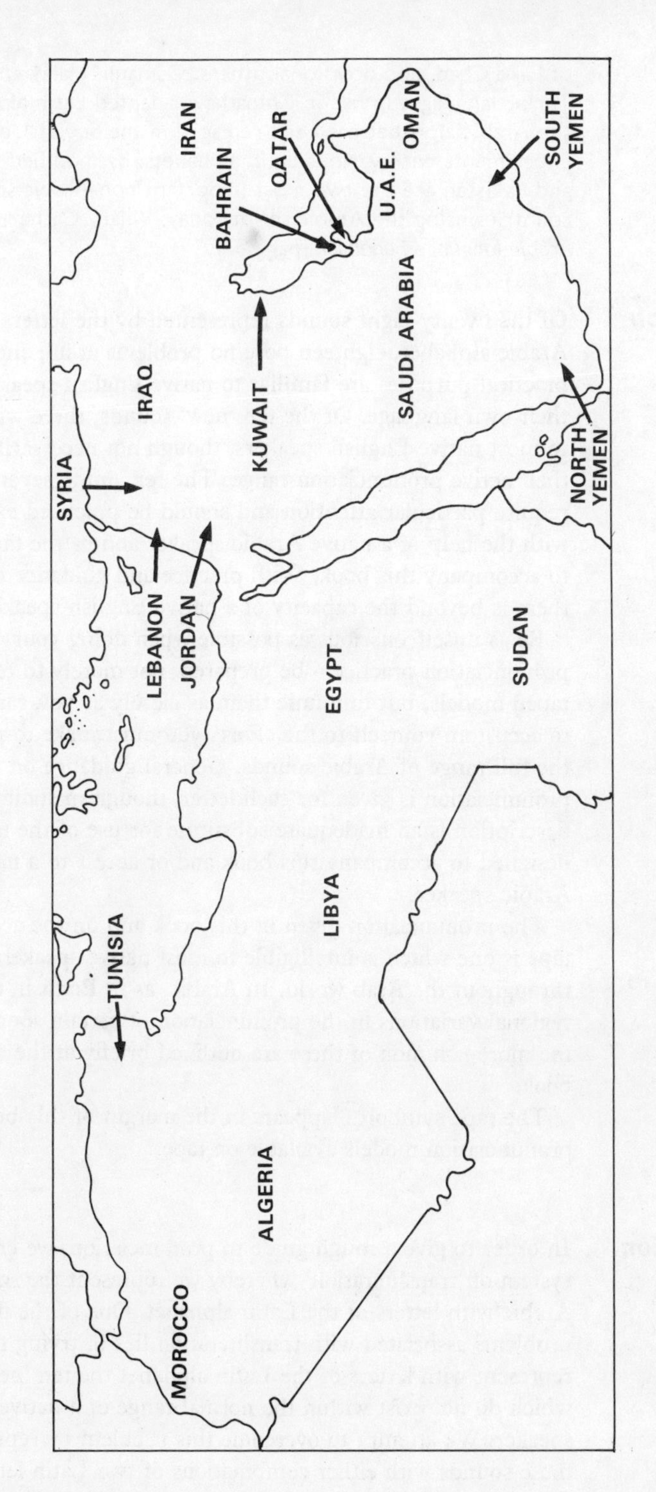


Map of the Arab World

of Lake Chad, and occasional others. Osmanli, Malay and all the Turkic languages in use in China have adapted Latin alphabets, while the Arabic alphabet has been replaced in the Soviet Union, after experiments with various Latin alphabets, by modified Cyrillic. Iran and Pakistan are the two most important non-Arabic speaking countries using the Arabic script today.' (Mary Catherine Bateson, *Arabic language handbook*, page 57)

## Pronunciation

Of the twenty-eight sounds represented by the letters of the Arabic alphabet, eighteen pose no problems at all, and for all practical purposes are familiar to native English speakers within their own language. Of the ten 'new' sounds, three will be familiar to most native English speakers, though not necessarily within their active pronunciation range. The remaining seven sounds require particular attention and should be practised extensively with the help of a native Arabic speaker and/or the tape designed to accompany this book. With practice and guidance none of them is beyond the capacity of a native English speaker.

Be as unselfconscious as possible when doing your pronunciation practice – be prepared, not merely to repeat the taped models, but to mimic them as closely as you can in order to accustom yourself to the efforts you must make to produce the full range of Arabic sounds. General guidance on pronunciation is given for each letter, though in some cases verbal description is an inadequate substitute for use of the tape designed to accompany this book and/or access to a native Arabic speaker.

The pronunciation given in this book and on the accompanying tape is one which is intelligible to most native speakers throughout the Arab world. In Arabic, as in English, there are regional variations in the pronunciation of certain sounds, and the more common of these are outlined briefly at the end of the book.

The tape symbol (T) appears in the margin of this book beside pronunciation models available on tape.

## Transliteration

In order to give a rough guide to pronunciation, we employ a system of 'transliteration' whereby we represent the sounds of Arabic with letters of the Latin alphabet. One of the many problems associated with transliteration lies in trying to represent with letters of the Latin alphabet the ten 'new' sounds which do not exist within the normal range of a native English speaker. We attempt to overcome this problem by representing these sounds with either combinations of two Latin letters, or a single Latin letter modified by underlining or a following colon.

There is no standard system of transliteration. Ours has been developed with regard to the exigencies of this book, and you will come across other systems which differ from it in various respects.

'The rendering of Arabic in Latin script involves problems more acute than are normal in the case of most non-Latin scripts. Even the primary need of assigning Latin alphabet equivalents to the Arabic phonemes, has never been decisively met; there are some half dozen competing systems in current use.' (A. F. L. Beeston, *The Arabic language today*, page 28)

Do not rely on transliteration: it is no more than an approximate guide and is no way a substitute for a sound knowledge of the Arabic alphabet and its pronunciation.

## Names of the letters

The first time you will see transliteration used in this book is to give guidance on the pronunciation of the names of the letters of the Arabic alphabet. In the study of any alphabet, it is important to distinguish between the *names* of the letters and the *sounds* represented by these letters.

In Arabic, the names of the letters are frequently written down (in grammar books, dictionaries, etc.) and their spelling is well-established. For comparison, consider the situation in English. If asked to spell the word 'big' out loud, most native speakers would *say* 'bee', 'eye', 'gee'. This *looks* very curious when written down, but is quite acceptable when delivered orally. Although each letter of the English alphabet has an established name, they are very rarely written down. A common exception is 'aitch' ('h'), which perhaps owes written existence (in England at least) to its use in the phrase 'to drop one's aitches'.

In learning Arabic, it is particularly useful to learn the names of the letters of the alphabet at the same time as learning to read, write and pronounce them. In order to help you in this task, the name of each new letter is given in transliteration as it is introduced. It would, of course, be very useful to give the names of the letters in the Arabic script from the very beginning. This is obviously not possible in the early stages since many of the names are spelt with letters whose written forms are only subsequently introduced.

There are three transliteration symbols we want you to familiarise yourself with and learn now, even before you have seen the corresponding Arabic letters, since they represent sounds which occur in the names of the first letters you will learn. They are as follows:

/a:/ Pronounced something like a lengthened version of the 'a' in 'ham' (in Standard English), or the first 'o' in 'doctor' (in Standard American).

/u:/ Pronounced like the 'u' in 'rude'.

/ ' / This symbol represents the 'glottal stop', a sound which occurs in English in, for example, the London Cockney pronunciation of 'tt' in words like 'bitter' and 'butter'. It is also used in English to eliminate ambiguity in certain sound sequences, e.g. 'I didn't ask for "some mice", I asked for "some ice",' where 'ice' begins with a glottal stop. The important point to notice is that although the sound we call the 'glottal stop' occurs frequently in English, it is not normally represented in writing. In Arabic it is both heard *and* written, though the symbol which represents it is not normally counted as a letter of the alphabet.

The names of some letters of the alphabet are given in Arabic in the writing practice sections of various units. A complete list appears with the alphabet table at the back of the book.

We do not introduce the letters in their traditional alphabetic order. We have chosen an order which, in the course of our teaching experience, we have found best suited to the needs of a non-Arabic speaker learning the alphabet.

### Tools of the trade: paper and pen

It is worth taking some care over choosing the materials you use when first attempting to write the Arabic script.

□ We recommend you use either plain paper with a sheet of heavy lined paper underneath to provide a horizontal line to follow across the page, or wide spaced, faint ruled paper.

□ Don't write on scraps of paper. Use large sheets of A4 paper, and keep all your written practice in a file so that you keep a record of your progress.

□ Don't cramp your writing – always allow yourself plenty of space.

□ For your first attempts use a fairly sharp HB pencil – keep a good pencil sharpener and a soft eraser handy. Use a pencil until you feel you have achieved some degree of proficiency in writing, then experiment with other types of pens, but make sure that whatever you use gives a smooth flow of ink and doesn't scratch.

□ Experiment with felt tipped pens of varying thickness, but avoid ball point pens – they are too sharp and uneven in their ink flow.

□ Be wary of using a much loved fountain pen that has been used to write English all its working life. It will be broken into your 'English' hand, and will not take kindly to a sudden reversal in its writing habits. If you are accustomed to using a fountain pen, invest in a new one and keep it exclusively for writing Arabic.

# Unit 1

The basic shape shared by the isolated form of these three letters is: ٮ

The basic shape with one dot below is *ba:'*. It is pronounced like the 'b' in '*b*ig', and is transliterated as /b/. ب

The basic shape with two dots above is *ta:'*. It is pronounced like the 't' in '*t*ongue', and is transliterated as /t/. ت

The basic shape with three dots above is *tha:'*. It is pronounced like the 'th' in '*th*ick'. ث
Notice that Arabic uses only one letter to represent a sound for which English needs two.

It may help you to distinguish between the pronunciation of these three letters if you remember that:

ب *ba:'* has one dot *b*elow

ت *ta:'* has *t*wo dots above

ث *tha:'* has *th*ree dots above

Remember that in handwritten Arabic:
two dots / •• / are written as a horizontal stroke / ▬ /
three dots / ∴ / are written as a small inverted 'v' / ^ /
which are made in a right to left movement.

***Isolated form***

Before attempting to write anything, look at this enlarged shape:

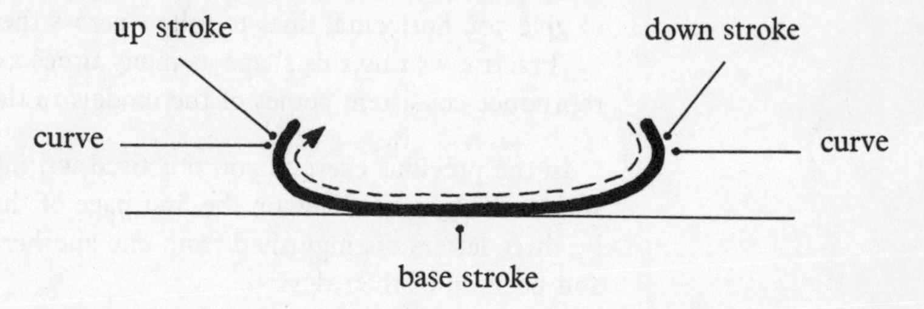

**Writing instructions** Note these features about the shape:

☐ It is made in one movement from right to left.

☐ The initial down stroke slopes to the left of upright.

☐ The curve of the down stroke into the base stroke is smooth and rounded.

☐ The base stroke sits on the line.

☐ The curve of the base stroke into the up stroke is smooth and rounded.

☐ The up stroke slopes to the right of upright.

☐ The height of the down stroke and the up stroke are roughly level.

**Writing practice**

Make copies of the models above. For your first attempt it might be helpful to trace over a few models to get the feel of the shape and the right to left movement before making any freehand attempts.

☐ The slight degree of variation between each of these models should give you an idea of the leeway you can allow yourself when first attempting to draw this shape.

☐ Always start your writing practice on the *right* of the page and work across to the left.

☐ If you are writing on lined paper, make sure to draw your examples sitting on the line as in the models above. If you are using plain paper, put a sheet of heavy lined paper underneath to give you horizontal lines to follow across the page.

☐ Practise writing this shape as many times as it takes you to reproduce consistent copies of the models in the book.

In the previous exercise you practised writing a basic isolated shape which, as you saw on the first page of this Unit, is shared by three letters distinguished from one another only by the number and position of their dots.

Remember that in handwritten Arabic:
two dots / •• / are written as a horizontal stroke / — /
three dots / ⁖ / are written as a small inverted 'v' / ^ /
which are made in a right to left movement.

**Writing practice** Make copies of the models below. For your first attempts it might be helpful to trace over a few models to get the feel of the shape.

☐ Say the name of each letter aloud each time you write it.

1 *ba:'* ب one dot below basic shape

| ب | ب | ب | ب | ب |
|---|---|---|---|---|

2 *ta:'* ت two dots above basic shape

| ت | ت | ت | ت | ت |
|---|---|---|---|---|

3 *tha:'* ث three dots above basic shape

| ث | ث | ث | ث | ث |
|---|---|---|---|---|

☐ Don't push your pen across the page – this will give your writing a forced, uneven look. Make the initial down stroke, and then as you gain more confidence, complete the base stroke and final up stroke by pulling your pen across the page in a single controlled flourish, flicking it up and slightly to the right at the end of the movement.

☐ Don't take your pencil off the paper until you have completed the final up stroke of each letter. Then go back and put in the dots, making the dot strokes / — / and / ^ / from *right to left*. At this stage it will almost certainly feel more natural for you to draw these dot strokes from left to right – resist the temptation and train yourself from the outset to think from right to left.

## Joining letters together

Now that you have learned to recognise and write the isolated forms of these three letters, we want to show you how they appear when they occur at the beginning, in the middle and at the end of a word. Remember, *Arabic is always written cursively*. It does not offer you the choice, which you have when using the Latin alphabet, of 'printing' your handwriting – that is, writing a word composed of unjoined letters. Not only do letters within a word join to each other, but they also undergo modifications according to whether they occur at the beginning, in the middle or at the end of a word. It will therefore be impossible for you to write a complete Arabic word using the three letters in this Unit until you have learned how to make all their modified forms.

We do not want you to practise incomplete combinations of letters which you will never need to write in normal circumstances, so read carefully through this Unit up to the introduction of the final form, but *don't* attempt to practise the initial and medial forms. Once you have learned how to make the final form you will be in a position to write complete word shapes using all three of these letters, and thereafter you can practise.

Let us approach the question of joining letters in Arabic by first considering, very briefly, how two letters of the Latin alphabet behave when they are written cursively. You will see that they must be modified according to their position in a word, though the modifications are not extensive:

OBSERVE

| | isolated | initial | medial | final |
|---|---|---|---|---|
| A | | ice | rice | ski |
| | i | i | i | i |
| B | | you | eye | buy |
| | y | y | y | y |

If we regard the isolated form of the letter as being the basic shape, you will notice that the other three forms (initial, medial and final) consist of the following:

**initial** basic shape plus one connecting line to the right
**medial** basic shape plus one connecting line from the left and one to the right
**final** basic shape plus one connecting line from the left

This process of modification exists in all cursive writing, though the actual degree of modification varies from script to script. In

Arabic it is not merely a matter (as with the 'i's' and 'y's' on page 26) of adding connecting lines to an otherwise unchanging basic shape – modifications must actually be made to the basic shape (i.e. the isolated form) of most letters before they can join to other letters.

The terminology in this book reflects the fact that *Arabic is always written cursively*, and that, most letters of the Arabic alphabet have four distinct though closely related forms:

**isolated form** When the letter stands alone, joined neither to a preceding letter nor to a following letter. This is the form in which all letters are first introduced throughout this book, and is the basic shape from which all other forms are derived.

**initial form** When the letter is joined to a following letter only.

**medial form** When the letter is joined to both a preceding and following letter.

**final form** When the letter is joined to a preceding letter only.

## Initial form

When these letters occur at the beginning of a word, only a fraction of the basic shape is written and they join to a following letter.

OBSERVE

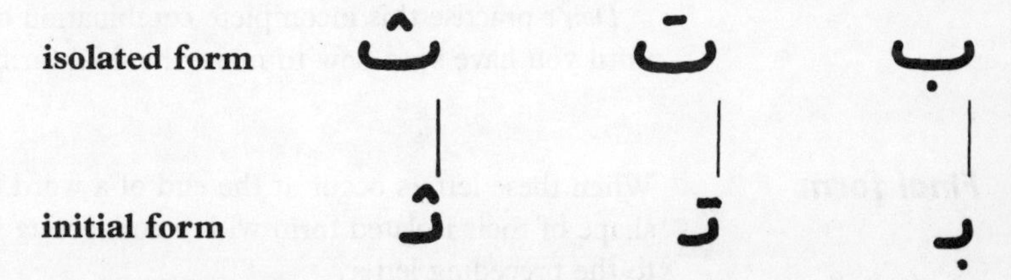


The part of the basic shape that is retained consists of the initial down stroke and a part of the base stroke which provides a connecting line to a following letter. The initial form should be between a quarter and a third of the length of the isolated form.

Note that in the isolated forms the dots appear centrally above or below the basic shape, whereas in the initial forms the dots are placed above or below the down stroke.

Don't practise this shape in isolation; you will never need to write it unless you are going to join it to a following letter.

## Medial form

When these letters occur in the middle of a word they retain the shape of their initial form, but with a connecting line to both preceding and following letters.

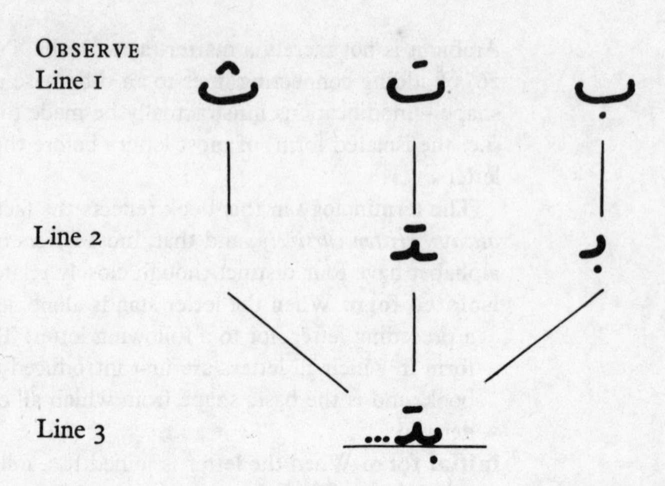


In the word diagrams in this book:

- ☐ Line 1 will show the isolated form of the letter to be used.
- ☐ Line 2 will show the form in which each letter appears in the word.
- ☐ Line 3 will show the completed word.

Since you have not yet seen how to write the final form of these letters, Line 2 of the word diagram above cannot show the final form of ث , nor can Line 3 show a complete word.

*Don't* practise this incomplete combination of letters – wait until you have seen how to make the final form.

## Final form

When these letters occur at the end of a word they retain the shape of their isolated form with a connecting line joining them to the preceding letter.

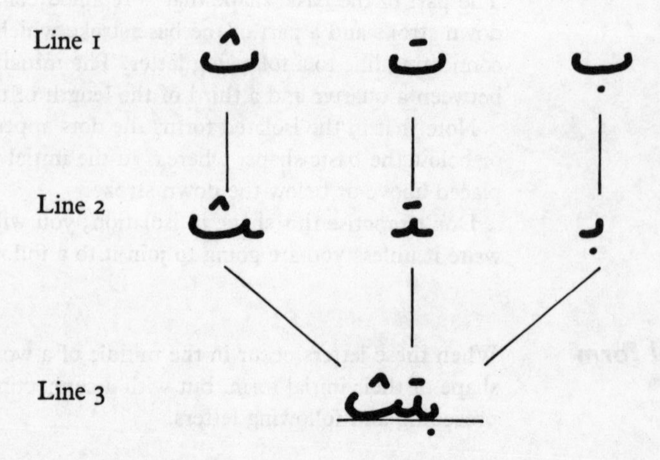

You are now in a position to write complete Arabic word shapes, but before producing any freehand attempts read the writing instructions below with close reference to the model in Line 3 of the word diagram.

**Writing instructions**

□ Make your initial بـ *ba:'* roughly one third the length of an isolated form:

□ From the base stroke of the initial بـ *ba:'* make the up stroke of the medial ـتـ *ta:'*, then retrace the down stroke over the up stroke almost to the horizontal line before veering away to provide the connecting line into the final ـث *tha:'*

□ Lead into the up stroke of the final ـث *tha:'*, then retrace the down stroke over the up stroke, again almost to the horizontal line, before completing the final up stroke in a controlled flourish up and to the right.

□ Try to keep the up strokes and down strokes vertical and roughly level.

Note that we haven't yet put in any dots. The cardinal rule is to produce the basic shape of a word first of all, and then go back and put the dots in from *right to left* once the basic word shape has been completed. Remember, also, to write the dot strokes themselves from *right to left:*

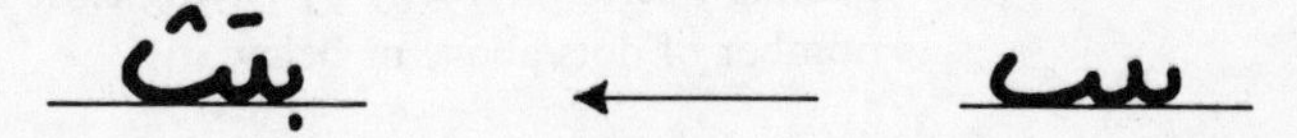

This is roughly analogous to our habit of writing a word and then going back to dot the 'i's' and cross the 't's':

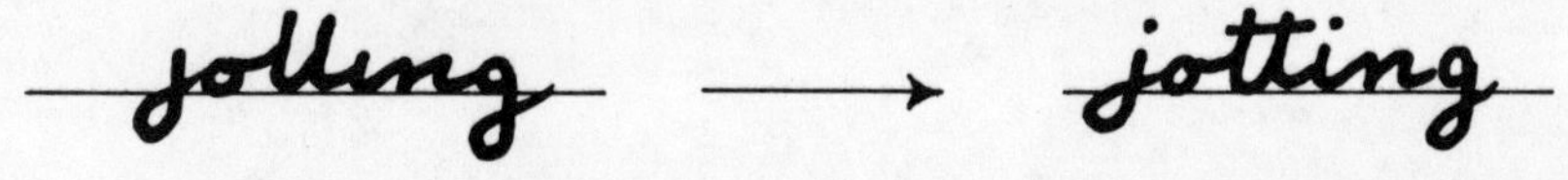


It is very important to be systematic in your dotting of letters. Doing it in the manner suggested above will help you to be thorough while at the same time enabling you to develop an easy right to left rhythm in your handwriting.

**Writing practice** Use the models below for writing practice, but don't make any attempt at pronouncing the words yet, just say the name of each letter as you write it.

In your writing practice you may find it helpful to use a trace and copy technique – trace the models in the book onto a blank sheet of paper to get a feel for the shapes, then copy these traced models to produce your own freehand attempts. Check regularly with the models in the book to make sure that you are not deviating too much from the acceptable range indicated by the slight degree of variation between them. These word shapes are made in one continuous movement without taking the pen off the paper. Don't break off in the middle of writing a letter. Always complete the basic word shape in one flowing motion.

بتث بتث بتث بتث بتث

بتث بتث بتث بتث بتث

Since the three letters of this Unit all share the same initial, medial and final forms, it is now possible for you to join them together in any order.

□ Trace and copy the models on page 31 with reference to the writing instructions given earlier in the Unit.

□ Remember to complete the basic shape of a word before going back to the beginning and putting the dots in from *right to left*.

□ Don't make any attempt at pronouncing the words yet; just say the name of each letter as you write it. Make sure you are naming a letter correctly by paying close attention to the number of dots above or below it.

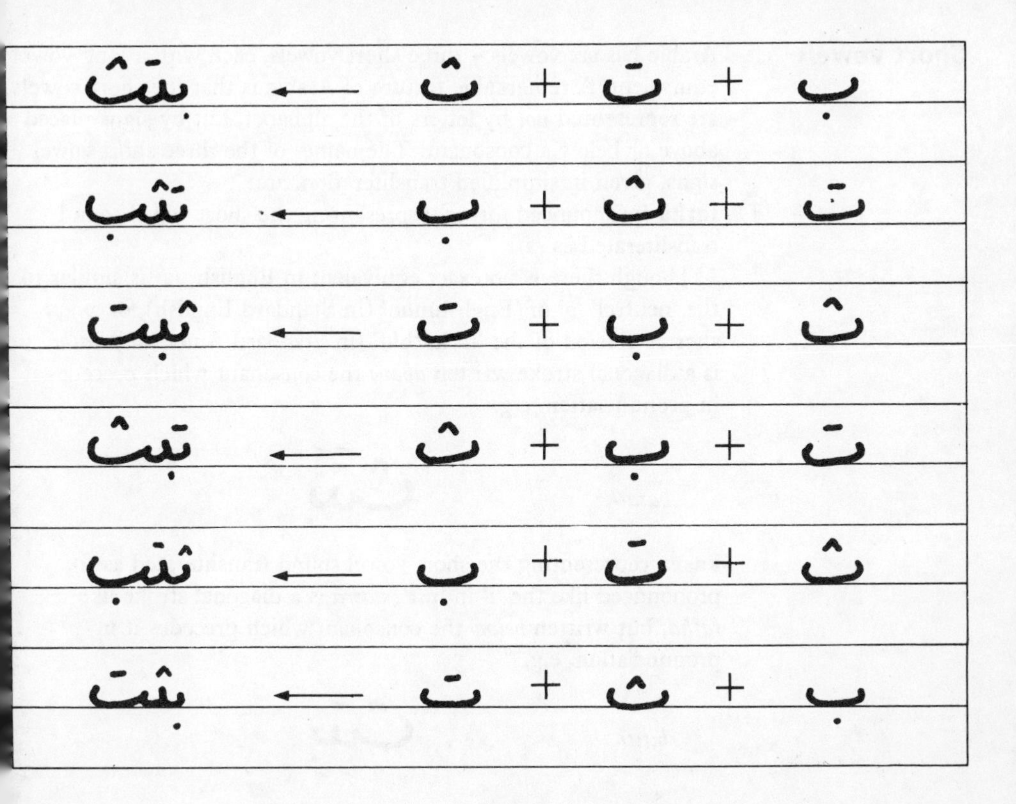


To achieve a natural looking hand from the outset it is worth taking time to practise these combinations of letters carefully. Do the following exercise regularly in these early stages to accustom your hand to moving smoothly and evenly from *right to left* across the page:

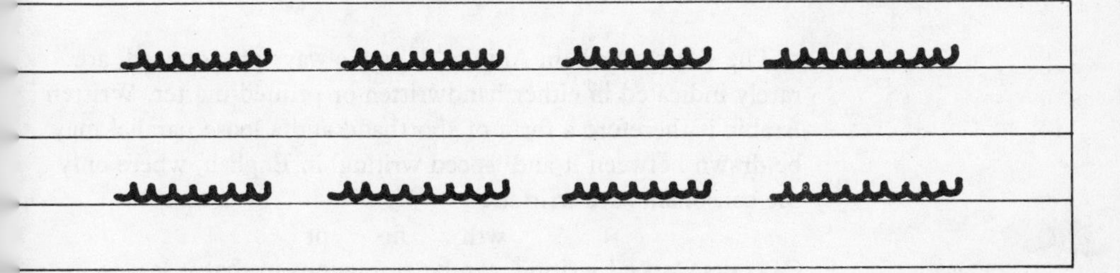

All you are in fact doing is making from right to left the shape you would be making from left to right if you wrote a long line of 'i's' or 'u's' joined together. Try to keep the upright strokes vertical and roughly level, and the connecting lines constant in length.

## Short vowels

Arabic has six vowels – three short vowels, each with a long vowel equivalent. A remarkable feature of Arabic is that the short vowels are represented *not* by letters of the alphabet, but by signs placed above or below a consonant. The names of the three short vowel signs, given in simplified transliteration, are:

Ⓣ **fatha** (pronounced *fat-ha*) representing the short vowel sound transliterated as /a/.

Though there is no exact equivalent in English, /a/ is similar to the 'neutral' 'a' of 'English*ma*n' (in Standard English), or a shorter version of the 'u' in 'b*u*t' (in Standard American). *fatha* is a diagonal stroke written *above* the consonant which precedes it in pronunciation. e.g.

*batath* 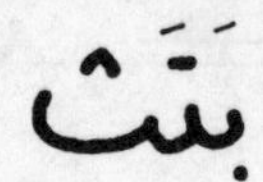

**kasra** representing the short vowel sound transliterated as /i/, pronounced like the 'i' in 'p*i*t'. *kasra* is a diagonal stroke like *fatha*, but written *below* the consonant which precedes it in pronunciation, e.g.

*bitith* 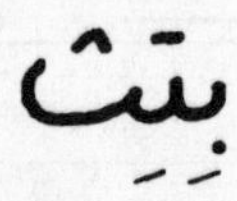

**damma** representing the short vowel sound transliterated as /u/, pronounced like the 'u' in 'p*u*t'. *damma* is an apostrophe-like shape written *above* the consonant which precedes it in pronunciation, e.g.

*bututh* 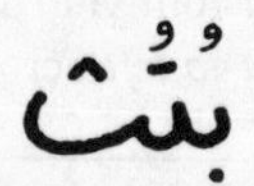

The short vowels in Arabic, though always pronounced, are rarely indicated in either handwritten or printed matter. Written Arabic is therefore a form of shorthand and a loose parallel may be drawn between it and 'speed writing' in English, where only the consonants are written:

wth flt pt

Of course 'speed writing' can be ambiguous in that it leaves some words open to several possible interpretations. The three letters of the first example would be clear in any context – they can only be read as 'with'. But, out of the context of a sentence should the second example 'flt' be read as 'flat'; 'flit'; 'felt'; 'fault'; 'float'; 'flute' or 'fleet'? Similarly, is 'pt' to be read as 'pat'; 'pet'; 'pout'; 'put'; 'pit'; 'pot'; 'peat' or 'pate'?

The possibility of such ambiguities arising out of the non-indication of short vowels is much slighter in Arabic. In common with all Semitic languages, Arabic depends primarily on the consonantal framework of a word for the determination of meaning. The short vowels (together with certain prefixes, interfixes and suffixes) have the secondary responsibility of determining the function of a word – whether it is a noun, an adjective or a verb, etc., and of fixing the exact shade of meaning. The three consonants 'k''t''b', for example, carry the concept of 'writing' whenever they occur in this order in an Arabic word. Thus any word containing these consonants will have some connection with the concept of 'writing', no matter what other letters it may contain. In English, on the other hand, vowels are just as important as consonants in the determination of meaning, and their removal from a word will usually lead to considerable ambiguity, as we saw on page 32.

In Arabic today, short vowels are not generally indicated in books, newspapers, magazines, advertisements or any handwritten material. They are, however, always used in editions of the Qur'an (to ensure consistency in pronunciation and interpretation), and often in poetry, where a certain exact pronunciation may be crucial to the success of a metre. They are also indicated in children's books, particularly those which are used in the early stages of learning to read and write their own script and language. Additional use of short vowel signs is limited to occasions where the kind of ambiguity discussed above in relation to 'speed-writing' is likely to occur in Arabic.

**Reading and writing practice** These are combinations of the three letters you have learned in this Unit with various combinations of the three short vowels.

Ⓣ ☐ Read each model aloud several times with reference to the tape drills, and/or your teacher. Pay attention to the number and position of the dots – make sure that you are correctly identifying each letter and short vowel sign, and the sound they represent.

☐ Repeat this drill until you can recognise and read each model without hesitation.

*Note:* These are not real words, but models for reading and writing practice only.

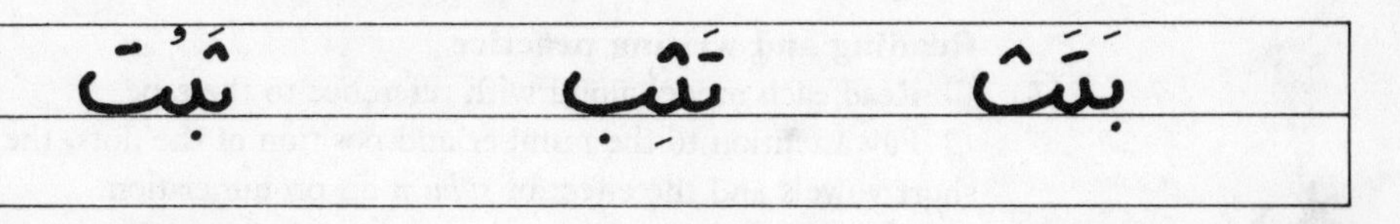


3 *thabut* 2 *tathib* 1 *batath*

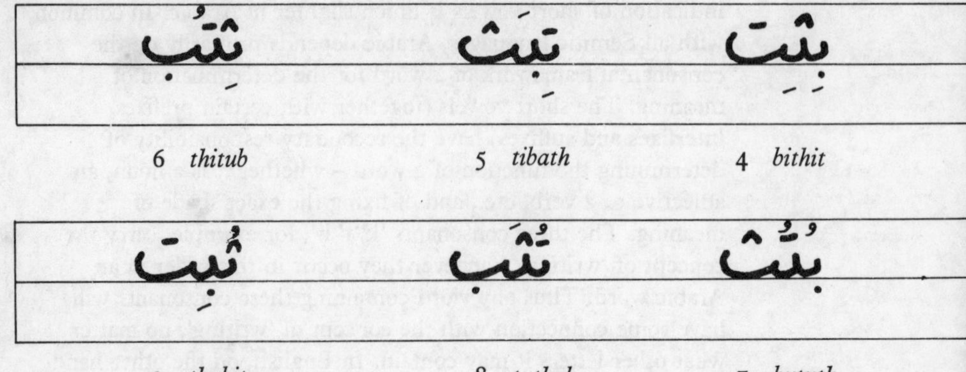


□ Use the models above for writing practice. Write each word in three stages – first complete the basic word shape, go back and put in the dots from right to left, and then go back again to the beginning of the word and put in the short vowel signs.
□ Practise writing these words until you can consistently reproduce a fair copy of the models in the book.

## Additional signs used in Arabic

1 *suku:n* ْ
This is the sign written above a consonant to show that there is no vowel between that consonant and the next one.

Ⓣ OBSERVE
Contrast

*thabat* ثَبَت

*thabt* ثَبْت

It may help you to remember the function of *suku:n* if you regard it as a small zero sign signifying 'zero vowel'. In fact, *suku:n* literally means 'silence' in Arabic.

**Writing instructions** '*suku:n*' is a small clock-wise circle.

**Reading and writing practice**

Ⓣ □ Read each model aloud with reference to the tape.
□ Pay attention to the number and position of the dots, the short vowels and the effect of *suku:n* on pronunciation.
*Note:* These are not real words, but models for reading and writing practice only.

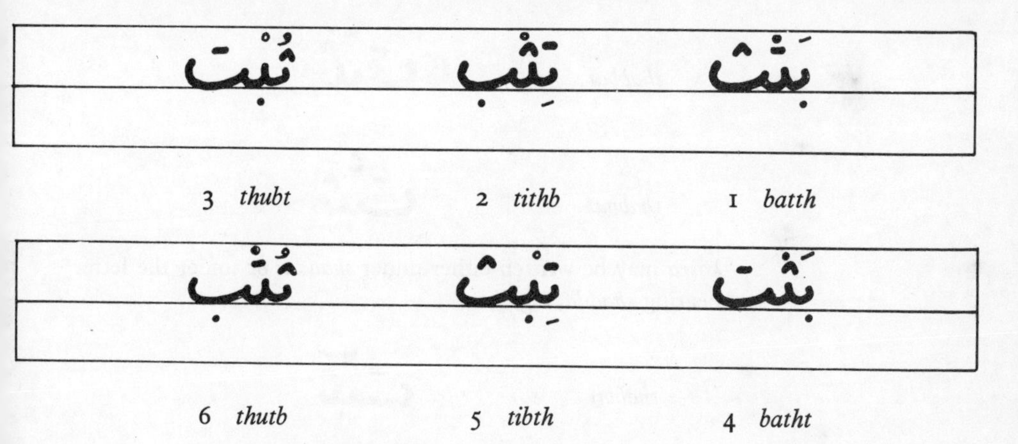


Ⓣ 2 *shadda* ّ

This is the sign written above a consonant to indicate that it is doubled in pronunciation. The Arabic name for this sign means 'emphasis' or 'stress'.

OBSERVE

Contrast *thabat* ثَبَت

*thabbat* ثَبَّت

Doubled consonant sounds do not occur within words in English – the spellings of words like 'letter', 'sadder', 'ribbon' belie the fact that only one consonant sound is pronounced in the middle of each word. Doubled consonants can occur in English when one word ending in a consonant is followed by a second word beginning with the same sound, as in 'tha*t t*ime', 'goo*d d*eal', and in compound words like 'nigh*t-t*ime' and 'boo*k-k*eeper'.

Arabic consonants, on the other hand, *can* be pronounced double within a single word – in fact the contrast of a doubled consonant in one word and the same consonant, undoubled, in another is often the sole feature of pronunciation distinguishing between two words with completely different meanings. It is therefore important to hear and reproduce the differences between doubled and single consonants, and the tape drills to this Unit highlight this point.

**Writing instructions** The *shadda* consists of three 'teeth' – like a small rounded 'w', but written from *right to left*. ّ

A doubled consonant in the middle of an Arabic word is always accompanied by a short vowel. *fatha* and *damma* are written above *shadda*, e.g.

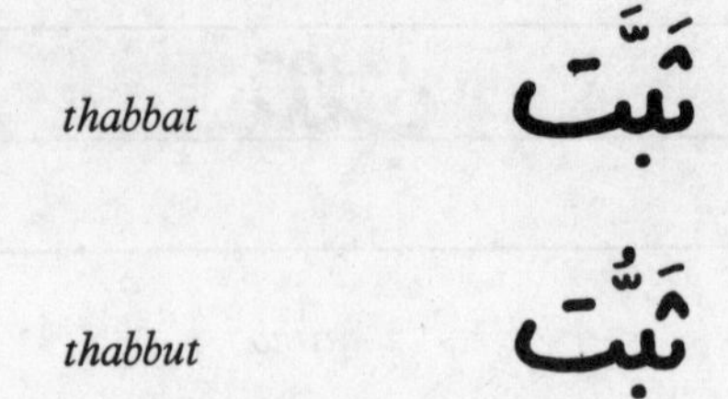


*kasra* may be written either under *shadda*, or under the letter bearing *shadda*, e.g.

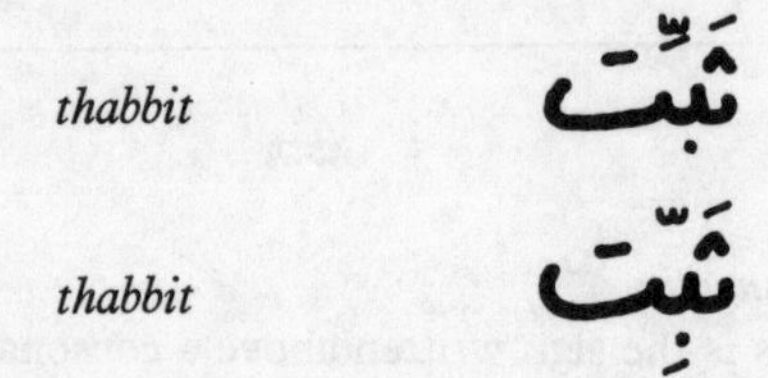


Like the short vowels, the signs *suku:n* and *shadda* are rarely indicated in either handwritten or printed matter, but *will* be marked throughout this book. Indication of the short vowels, *suku:n*, and *shadda*, is essential for the purposes of non-Arabic speakers in the early stages of learning to read and write the Arabic script.

**Reading and writing practice**

Ⓣ ☐ Read each model aloud with reference to the tape.

☐ Pay attention to the number and position of the dots, the short vowels and the effect of *shadda* on pronunciation.

| ثُبُّت | تِثِّب | بَتَّث |
|---|---|---|
| 3 *thubbut* | 2 *tiththib* | 1 *battath* |
| ثَتُّب | تَبِّث | بَثَّت |
| 6 *thattub* | 5 *tabbith* | 4 *baththat* |

☐ Use these models for writing practice. Remember – write each word in three stages; first complete the basic word shape, go back and put in the dots from *right to left*, and then go back again to the beginning of the word and put in the short vowel signs and *shadda*.

*Note:* The words on page 36 are not real words, but models for reading and writing practice only.

'Before and during early Islamic times, Arabic writing was quite faulty. There was no system at all for writing the vowels, and the diacritical marks for distinguishing similar letters didn't exist. This was a difficult situation and led to the introduction of dots for distinguishing identical consonants and for indicating the three short vowels (*u*, *a* and *i*). The dotted vowels were written in coloured ink, usually red, while other consonants and consonantal dots were written in black. The dots for vowels were placed in or beside the character for *u*, above it for *a*, and below it for *i*. These dots were cumbersome, though, and were eventually replaced by more viable signs. One was in the form of a comma placed above the consonant to indicate *u*; another was a slanting dash above the consonant for *a*; and the last was another slanting dash below the consonant for an *i*. At this time other diacritical marks were also introduced. Among these are . . . the *shadda* for doubling a consonant, and the *suku:n* for marking an unvowelled consonant. Not until after the seventh century was the script form gradually fixed.' (Anwar G. Chejne, *The Arabic language: its role in history*, page 28)

***Pronunciation drill*** Ⓣ

**Contrast single and doubled consonants**

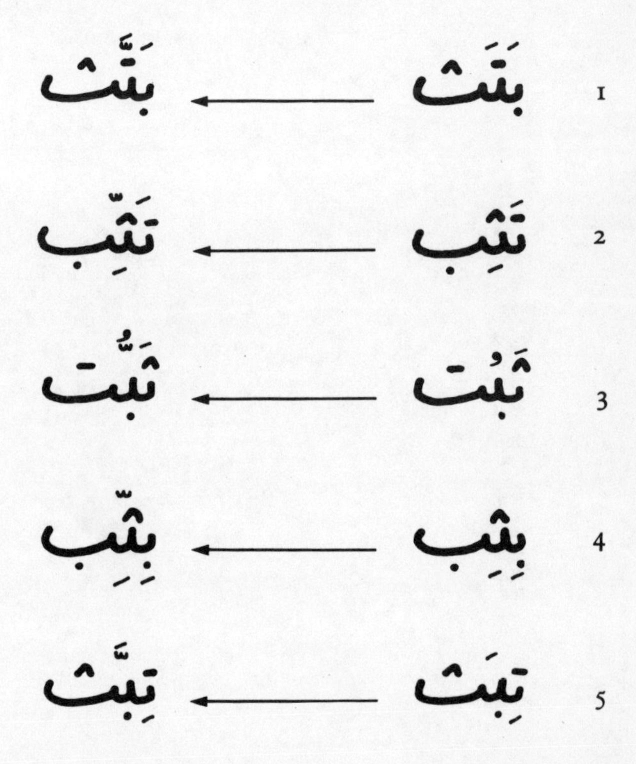

| | | | |
|---|---|---|---|
| 6 | ثِتُب | ← | ثِتُّب |
| 7 | بَتُث | ← | بَتُّث |
| 8 | تُثَب | ← | تُثَّب |
| 9 | ثُبِت | ← | ثُبِّت |

# Unit 2

The name of this letter is *nu:n*. It is pronounced like the 'n' in '*n*eck', and is transliterated as /n/.

### Isolated form

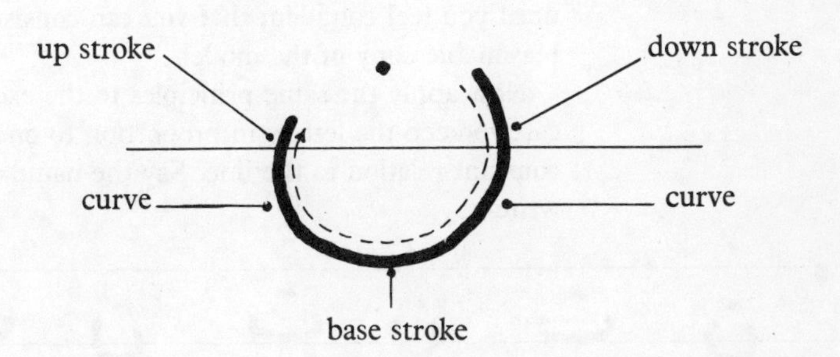


**Writing instructions** Compare the isolated forms of

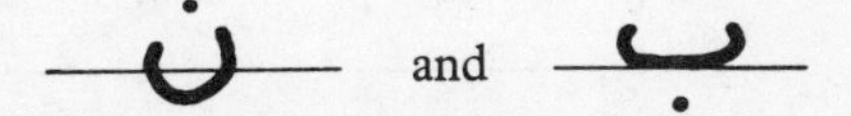


You can see that there is a degree of resemblance between the two. However, ن *nu:n* does differ from ب *ba:'* in several important respects:

☐ The initial down stroke is longer, though still sloping to the left of upright.

☐ The curve of the down stroke into the base stroke is still smooth and rounded, but the base itself is somewhat bulbous and sinks below the line, while the base of ب *ba:'* is more or less flat and sits on the line.

☐ The curve of the base stroke into the final up stroke is still smooth and rounded, but the final up stroke is longer – roughly the same length as the initial down stroke.

□ The single dot is placed just above and between the two upright strokes.

**Reading and writing practice** Say the name of the letter each time you write it.

Make copies of the models above. It might be helpful to trace over a few models to get the feel of the shape before making your first freehand attempts. The slight degree of variation between each of the models should give you a guide to the amount of leeway you can allow yourself when drawing this shape for the first time. After three or four attempts always go back and check your examples with the models in the book. Practise the shape until you feel confident that you can consistently produce a reasonable copy of the models.

Now apply the same principles to the exercise below, taking care to keep the letters in proportion to one another, and in constant relation to the line. Say the name of each letter as you write it.

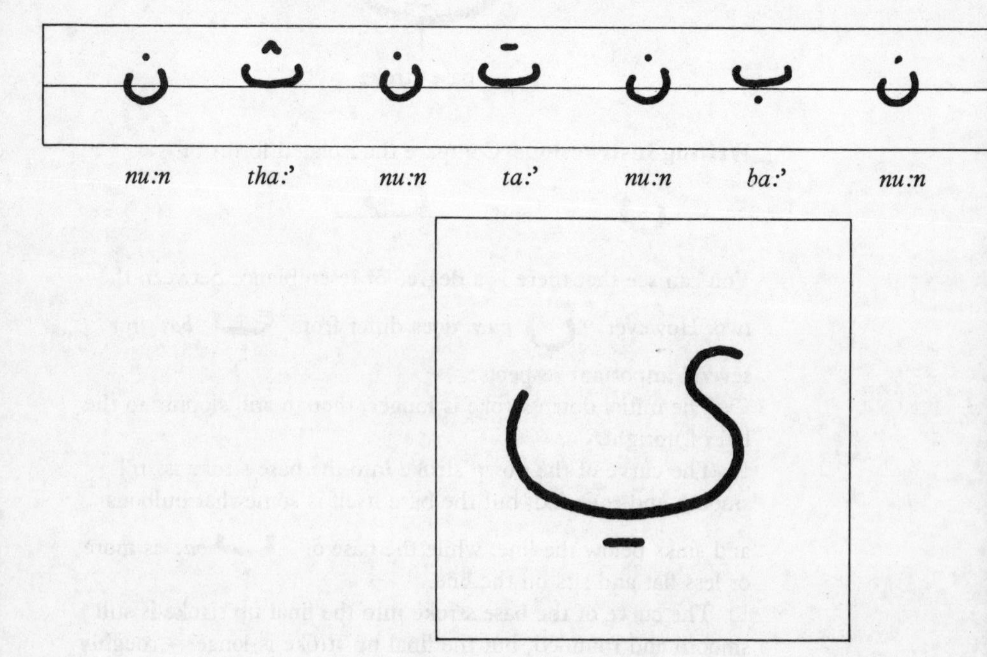


The name of this letter is *ya:'*. Though it poses no actual pronunciation problems to the English speaker, it requires particular attention since it represents two different sounds – a vowel and a consonant, depending partly on its position in a word and partly on the sounds which occur adjacent to it.

☐ When it occurs at the beginning of a word it is always a consonant, pronounced like the 'y' in '*y*oung', and transliterated as /y/.

☐ When it occurs in the middle of a word it can be either the consonant /y/ or a long vowel pronounced like the 'ee' in 's*ee*p', and transliterated as /i:/. This is the long vowel sound corresponding to the short vowel /i/ represented by *kasra.* (Note that we use a colon in our transliteration system to distinguish the long vowel sound from its corresponding short vowel.)

This is an instance of Arabic using a single letter to represent two sounds for which English uses a number of different letters and combinations of letters ('y' as in 'young'; 'ee' as in 'seep'; 'ea' as in 'bead'; 'ie' as in 'fiend'; and 'ei' as in 'received').

☐ At the end of a word ي is always the long vowel /i:/.

## *Isolated form*

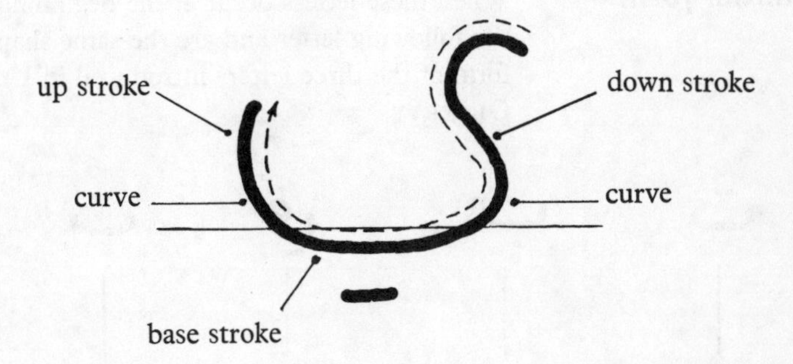


**Writing instructions** The isolated form of ي is identical to the isolated form of ن except for its initial down stroke and the number and position of the dots. The down stroke of ي *ya:*' begins with a 'c' shaped hook leading smoothly into the base stroke. The two dot stroke / ▬ / is placed centrally below the base line.

**Reading and writing practice**

☐ Make copies of the models on page 41, saying the name of the letter each time you write it. Trace over a few of the models before making any freehand attempts.
☐ Remember to write from *right to left* across the page, and allow plenty of space for each example.
☐ Keep your examples in constant relation to the horizontal line, real or imaginary. Monitor your own progress – go back after every few attempts and check with the models in the book.
☐ Compare and contrast the letters you have learned so far. Use the models for writing practice, and say the name of each letter as you write it.

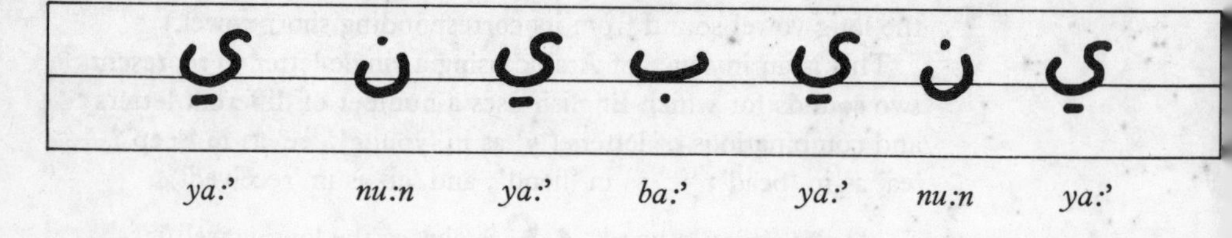


*ya:ʾ* *nu:n* *ya:ʾ* *ba:ʾ* *ya:ʾ* *nu:n* *ya:ʾ*

**Initial form**

When these letters occur at the beginning of a word they join to the following letter and are the same shape and size as the initial form of the three letters introduced in Unit 1.

OBSERVE

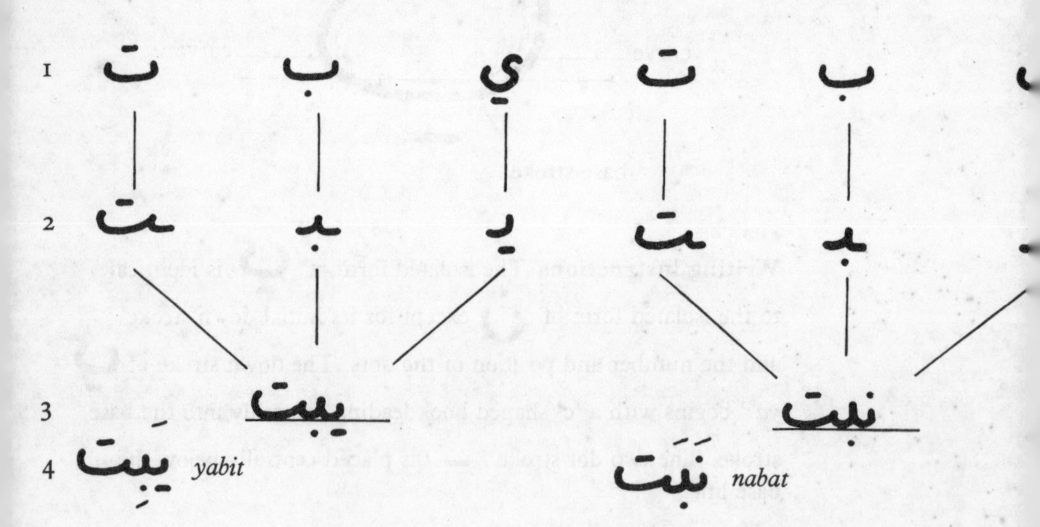


Line 4 shows the word from the word diagram both in Arabic, complete with short vowels, and in transliteration.

Notice that the initial forms of all five letters you have seen so far are identical in shape, distinguished from one another *only* by the number and position of dots which go with them.

| initial form | | isolated form | name of letter |
|---|---|---|---|
| one dot below | ...بـ | ب | *ba:'* |
| two dots above | ...تـ | ت | *ta:'* |
| three dots above | ...ثـ | ث | *tha:'* |
| one dot above | ...نـ | ن | *nu:n* |
| two dots below | ...يـ | ي | *ya:'* |

It is therefore extremely important to place dots carefully, making sure that you put the correct number (one, two or three) in the correct place (either above or below the letter). Mis-dotting just one letter can radically alter the meaning of a word.

**Writing instructions**
Same as for initial form of ب *ba:'* ت *ta:'* and ث *tha:'*.

**Reading and writing practice**

Ⓣ □ Read and pronounce the models below with reference to the tape. Bear in mind that ي *ya:'* at the beginning of a word is always the consonant /y/, and pay particular attention to dots, short vowels and other signs.

□ For writing practice start by tracing the models fairly quickly, and as smoothly as possible, onto a blank sheet of paper. This will help you to get a feel for the overall shape of the words. Then produce your own freehand attempts, remembering to complete the basic shape of a word before going back to put in first the dots, and then the short vowels, *shadda*, and *suku:n*, all from *right to left*.

(*Note:* Examples 1 and 2 are from the word diagram on page 42. Examples 3 to 8 are the same combinations of letters using the other short vowels and signs you have learnt.)

| يُبِّت | نَبَّت | يَبِت | نَبَت |
|---|---|---|---|
| 4 *yubbit* | 3 *nabbat* | 2 *yabit* | 1 *nabat* |

نَبْت يَبَّت نُبِت يَبْت

8 *yabt* 7 *nubit* 6 *yabbat* 5 *nabt*

□ Always start your writing practice on the right of your practice page and work across to the left. Keep the letters of each word in proportion to one another and in constant relation to the line. Don't cramp your examples too closely together – allow yourself plenty of space.

**Medial form**

When these letters occur in the middle of a word they have the same shape and size as the medial form of ب ت and ث and join to both the preceding and following letters.

OBSERVE

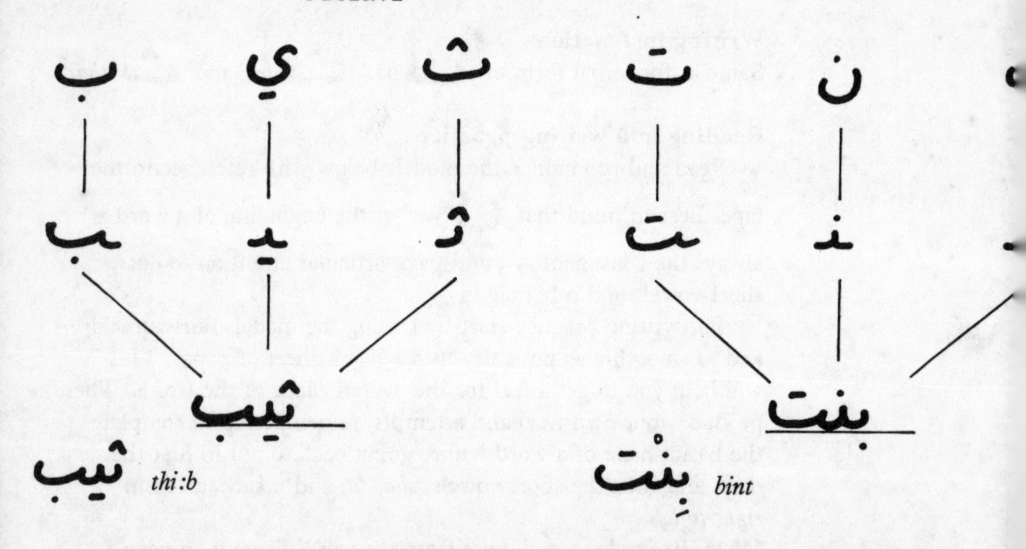


Notice that the medial forms of all five letters you have learned so far are identical in shape, distinguished from one another *only* by the number and position of dots that go with them.

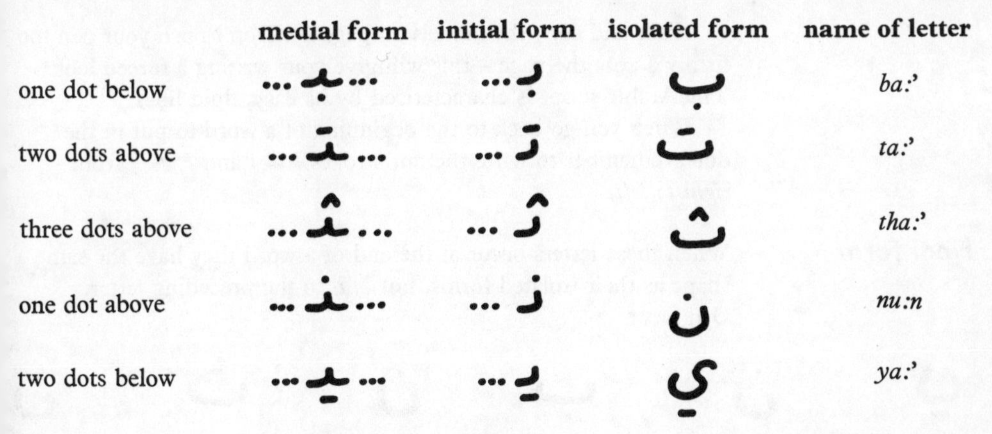

| | medial form | initial form | isolated form | name of letter |
|---|---|---|---|---|
| one dot below | ...ـبـ... | ...بـ | ب | *ba:'* |
| two dots above | ...ـتـ... | ...تـ | ت | *ta:'* |
| three dots above | ...ـثـ... | ...ثـ | ث | *tha:'* |
| one dot above | ...ـنـ... | ...نـ | ن | *nu:n* |
| two dots below | ...ـيـ... | ...يـ | ي | *ya:'* |

Once again, this emphasises the importance of careful and accurate dotting of letters.

**Writing instructions** Same as for medial form of ب *ba:'* ت *ta:'* and ث *tha:'*.

**Reading and writing practice**

Ⓣ □ Read and pronounce the models below with reference to the tape.

Remember that ي in the middle of a word can represent either the consonant /y/ or the long vowel /i:/.

□ When it is either preceded or followed by a vowel ي is always pronounced as the consonant /y/. (See examples 7 and 8)

□ When it is neither preceded nor followed by a vowel ي is pronounced as the long vowel /i:/. (See examples 2, 3, 4 and 6)

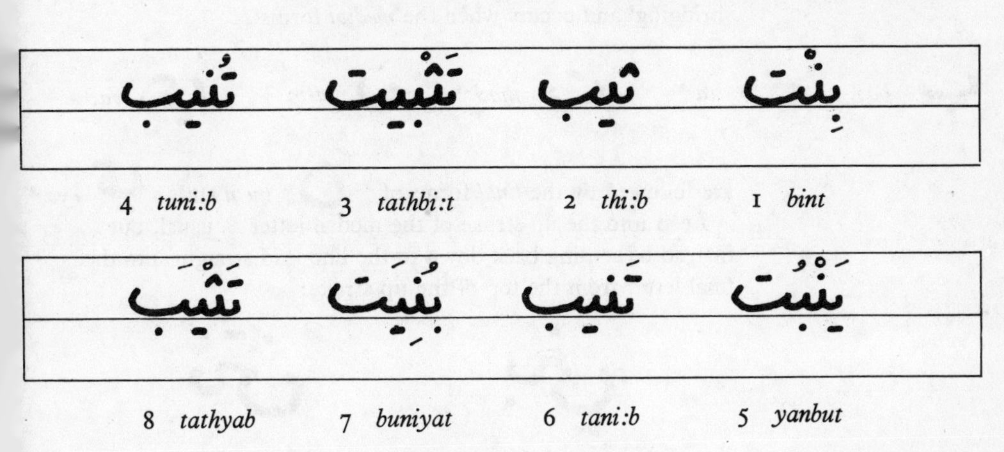

4 *tuni:b* 3 *tathbi:t* 2 *thi:b* 1 *bint*

8 *tathyab* 7 *buniyat* 6 *tani:b* 5 *yanbut*

□ Trace and copy the models on page 45. Don't push your pen too firmly across the page – this will give your writing a forced look. The Arabic script is characterised by its easy, fluid lines.
□ When you go back to the beginning of a word to put in the dots, remember to write the dot strokes / ▬ / and / ^ / from *right to left*.

***Final form***

When these letters occur at the end of a word they have the same shape as their isolated forms, but join to the preceding letter.
OBSERVE

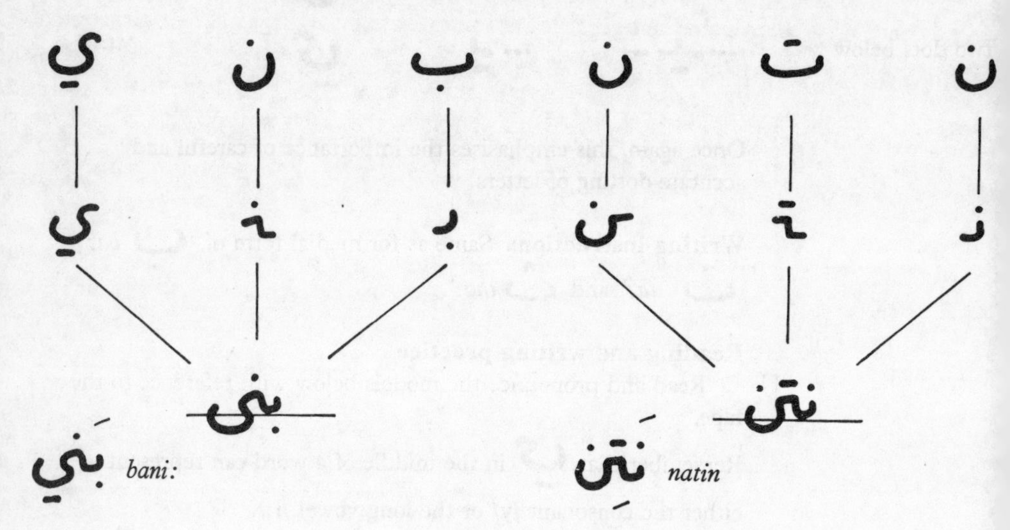


**Writing instructions – Bridging** Look carefully at the modification in the shape of medial ت *ta:'* and ن *nu:n* when followed by final ن *nu:n* and final ي *ya:'* in the examples in the word diagrams above. This modification is called 'bridging' and occurs when the *medial* forms of

are followed by the *final* forms of ن *nu:n* and ي *ya:'*.
Lead into the up stroke of the medial letter as usual, but instead of coming back down to the line lead straight into the final letter from the top of the up stroke:

This bridging technique is by no means compulsory. The examples on page 46 can be quite acceptably written without any modification to the medial form:

Bridging is, however, a very common feature of handwritten Arabic and will therefore be used throughout this book. Practise it extensively – it is a short cut to developing a more cursive and natural style.

**Reading and writing practice**

Ⓣ ☐ Read and pronounce the words below with reference to the tape. Remember that ي *ya:'* at the end of a word is always the long vowel /i:/.

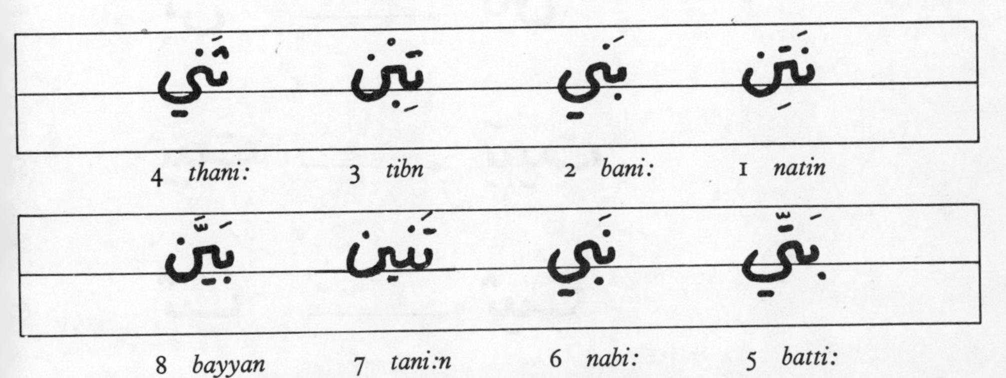

4 *thani:* 3 *tibn* 2 *bani:* 1 *natin*

8 *bayyan* 7 *tani:n* 6 *nabi:* 5 *batti:*

☐ Trace and copy the models pronouncing each word as soon as you have completed it. Check your examples frequently with the book, paying particular attention to dots (number and position), short vowels and other signs.

**Pronunciation drill** Ⓣ

**Contrast the short and long vowel sounds /i/ and /i:/.**

| /i:/ | | /i/ | |
|---|---|---|---|
| تيب | ← | تِب | 1 |
| بين | ← | بِن | 2 |
| بيت | ← | بِت | 3 |
| ثين | ← | ثِن | 4 |
| يَبيت | ← | يَبِت | 5 |
| ثيب | ← | ثِب | 6 |
| تَثْبيت | ← | تَثْبِت | 7 |
| تَنيب | ← | تَنِب | 8 |

# Unit 3

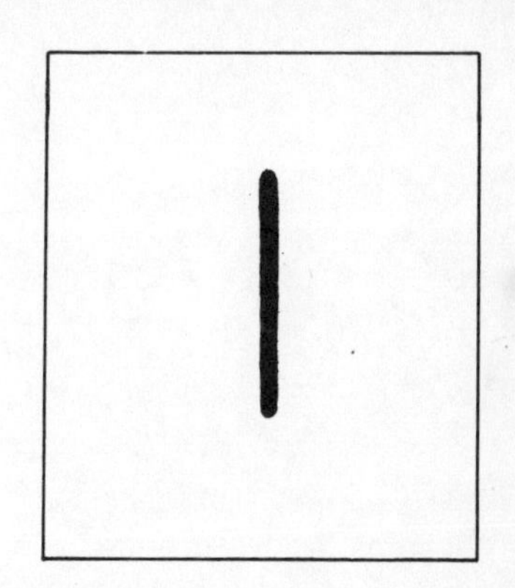

The name of this letter is *alif*. It is the letter you have seen transliterated as /a:/ in the names of the letters ب *ba:'* ت *ta:'* and ث *tha:'*. There is no precise equivalent in English, so pay particular attention to the tape drills and/or your teacher's pronunciation. For rough guidance consider /a:/ similar to the 'a' in 's*a*d', but longer in duration. This is the long vowel sound corresponding to the short vowel /a/ represented by *fatha*.

## Isolated form

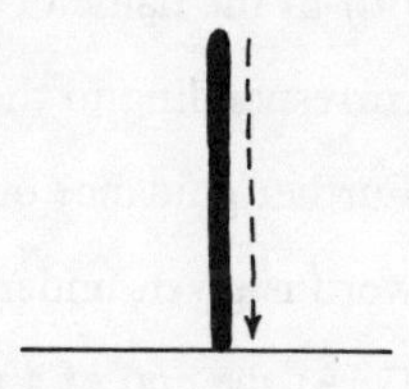

**Writing instructions** This letter is written in a single down stroke about three times the height of the initial down stroke of ب *ba:'*. It stands on the line.

**Reading and writing practice** Trace and copy the models below. Notice the size of ا *alif* in relation to the letters you have already learned. Say the name of each letter as you write it.

*alif* *ya:'* *alif* *nu:n* *alif* *ba:'* *alif*

The name of this letter is *wa:w*. Like ي *ya:'* it may be either a consonant or a long vowel, and therefore requires particular attention.

□ When it occurs at the beginning of a word it is always a consonant, pronounced like the 'w' in '*w*et' and transliterated as /w/.

□ When it occurs in the middle of a word it can be either the consonant /w/ or a long vowel pronounced like the 'u' in 'r*u*de'. As a long vowel it is the letter you have seen transliterated as /u:/ in the name of the letter ن *nu:n*. It is the long vowel corresponding to the short vowel /u/ represented by *damma.* Further guidance on the pronunciation of و in the middle of a word is given under medial position.

□ At the end of a word و is always the long vowel /u:/.

This is another example of Arabic using a single letter to represent two sounds for which English uses a number of different letters and combinations of letters ('w' as in '*w*et'; 'u' as in 'r*u*de'. 'oo' as in 's*oo*n', 'ui' as in 'fr*ui*t').

## *Isolated form*

**Writing instructions** This letter has a 'head' and a 'tail'. To get the characteristic sweep of the tail, first draw the clockwise circle of the head, then allow your pen to flick down and across in a controlled flourish. The head sits on the line and the tail extends below the line.

**Reading and writing practice** Trace and copy the models below. Say the name of the letter each time you write it.

Look at the two new letters in proportion to the letters from Units 1 and 2:

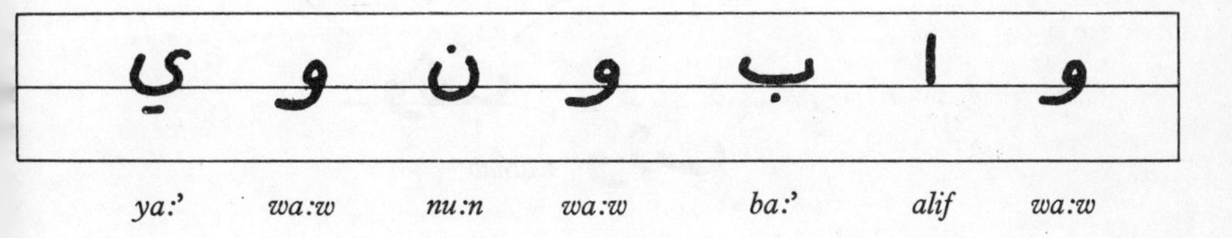


Use this proportion guide as an exercise for writing practice. Trace and copy the letters keeping them in constant proportion to one another, and in correct relation to the line. Say the name of each letter as you write it.

### *Initial position*

All the letters you learned in Units 1 and 2 join to both preceding and following letters within a word. The two letters introduced in this Unit, however, can *never* join to a following letter, and we refer to them as 'non-connectors'. There are six non-connectors in the Arabic alphabet. When they occur at the beginning of a word they *always* stand alone in their isolated form.

There is no word diagram for initial ا *alif* since this letter only occurs at the beginning of a word under special circumstances, which will be explained shortly.

OBSERVE

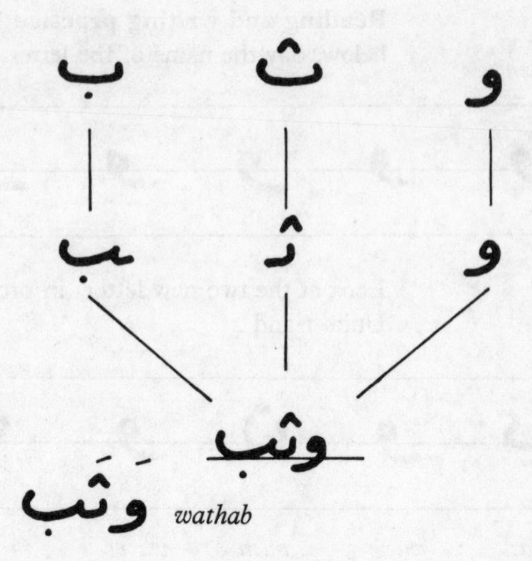


Up to this Unit any letter occurring at the beginning of a word (initial position) has automatically appeared in its initial form, in the middle of a word (medial position) in its medial form, and at the end of a word (final position) in its final form. Now that we have introduced the first two non-connectors, however, you will appreciate that there is not always a direct correspondence between 'position' and 'form'. In the word diagram above, for example, notice that though ثـ is in the middle of the word – i.e. in a medial *position* – it appears in its initial *form* because it is preceded by a non-connector. Similarly, و is in an initial *position* but, because it never joins to a following letter, appears in its isolated *form*.

**Writing instructions**

Same as for isolated form.

**Reading and writing practice**

Ⓣ ☐ Read and pronounce aloud the words below with reference to the tape. Remember that و at the beginning of a word is always the consonant /w/.

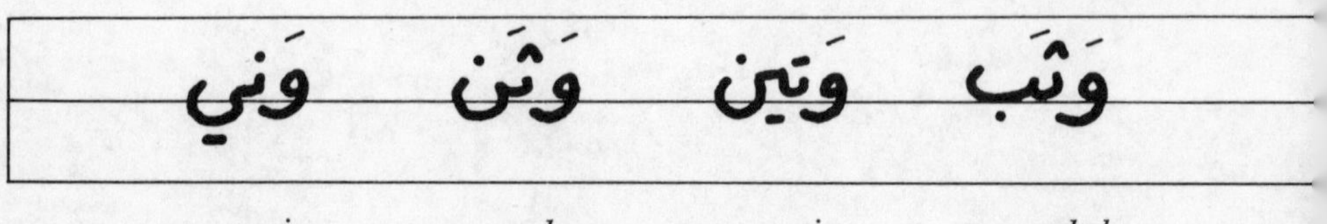


4 *wani:* 3 *wathan* 2 *wati:n* 1 *wathab*

☐ Now trace and copy the models. Monitor your progress by going back and checking your examples with the models in the book after every two or three attempts.

☐ Pronounce each word several times after you have written it – make sure you are correctly identifying the three short vowels and the sounds they represent.

☐ Note the spacing within these words – don't squash a non-connector too close to a following letter, but don't let too much of a gap open up. The degree of variation between the models should give you an idea of the leeway you can allow yourself. The occurrence of a non-connector is the only occasion you should take your pen off the paper in the middle of writing a word.

***Medial position*** Note again that the two letters introduced in this Unit can *never* join to a following letter. When they occur in the middle of a word they join to a preceding letter only.

OBSERVE

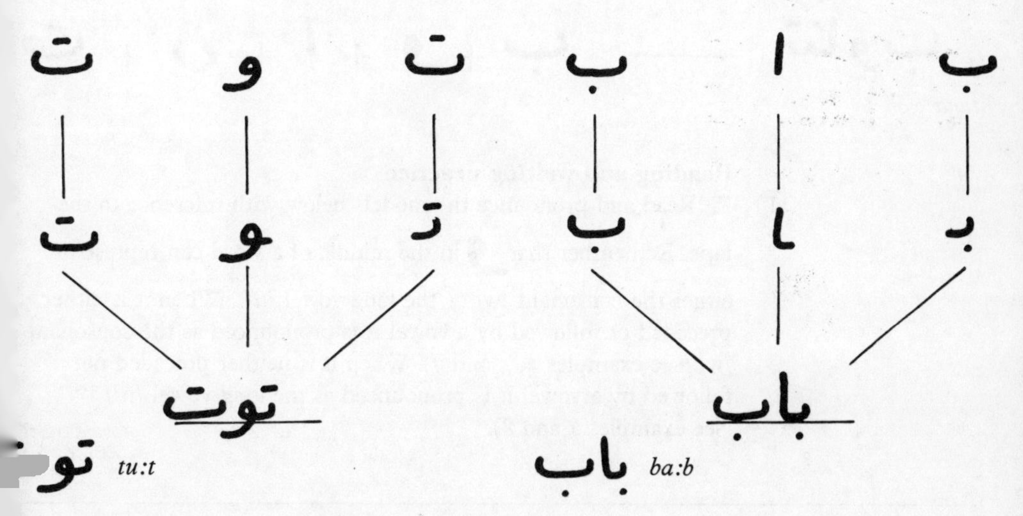


**Writing instructions** When ا *alif* joins to a preceding letter you write it as an up stroke leading out of the connecting line from the preceding letter, without taking your pen off the paper:

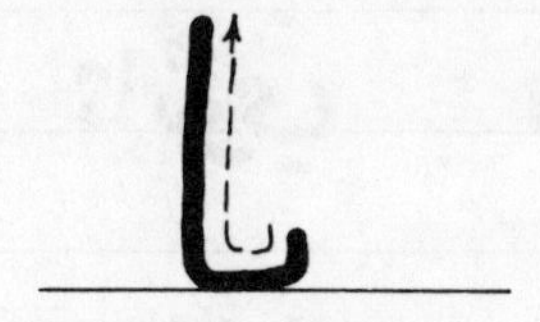

When و *wa:w* joins to a preceding letter you lead into the anti-clockwise circle of the head with the connecting line from the preceding letter:

If two non-connectors such as these appear one after the other within the same word, the second of them will always remain unconnected and in its isolated form:

ب + و + ا + ب ← بَوّاب

*bawwa:b*

ت + ن + ا + و + ب ← تَناوَب

*tana:wab*

**Reading and writing practice**

Ⓣ □ Read and pronounce the models below with reference to the tape. Remember that و in the middle of a word can represent either the consonant /w/ or the long vowel /u:/. When it is either preceded or followed by a vowel it is pronounced as the consonant /w/ (see examples 3, 4 and 7). When it is neither preceded nor followed by a vowel it is pronounced as the long vowel /u:/ (see examples 2 and 8).

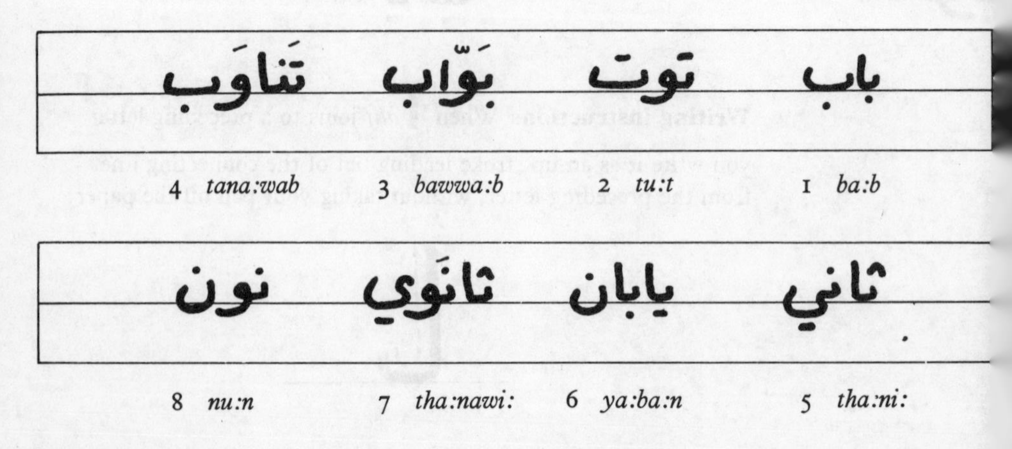

□ Trace and copy the models, pronouncing each word as soon as you have completed it. Try to keep the ا *alif* upright. Make sure you are keeping all the letters in proportion to one another and in correct relation to the line. Pay particular attention to the spacing within these words – don't squash a non-connector too close to a following letter, but don't allow too wide a gap to open up. Keep practising until you can consistently produce reasonable copies of the models in the book.

***Final position*** When these two letters occur at the end of a word they join to the preceding letter, retaining the shape of their medial form.
OBSERVE

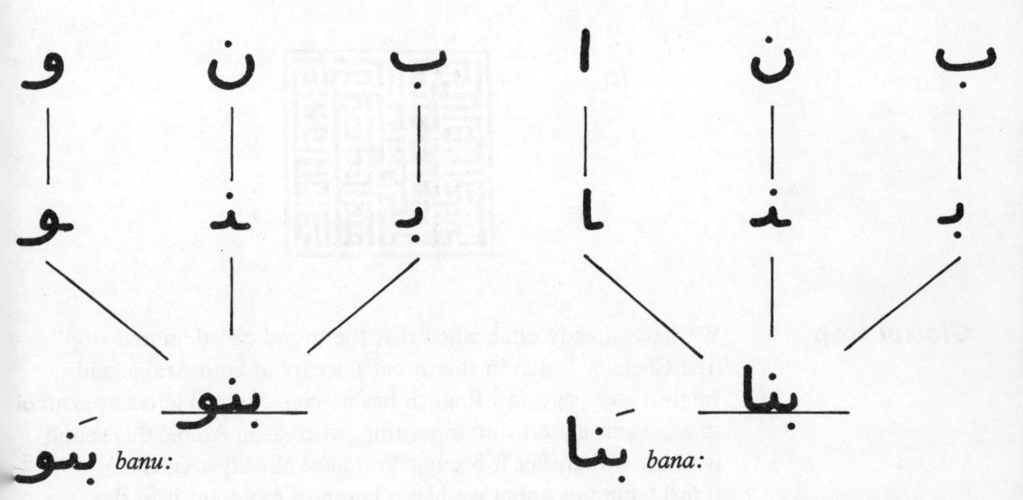


**Writing instructions** The final forms of these two letters are in all respects identical to their medial forms.

**Reading and writing practice**

Ⓣ □ Read and pronounce the words below with reference to the tape. Remember that و *wa:w* at the end of a word is always the long vowel /u:/.

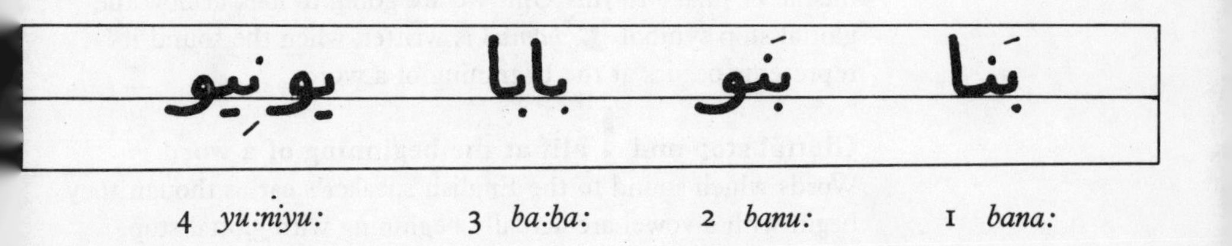


4 *yu:niyu:* 3 *ba:ba:* 2 *banu:* 1 *bana:*

☐ Trace and copy the models, pronouncing each word as you complete it.
☐ Monitor the size of your writing by careful reference to the book. Practise each word as many times as it takes for you to produce a consistent copy of the model in the book, and try to keep your examples in constant relation to the horizontal line. Make particularly sure that you don't join a non-connector to a following letter.

☐ Notice that unlike the letters from Units 1 and 2 (which have four forms), ا *alif* and و *wa:w* have only two forms – either standing alone, or joined to a preceding letter. This is also the case with the four remaining non-connectors which you will see in the next two Units.

**Glottal stop**

We have already established that the sound called 'glottal stop' (the Cockney 'catch in the throat') occurs in both Arabic and English (see page 22). English has no conventional letter or symbol to represent glottal stop in writing, whereas in Arabic this sound *is* written whenever it occurs. You have already seen the transliteration symbol we have chosen to represent it in the names of the letters

ب *ba:'* ت *ta:'* ث *tha:'* ي *ya:'*

The Arabic symbol for glottal stop is ء , called *hamza*. It is not a letter in its own right, but a symbol which usually appears in conjunction with a letter acting as a support or 'seat'. The choice of seat for ء *hamza* depends on a number of factors, including its position in a word (i.e. whether it is initial, medial or final). In this Unit we are going to look at how the glottal stop symbol ء *hamza* is written when the sound it represents occurs at the beginning of a word.

**Glottal stop and ا alif at the beginning of a word**
Words which sound to the English speaker's ear as though they begin with a vowel are actually beginning with glottal stop,

which is a consonant. In fact Arabic words always begin with a consonant – when you hear a word which seems to begin with a vowel sound you will know that the initial consonant in that case is ء *hamza*.

ء *hamza* at the beginning of a word is always written either above or below ا *alif*. The ا *alif* itself is *not* pronounced – it serves merely as a silent seat for ء *hamza* which cannot be written on its own at the beginning of a word.

Initial ء *hamza* is always accompanied by a short vowel which immediately follows it in pronunciation. If the accompanying short vowel is either *fatha* or *damma*, then ء *hamza* is written above ا *alif* and the vowel is in turn written above *hamza*.

OBSERVE

'*uthbut* أُثْبُت  '*ant* أَنْت

If the accompanying short vowel is *kasra*, then ء is written *below* ا and the vowel is in turn written below ء.

OBSERVE

'*inba:t* إِنْبات

It is important to remember that the ا which always accompanies initial ء is *not* pronounced – it serves simply as a silent support, or 'seat'.

**Writing instructions** To make the glottal stop symbol *hamza* write a very small 'c' shape with the addition of a short right to left base stroke:

**Reading and writing practice**

Ⓣ □ Read and pronounce the words on page 58 with reference to the tape.

□ Trace and copy the examples. Complete the basic word shape, then go back and put in first the dots, and then the short vowels, *suku:n*, and *hamza*, all from *right to left*. Pronounce each word several times as soon as you have completed it.

| أَنا | إِنْبات | أُثْبُت | أَنْتَ |
|---|---|---|---|
| 4 *'ana:* | 3 *'inba:t* | 2 *'uthbut* | 1 *'ant* |

| إِبْثاث | أُنْثَوِي | إِثْبات | أَبو |
|---|---|---|---|
| 8 *'ibtha:th* | 7 *'unthawi:* | 6 *'ithba:t* | 5 *'abu:* |

***Pronunciation drill*** Ⓣ **Contrast the short and long vowel sounds /a/ and /a:/ /u/ and /u:/**

| /u:/ | | /u/ | | /a:/ | | /a/ |
|---|---|---|---|---|---|---|
| توت | ← | تُت | 7 | باب | ← | بَب |
| نون | ← | نُن | 8 | بان | ← | بَن |
| ثوب | ← | ثُب | 9 | تاب | ← | تَب |
| بون | ← | بُن | 10 | ثان | ← | ثَن |
| ثُبوت | ← | ثُبُت | 11 | بوّاب | ← | بَوَّب |
| بُتون | ← | بُتُن | 12 | ثانى | ← | ثَنِي |

# Unit 4

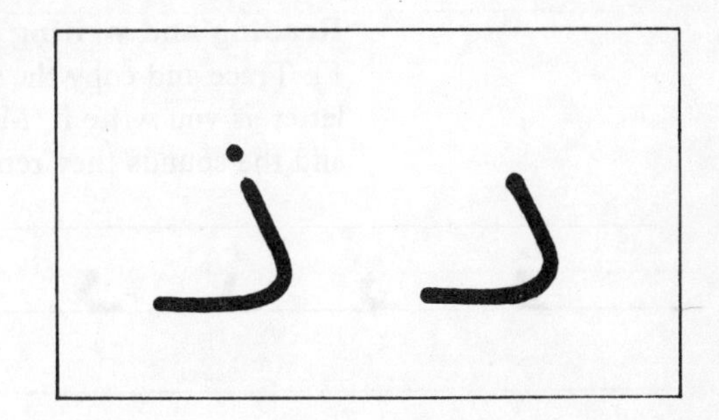

The basic shape shared by the isolated forms of these two letters is: د

The basic shape alone is *da:l.*

It is pronounced like the 'd' in '*d*eep', and is transliterated as /d/.

The basic shape with one dot above is *dha:l.* ذ

It is pronounced like the 'th' in '*th*is', and transliterated as /dh/. This is the second instance of Arabic using only one letter to represent a sound for which English needs two.

Notice that Arabic uses ث *tha:'* and ذ *dha:l*

for two sounds which are represented as a single combination of letters in English:

'th' in '*th*ick' is ث *tha:'*, transliterated as /th̆/.

'th' in '*th*is' is ذ *dha:l*, transliterated as /dh/.

## *Isolated form*

This is the basic shape shared by these two letters in their isolated forms:

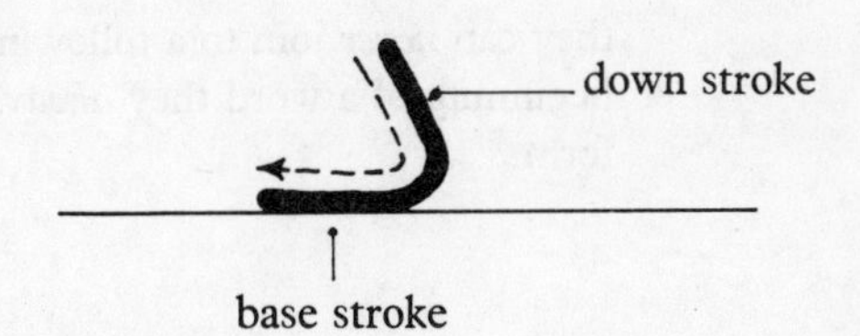


**Writing instructions** The down stroke and the base stroke are roughly the same length – about twice as long as the initial down stroke of ب *ba:'* – and meet at a rounded angle, with the base stroke sitting on the line and the down stroke leaning slightly to the left of upright.

The two letters are distinguished from one another by a single dot.

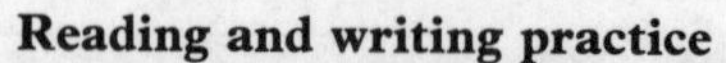

**Reading and writing practice**

☐ Trace and copy the models below, saying the name of each letter as you write it. Make sure you can identify both letters and the sounds they represent.

☐ Notice the slight variations in size – this is the kind of range you can allow yourself when first writing these letters.

☐ Don't make the down stroke too vertical or too acute, and keep the angle between the down stroke and the base stroke rounded – Arabic handwriting is characterised by its smooth curves and graceful lines.

Look at these two new letters in proportion to the other seven letters you have learned.

☐ Trace and copy the models, paying particular attention to the position of each letter in relation to the line.

☐ Say the name of each letter aloud as you write it, always working from *right to left* across the page.

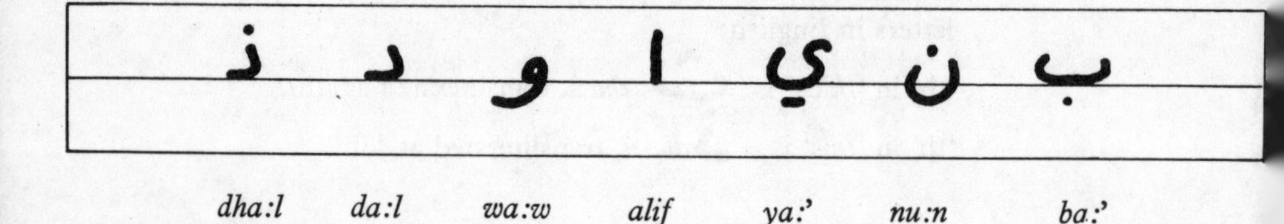


## Initial position

These letters, like ا *alif* and و *wa:w*, are 'non-connectors' – they can *never* join to a following letter. When they occur at the beginning of a word they *always* stand alone in their isolated form.

OBSERVE

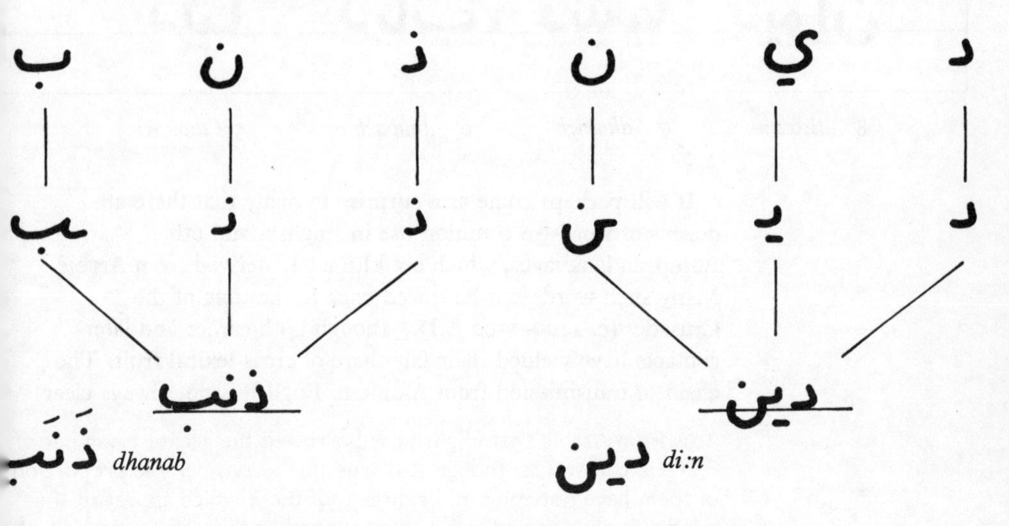


**Writing instructions** Same as for isolated form.

**Reading and writing practice**

Ⓣ ☐ Pronounce the words below with reference to the tape.
Remember that medial ي *ya:'* and و *wa:w* may be either the consonants /y/ and /w/ – (see examples 5 and 8), or the long vowels /i:/ and /u:/ – (see examples 1, 4 and 7).

☐ Trace and copy the models, pronouncing each word as soon as you have completed it. Don't squash non-connectors too close to following letters, but on the other hand don't let too much of a gap open up.

☐ Monitor your examples after every two or three efforts. Take the size of the writing in the book as a rough guide, but experiment with your own writing until you arrive at a size which you personally feel comfortable with, and then try to be consistent. Most important of all at this stage is to keep the letters within any one word in proportion to one another.

☐ Keep practising until you can consistently reproduce a reasonable copy of the models.

| دون | ذات | ذَنَب | دين |
|---|---|---|---|
| 4 *du:n* | 3 *dha:t* | 2 *dhanab* | 1 *di:n* |

دُنْيا ذُباب ذَنيب ديوان

8 *di:wa:n* 7 *dhani:b* 6 *dhuba:b* 5 *dunya:*

It will perhaps come as a surprise to many that there are dozens of words in common use in English, and other European languages, which are ultimately derived from Arabic. Many such words can be traced back to the time of the Crusades (c. 1100–1300 A.D.), though both earlier and later contacts have yielded their fair share of cross-lexical fruit. The chain of transmission from Arabic to English is not always clear:

'It is from Arabic that English has borrowed the greatest number of Eastern loan-words, though it is true that a considerable proportion of them have not come to us direct. Of those which appear in the middle English period, most have reached us through French (which often learnt them from Spanish), some perhaps directly from Spanish. The increasing trade with the Arabic speaking peoples of North Africa during the later fourteenth century, and in the sixteenth century trade and exploration further East gave us a new source of Arabic loans: the Arabic element in the dialects of India.' (Mary S. Serjeantson, *A history of foreign words in English*, page 213).

Similarly, Arabic has adopted a large number of words from English and other European languages. Such words, along with other points of interest, are briefly annotated wherever they occur in the writing practice sections of this and subsequent Units. We have included these items not as an exercise in vocabulary acquisition, but in an attempt to make learning the Arabic script more relevant and interesting by showing it used to write words which will for the most part be familiar to you as an English speaker.

**Points of interest** (The numbered points of interest correspond to the numbered examples in the writing practice. Transliteration is only given in the points of interest when the Arabic word used involves some modification of the corresponding writing practice example.)

8 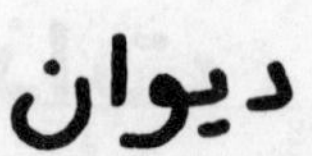

Originally a Persian word adopted by the Arabs with the meaning 'council of state; council chamber; office'. Passed into

English c. 1600 and today is used to describe a couch or kind of bed. Also entered several European languages meaning 'customs; customs house' (French 'douane'; Spanish 'aduana'; Italian 'dogana').

ديواني

*di:wa:ni:* is derived from the above and is the name of a style of Arabic script used by the Ottoman Turks for official court correspondence, and still used today for decorative purposes.

The word ديواني *di:wa:ni:* written in 'diwani' script.

**Medial position** These letters are non-connectors and can never join to a following letter. When they occur in the middle of a word they join to the preceding letter only.

OBSERVE

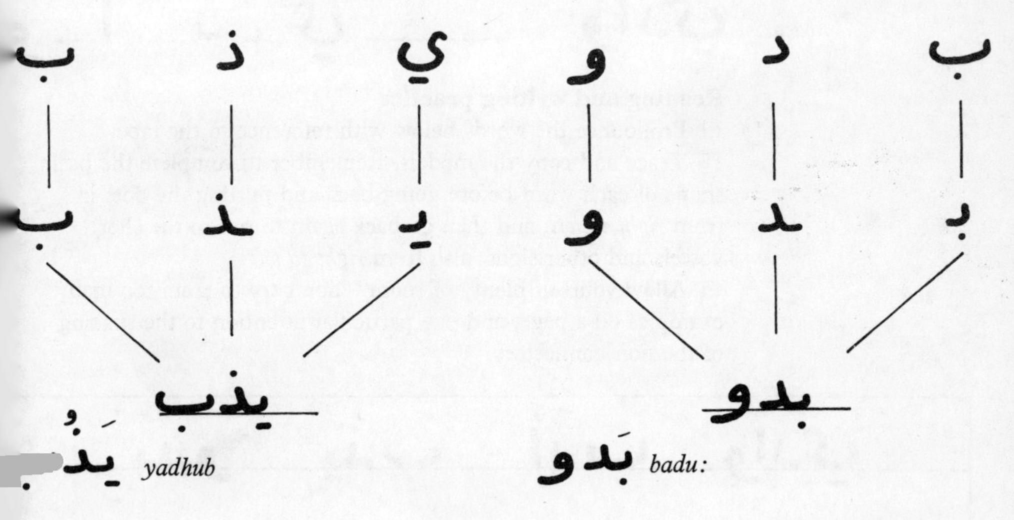

**Writing instructions** Lead into an up stroke the height of isolated ذ / ـذ with the connecting line from the preceding letter, then retrace the down stroke over the upstroke almost to the line before veering away to the left to form the base stroke:

If you retrace the down stroke to the line before leading into the base stroke, the resultant shape (though perfectly legible) will be too stylised and angular.

Avoid this: 

Remember that if any two non-connectors appear one after the other within a word, the second of them will always remain unconnected and in its isolated form.

In a word containing three letters of which the first two are non-connectors, *all three* will stand alone in their isolated forms:

*'adab* 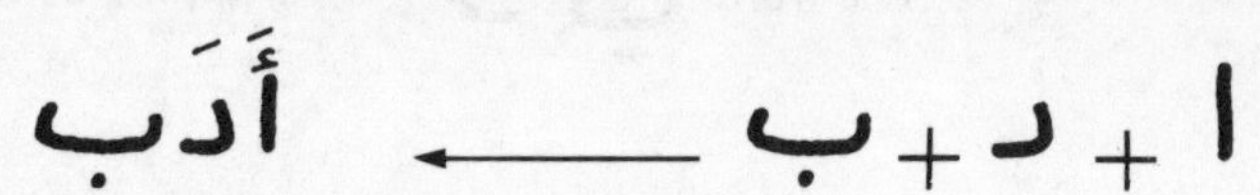

Similarly, in four letter words, in which the first three letters are non-connectors, *all four* will stand alone in their isolated forms:

*wa:di:* وادي ← ي + د + ا + و

**Reading and writing practice**

Ⓣ ☐ Pronounce the words below with reference to the tape.

☐ Trace and copy the models. Remember to complete the basic shape of each word before going back and putting the dots in from *right to left*, and then go back again to put in the short vowels and other signs, also from *right to left*.

☐ Allow yourself plenty of room – don't try to cram too many examples on a page, and pay particular attention to the spacing of the non-connectors.

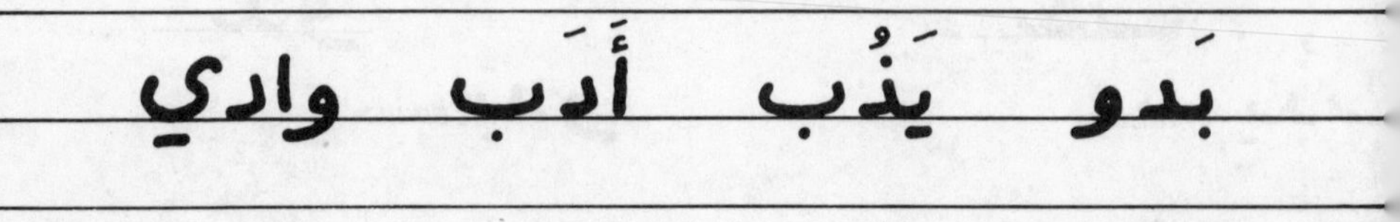

4 *wa:di:* 3 *'adab* 2 *yadhub* 1 *badu:*

بادِن تَذْويب بَدين تَدْوين

8 *tadwi:n* 7 *badi:n* 6 *tadhwi:b* 5 *ba:din*

**Points of interest:**

1 بَدو

'desert, nomads', from which English 'bedouin' is derived.

4 وادي

'river (bed)', from which English 'wadi' is derived. Also passed into Spanish as part of the name of the river 'Guadalquivir' – a corruption of the Arabic *al-wa:di: al-kabi:r*, 'the big river'.

***Final position***

The final forms of these two letters are in all respects identical to their medial forms.

OBSERVE

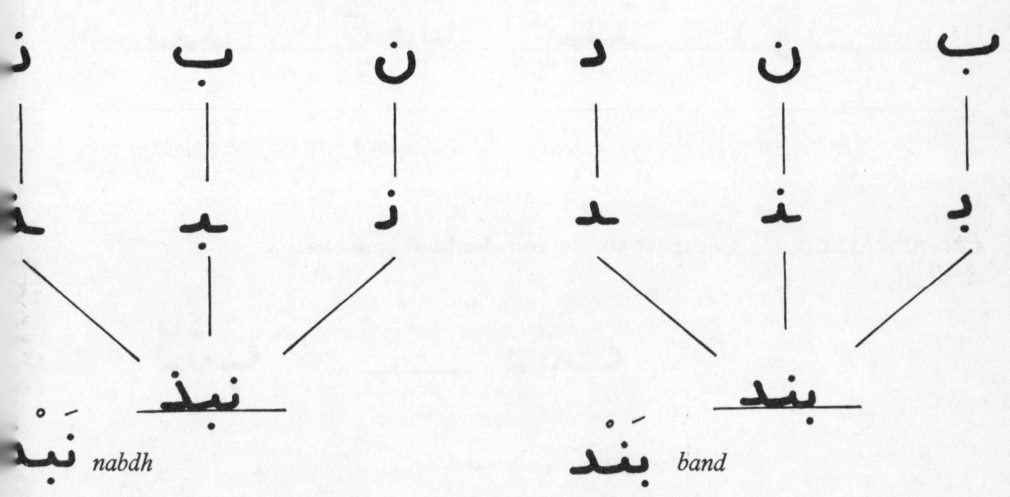


**Writing instructions** Same as for medial form. If final ـذ / ـد are preceded by a non-connector, they stand alone in their isolated form.

*wada:d* وداد ← د + ا + د + و

*'inba:dh* إنْباذ ← ذ + ا + ب + ن + ا

**Reading and writing practice**

Ⓣ ☐ Pronounce the words below with reference to the tape.

☐ Trace and copy the models. Make sure that you are identifying each letter correctly by paying particular attention to the number and position of the dots.

☐ Check your examples with the models in the book after every two or three attempts, and make especially sure that you haven't inadvertently joined a non-connector to a following letter.

| إنْباذ | وَداد | نَبْذ | بَنْد |
|---|---|---|---|
| 4 *'inba:dh* | 3 *wada:d* | 2 *nabdh* | 1 *band* |

| دود | نَبيذ | تَبْديد | بَدَّد |
|---|---|---|---|
| 8 *du:d* | 7 *nabi:dh* | 6 *tabdi:d* | 5 *baddad* |

**Pronunciation drill** Ⓣ

**Contrast single and doubled consonants.**

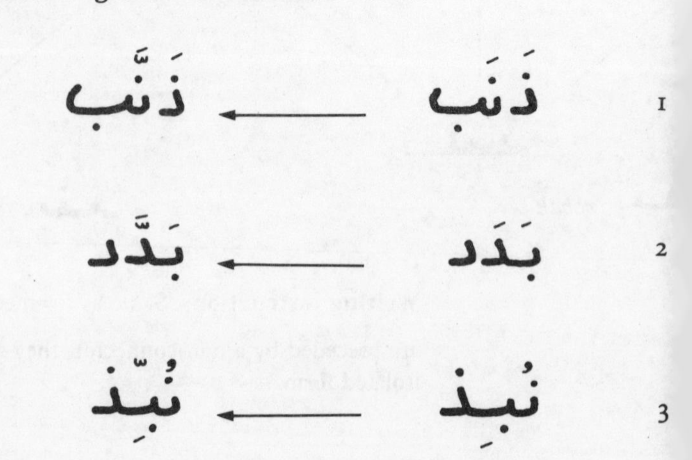

4 نَواب ← نَوّاب

5 دُنَت ← دُنَّت

6 بَيَن ← بَيَّن

7 ثُبِت ← ثُبِّت

8 بُذُب ← بُذُّب

# Unit 5

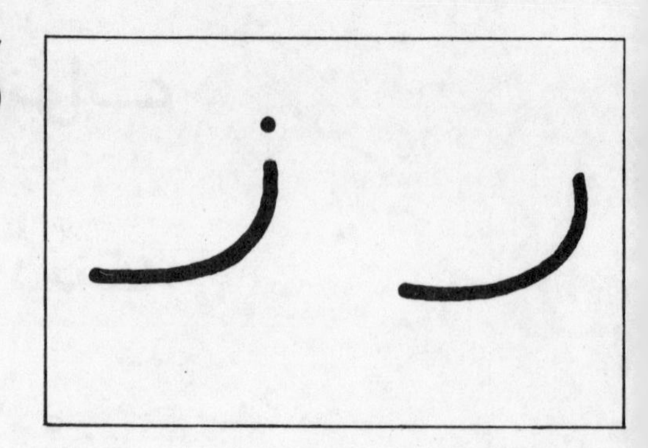

The basic shape shared by the isolated forms of these two letters is ر

The basic shape alone is *ra:'*.
It is transliterated as /r/ and pronounced by tapping the tongue once quickly behind the upper gum. This sound has no equivalent in English but does occur frequently in other European languages, as in Spanish 'caro' ('dear'), and 'pero' ('but').

It is very important for you to pay close attention to the tape drills and/or your teacher's pronunciation in order to train your ear and tongue to reproduce this sound.

The basic shape with one dot above is *za:y*. ز

It is pronounced like the 'z' in 'zip', and transliterated as /z/.

## Isolated form

This is the basic shape shared by these two letters in their isolated forms:

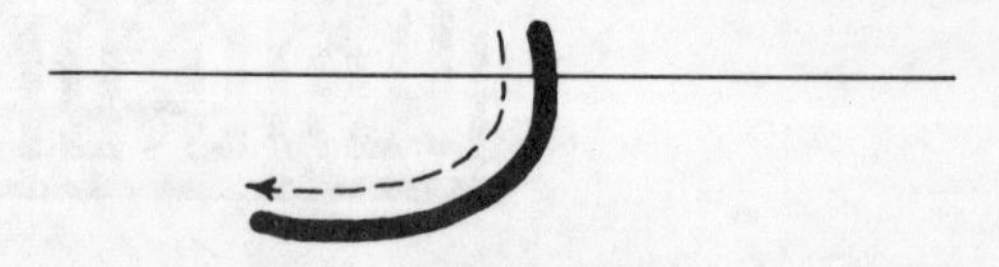

**Writing instructions** The ر/ز shape is identical to و *wa:w*, but without the 'head'. Use the same technique suggested for و to get the curve of ر and ز. Press firmly on the page at the point where you begin the letter, just above the line, then allow your pen to flick down and across to the left in a controlled flourish below the line.

These two new letters are distinguished from one another only by a single dot above the basic shape.

**Reading and writing practice** Trace and copy the models below, saying the name of each letter aloud as you write it. Keep your examples in constant relation to the line. Practise as long as it takes for you to consistently produce a fair copy of the models in the book. Make sure you can identify both letters and the sounds they represent.

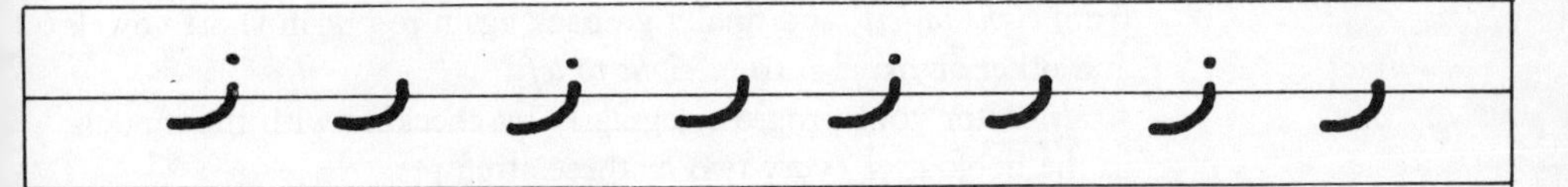

Look at these two new letters in proportion to the other nine letters you have learned.

***Initial position*** These letters complete the group of six non-connectors in the Arabic alphabet.

Like ا *alif*, و *wa:w*, د *da:l* and ذ *dha:l* they can *never* join to a following letter. When they occur at the beginning of a word they *always* stand alone in their isolated form.

OBSERVE

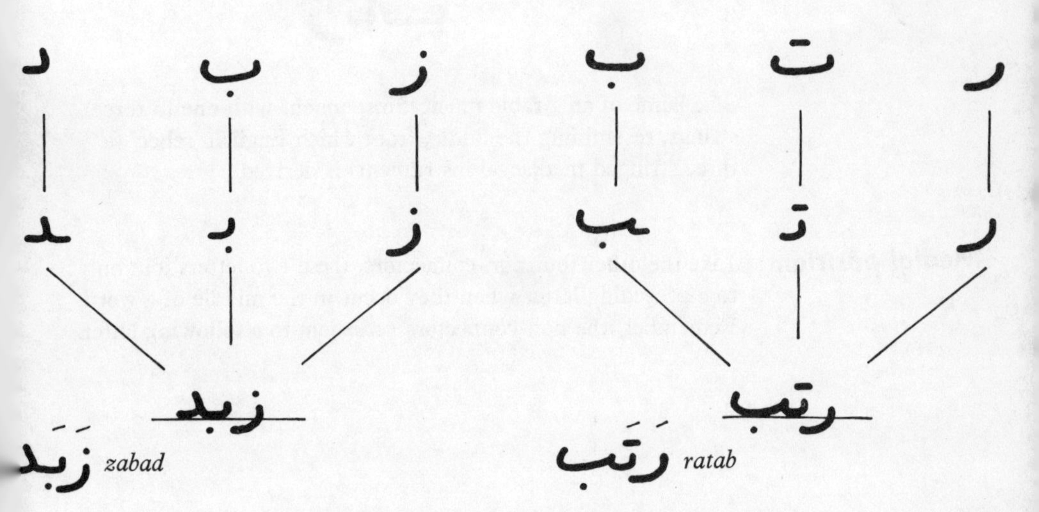


**Writing instructions** Same as for isolated form.

**Reading and writing practice**

Ⓣ ☐ Pronounce the words below with reference to the tape.

☐ Trace and copy the models. Don't leave too wide a gap between a non-connector and a following letter, and try to keep the letters within any one word in proportion to one another.

☐ Remember to write each word in three stages: first complete the basic shape of the word, then go back and put in the dots from *right to left*, and finally go back again to put in short vowels and other signs, also from *right to left*.

☐ Monitor your progress regularly by checking with the models in the book after every two or three attempts.

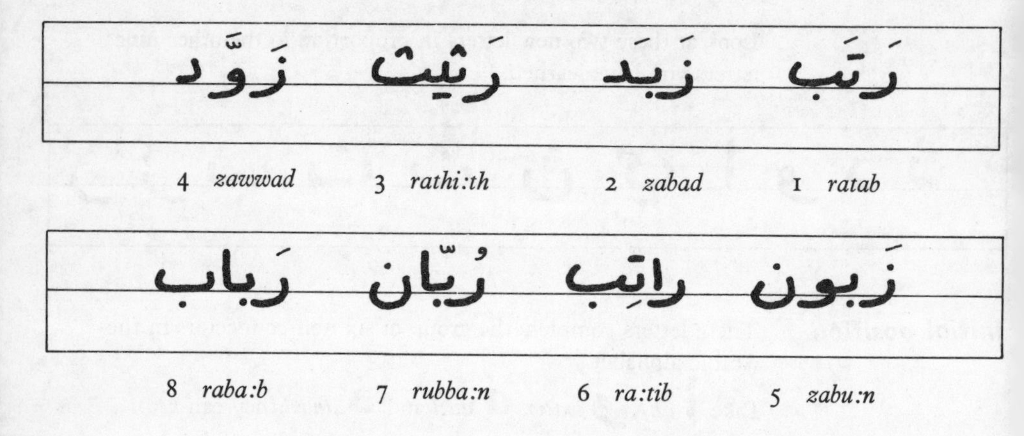


**Points of interest**

8

The name of an Arabic musical instrument with one to three strings, resembling the fiddle, from which English 'rebec' (a three stringed mediaeval instrument) is derived.

**Medial position**

Like the other four non-connectors, these two letters join only to a preceding letter when they occur in the middle of a word. Remember, the non-connectors *never* join to a following letter.

Observe

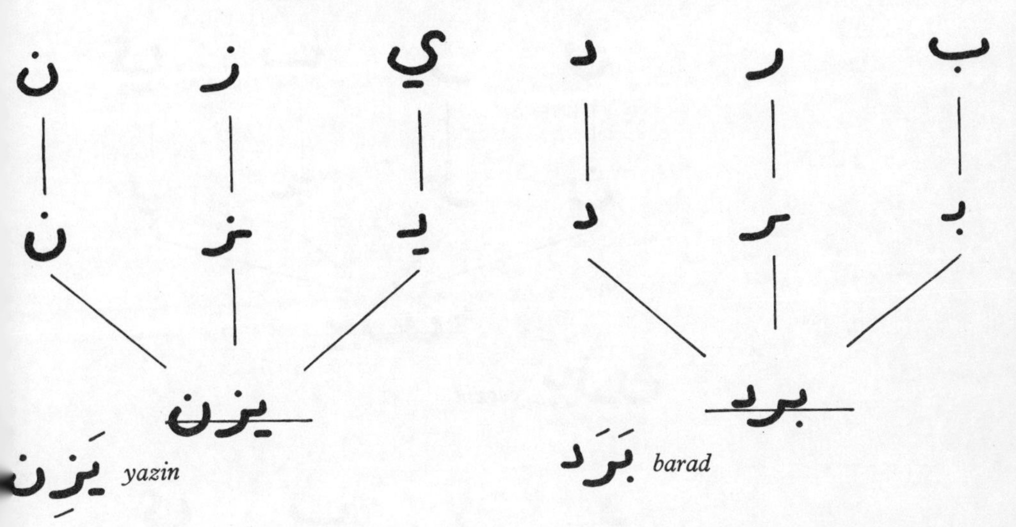

**Writing instructions** Lead into the top of ر/ز with the connecting line from the preceding letter, then complete the shape in a controlled flourish to the left below the line.

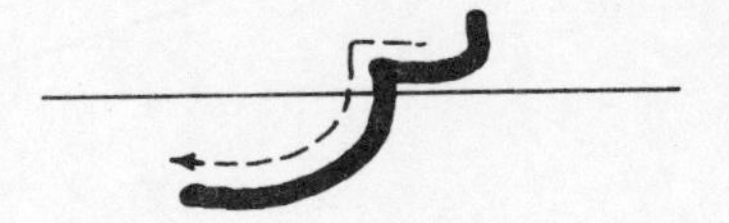

There are two other possible ways of writing the ر/ز shape when it occurs in the middle of a word.

1 **Bridging** When medial ر/ز follow a medial

(i.e. in a word of four letters or more), the 'bridging' modification occurs.

OBSERVE

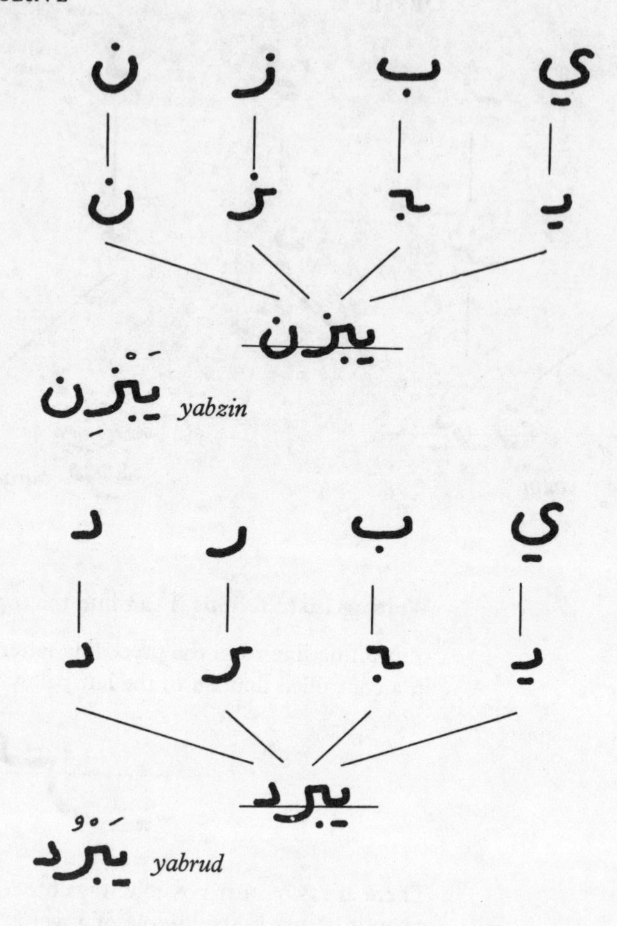


**Writing instructions** Lead into the up stroke of the medial letter as usual, but instead of coming back down to the line, lead straight into ز/ر from the top of the up stroke:

This bridging technique is by no means compulsory. The examples from the word diagrams above can be quite acceptably written without any alteration to the medial form:

Bridging is, however, a very common feature of handwritten Arabic and will therefore be used throughout this book. Practise it extensively – an ability to use it with ease will help you on your way to developing a natural and more cursive style. Note the similarity with bridging before final ن *nu:n* and ي *ya:'* (see Unit 2, page 46).

2 When medial ز/ر follow a non-connector, they stand alone in their isolated form.

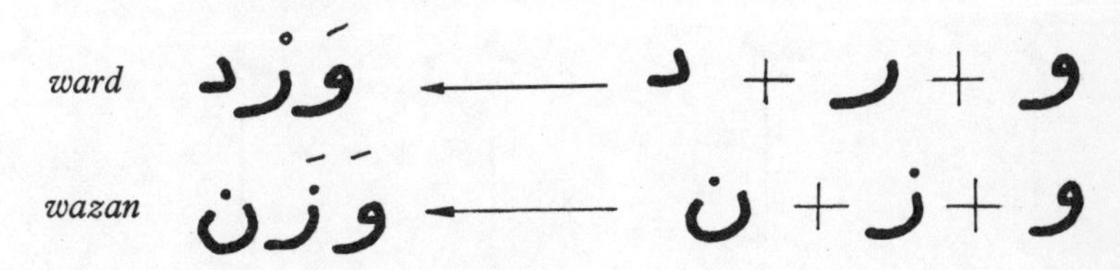


**Reading and writing practice**

Ⓣ □ Pronounce the words below with reference to the tape.

رّ /rr/ is a 'trill'. This sound does not occur in English, but is found in other European languages e.g. Spanish 'pe*rr*o' ('dog'). In pronouncing examples 5, 7 and 10 below, pay particular attention to the tape and/or your teacher's pronunciation.

□ Trace and copy the models – practise the bridging technique. Make sure you don't inadvertently join a non-connector to a following letter.

By now you should be establishing a more or less consistent size of handwriting. Take the size of the writing in the book as a rough guide – if your examples are consistently larger than the models in the book, scale your writing down a little.

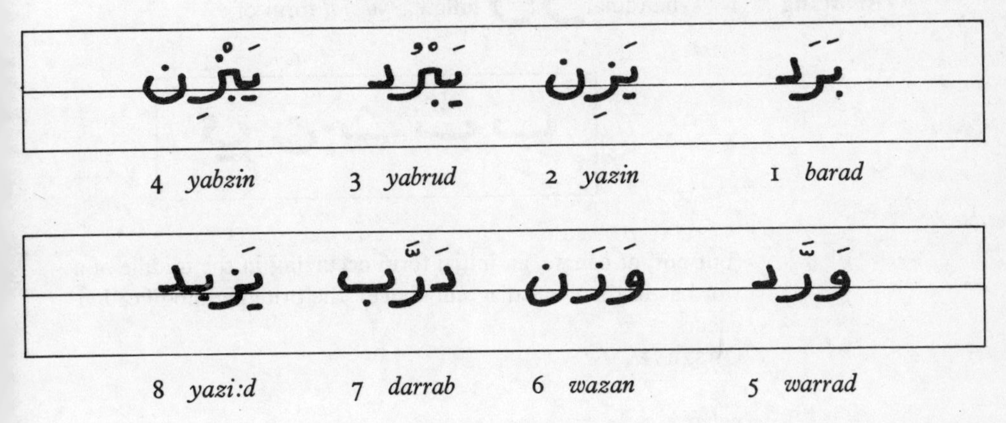

| تُراب | تَدْرِيب | بَرَّد | تَرَدُّد |
|---|---|---|---|

12 *tura:b* 11 *tadri:b* 10 *barrad* 9 *taraddud*

**Final position** When these letters occur at the end of a word they join to the preceding letter, retaining the shape of their medial form.

OBSERVE

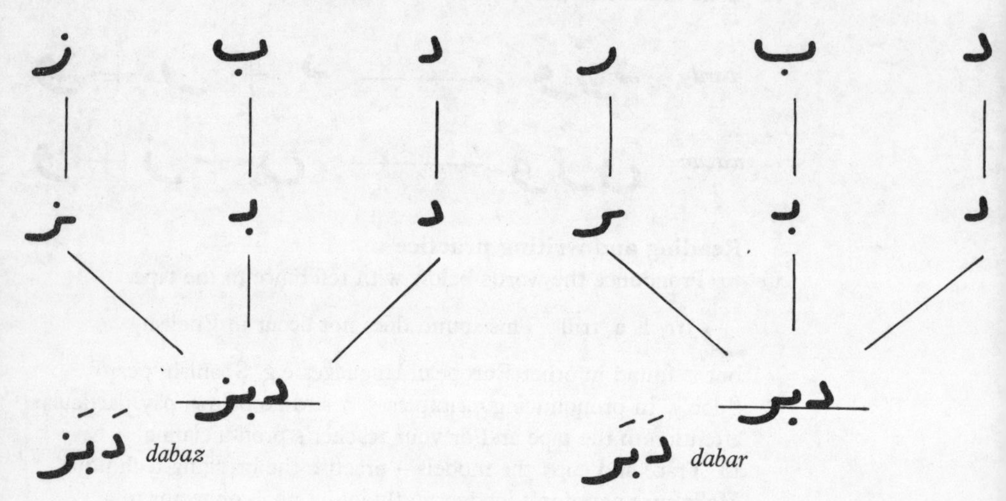


**Writing instructions** Same as for medial form.

As in the medial form, there are two other possible ways of writing the ز/ر shape when it occurs at the end of a word:

**Bridging** 1 When final ز/ر follow a *medial* form of

ب ت ث ن ي

(but not, of course, an initial form occurring in the middle of a word as in the word diagram above), the bridging modification occurs.

OBSERVE

*nabar*

ن + ب + ر ⟵ نَبَر

*nabaz* نَبَز ← ز + ب + ن

2 When final ز/ر follow a non-connector, they stand alone in their isolated form.

OBSERVE

*na:dir* نادِر ← ر + د + ا + ن

*ba:riz* بارِز ← ز + ر + ا + ب

**Reading and writing practice**

Ⓣ ☐ Pronounce each word below with reference to the tape.

☐ Trace and copy the models. Don't forget to complete the basic shape of a word before going back to put in first the dots, and then the short vowels, *shadda*, and *suku:n*, all from *right to left*.

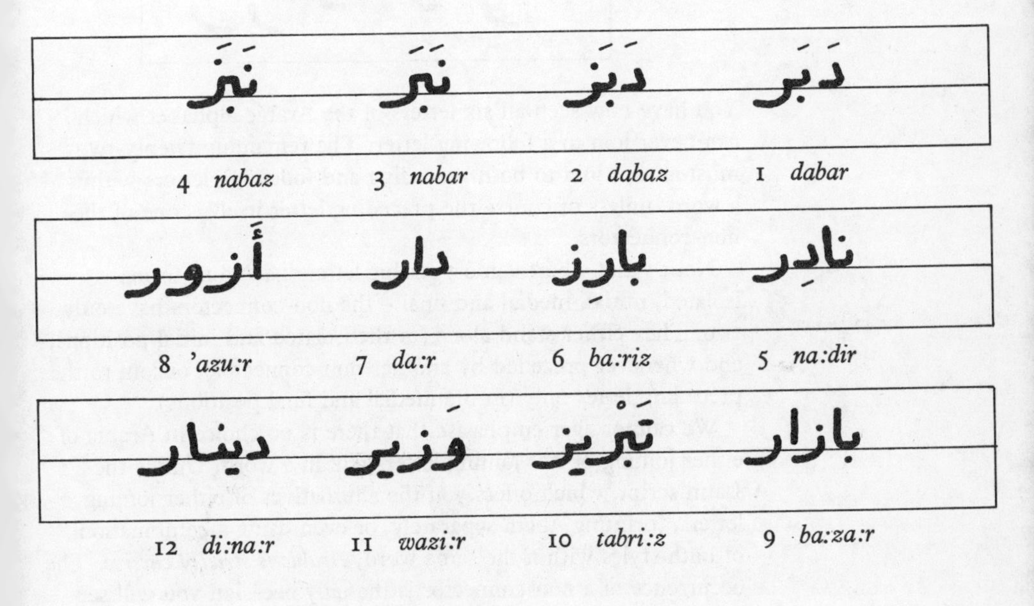


**Points of interest**

9 بازار

'bazaar' – passed into English from Persian via Turkish or Arabic.

10

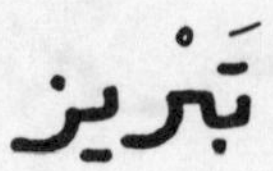

'Tabriz' – a city in North West Iran, the capital of Azerbaijan province.

11

'minister' – passed into English via Turkish as 'vizir'.

12

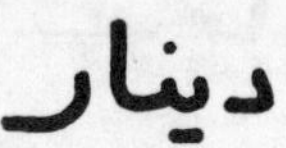

'dinar'. Unit of currency in various parts of the Arab world. Originally a Latin word which passed into Arabic. Note similarity with Spanish 'dinero' ('money').

## The six non-connectors

You have now seen all six letters of the Arabic alphabet which can never join to a following letter. The remaining twenty-two must always join to both preceding and following letters within a word, unless of course the preceding letter itself is one of the non-connectors.

Notice that whereas most Arabic letters have four forms – isolated, initial, medial and final – the non-connectors have only two. They either stand alone (in the isolated and initial positions, and whenever preceded by another non-connector), or join to the preceding letter only (in the medial and final positions).

We cannot over emphasise that there is no choice in Arabic of either joining or not joining letters within a word. Unlike the Latin script, which offers you the alternatives of either joining letters, 'printing' them separately, or even using a combination of both styles within the same word, *Arabic is strictly cursive.* The occurrence of a non-connector is the only occasion you will see a space between two consecutive letters within a word, and the only time you should take your pen off the paper in the middle of writing a word.

**_Pronunciation drill_** Ⓣ

**Contrast** ر **and** رّ

1 دَرَب ← دَرَّب

2 نُرُب ← نُرُّب

3 بَرَد ← بَرَّد

4 وَرَد ← وَرَّد

5 وَرِث ← وَرِّث

6 بَرَز ← بَرَّز

# Unit 6

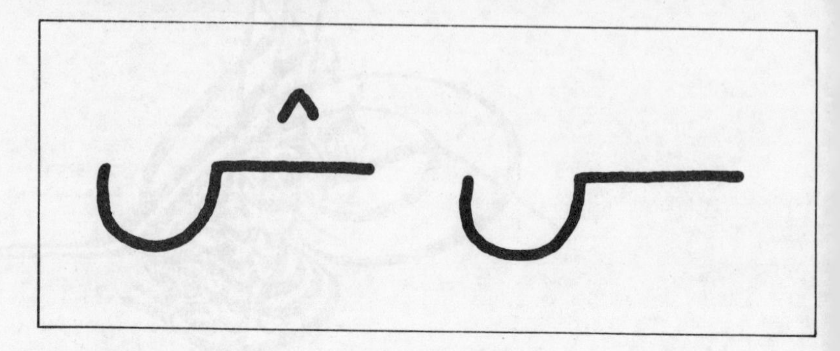

The basic shape shared by the isolated form of these two letters is: س
The basic shape alone is *si:n*.
It is pronounced like the 's' in '*s*ock', and transliterated as /s/.
The basic shape with three dots above is *shi:n*. ش
It is pronounced like the 'sh' in '*sh*unt', and transliterated as /sh/.

This is another instance of English using two letters to represent a sound for which Arabic needs only one – compare with ث and ذ .

## *Isolated form*

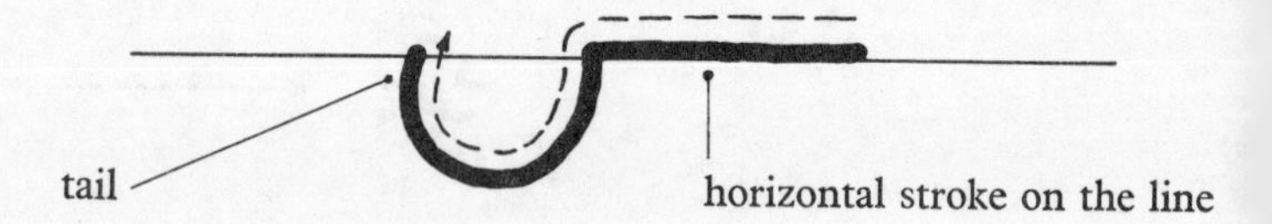


**Writing instructions** The س / ش shape has two elements – a straight horizontal stroke lying on the line, about the same length as the base stroke of isolated ب and a tail the same shape and size as ن descending below the line. The two letters are distinguished from one another by the dot stroke / ^ /.

**Reading and writing practice** Trace and copy the models on page 79, saying the name of each letter aloud as you write it. Remember to write the dot stroke / ^ / from *right to left*.

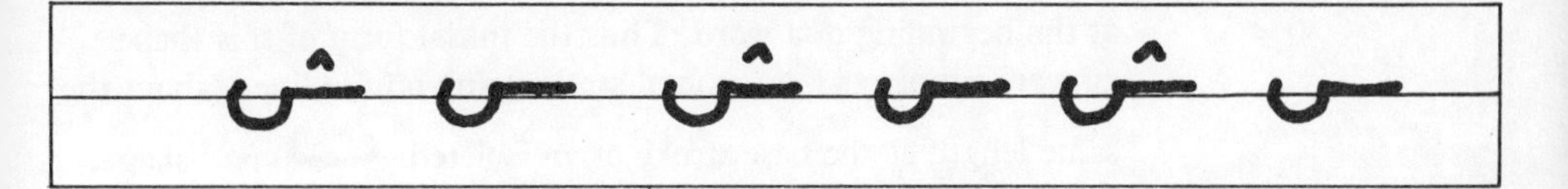

Look at these two new letters in proportion to the letters you have already seen.

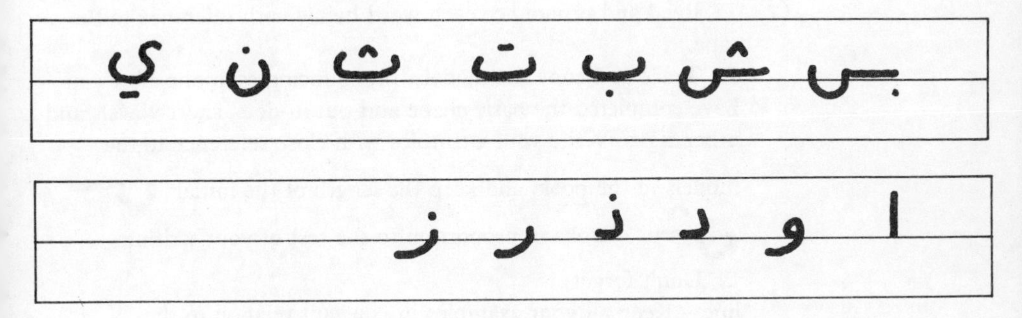

**Initial position** When these letters occur at the beginning of a word, they lose their 'tail' and join to the following letter, appearing simply as a straight line.

OBSERVE

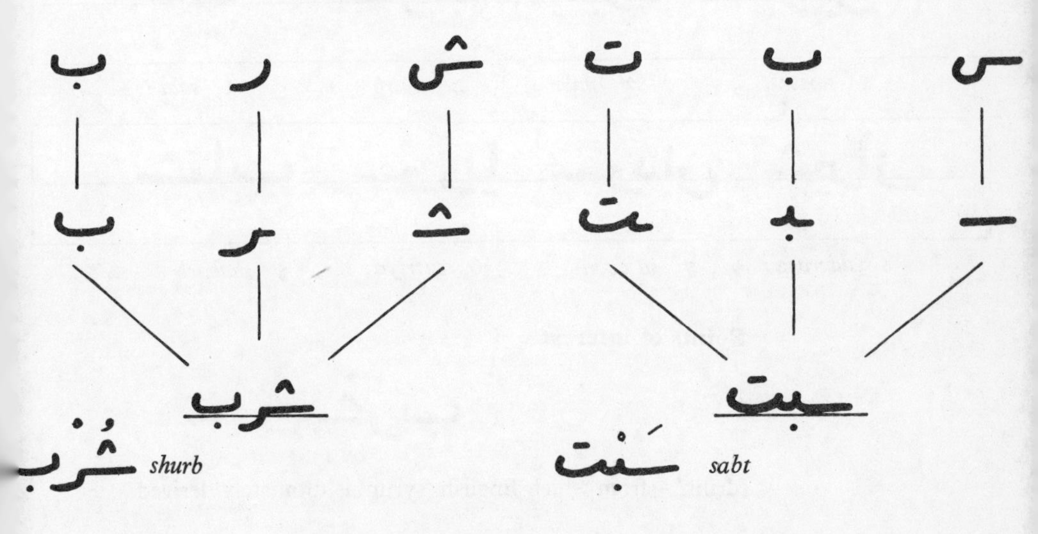

شُرْب *shurb*

سَبْت *sabt*

**Writing instructions** س *si:n* and ش *shi:n* are the first letters you have seen with a tail (apart from the non-connectors ز ر و)

Letters with tails in their isolated form lose them when they occur at the beginning of a word. Thus the initial form of this shape appears simply as a horizontal stroke lying on the line – about the same length as the base stroke of an isolated ب *ba:'* shape, and joining to a following letter.

**Reading and writing practice**

(T) □ Read and pronounce each word below with reference to the tape.

□ Trace and copy the models, pronouncing each one after you have completed the basic shape and put in dots, short vowels and other signs. Write your examples with close reference to the models in the book, and keep the length of the initial سـ / شـ stroke in proportion to the rest of your writing.

□ Don't forget:

line – Keep all your examples in constant relation to the horizontal line.

size – Keep all the letters in proportion to one another.

dots – Have you put the right number in the right place?

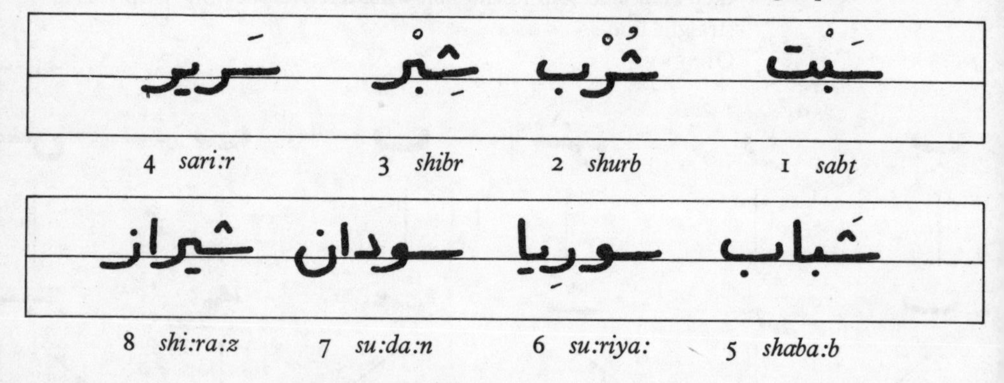


**Points of interest**

2 شُرْب

'drink' – from which English 'syrup' is ultimately derived.

6 سورِيا

'Syria'

7 سودان

'Sudan'

8 شیراز

'Shiraz' – a city in North West Iran.

**Medial position** When these letters occur in the middle of a word they retain the shape of their initial form and join to both the preceding and following letters.

OBSERVE

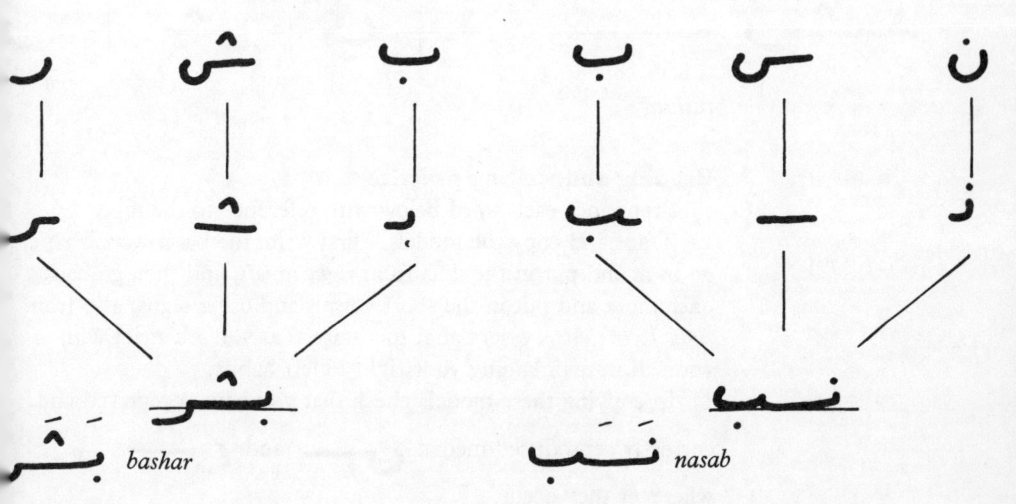


**Writing instructions** Letters with tails always lose them in their medial forms. (except for the non-connectors ز ر و ).

Lead into the horizontal stroke of the medial form with the connecting line from the preceding letter. It is the same length as the initial form, and appears simply as a horizontal stroke lying on the line.

The importance of maintaining a constant and proportionate length for the horizontal stroke of medial س / ش is illustrated by the examples on page 82. Apart from the short vowel signs (which are unmarked in most situations), the only distinguishing feature between two words with completely different meanings, is the length of the medial line.

*bar* بَر *basar* بَسَر

When preceded by one of the non-connectors medial ـسـ and ـشـ appear in their initial form and join to the following letter only:

د + س + ت + و + ر ← دُسْتور

*dustu:r*

ر + ش + ي + د ← رَشيد

*rashi:d*

**Reading and writing practice**

Ⓣ ☐ Pronounce each word below with reference to the tape.

☐ Trace and copy the models – first write the basic word shape, go back and put in the dots from *right to left*, and then go back once more and put in the short vowels and other signs, also from *right to left*. It is essential at this stage that you are strict with yourself in maintaining your right to left habits.

☐ In copying these models check that you have recognised and correctly reproduced medial ـسـ and ـشـ wherever they occur.

☐ Make sure that you don't inadvertently join a non-connector to a following letter.

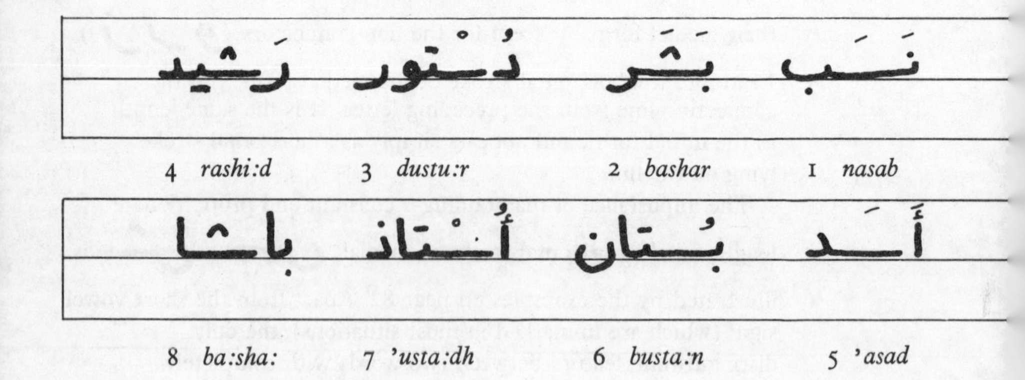

## Points of interest

4 رَشيد

A name well-known in the West through 'Harun ar-Rashid', the Abbasid Caliph who ruled the Islamic Empire from Baghdad at the height of its wealth and splendour (786–809).

7 أُسْتاذ

'master, teacher, professor', passed into Spanish as the polite form of address 'usted'.

8 باشا

'pasha', an honorific title which passed from Turkish into English and Arabic. Both English and Turkish have a 'p' sound, Arabic does not, and substitutes /b/ in words it adopts from other languages.

**Final position**

When these letters occur at the end of a word they have the same shape as their isolated form but join to the preceding letter. OBSERVE

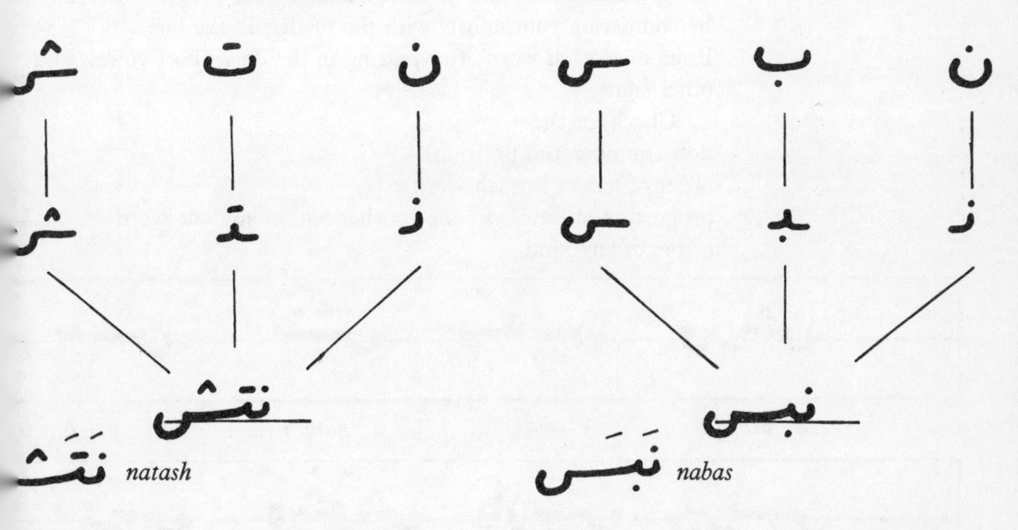

**Writing instructions** Letters which have a tail in their isolated form lose the tail in the initial and medial forms, but regain it in the final form. Lead into the horizontal stroke of final ـس / ـش with the connecting line from the preceding letter. Make the length of the horizontal stroke the same length as the horizontal stroke in the initial and medial forms and add the tail to complete the letter. It is very important to maintain a constant length for the horizontal stroke of initial, medial and final ـس and ـش .

When preceded by one of the non-connectors final ـس and ـش stand alone in their isolated form:

*suds* سُدْس ← س + د + س

*warash* وَرَش ← ش + ر + و

**Reading and writing practice**

Ⓣ ☐ Read and pronounce each word with reference to the tape.
☐ Trace and copy the models. Monitor your progress carefully by comparing your efforts with the models in the book. Pronounce each word after putting in the dots, short vowels and other signs.
☐ Check for the
dots (number and position)
order of letters in each word
proportion of letters to one another within any one word
errors of any kind

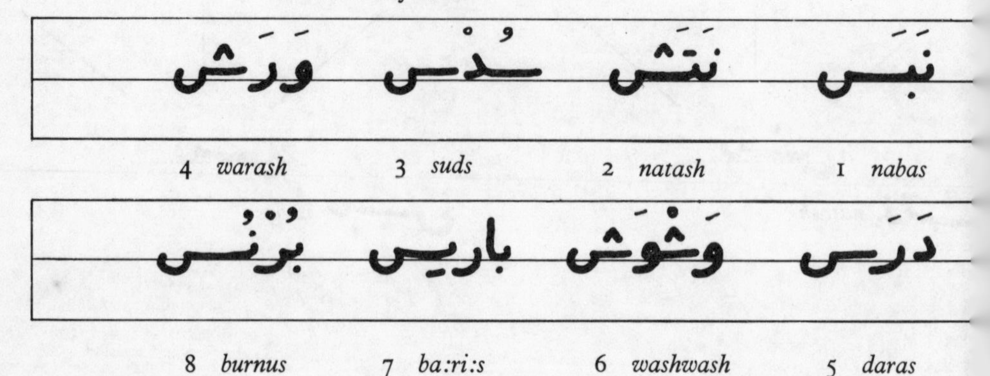

**Points of interest**

7 باريس

'Paris' – notice again that Arabic substitutes /b/ for 'p' in words adopted from other languages.

8

A hooded cloak, worn particularly in North Africa, from which English 'burnous' is derived.

***Note on vowels – diphthongs*** Ⓣ

You are already familiar with the three short vowels (represented by the signs *fatha*, *kasra* and *damma*) and the three long vowels (represented by the letters ا *alif*, ي *ya:'* and و *wa:w*). There are two further vowel sounds in Arabic, represented by combinations of *fatha* with ي and و.

They are diphthongs.

i) The first of these diphthongs is pronounced somewhere between the 'a' in 'f*a*te' and the 'i' in 'b*i*te'. It is represented by *fatha* followed by ي with *suku:n*, and is transliterated as /ay/.

OBSERVE

*bi:t* بيت

Contrast the pronunciation of the same combination of letters with *fatha* on the ب *ba:'* and *suku:n* on the ي *ya:'*.

*bayt*

ii) The second diphthong is pronounced somewhat like the 'ow' in 'how'. It is represented by *fatha* followed by و *wa:w* with *suku:n*, and is transliterated as /aw/.

OBSERVE

*thu:r*

Contrast the pronunciation of this same combination of letters with *fatha* on the ث *tha:'* and *suku:n* on the و *wa:w*.

*thawr*

**Printed Arabic**

Up to now you have seen only handwritten forms of letters of the Arabic alphabet. In this Unit we are going to introduce a printed style of Arabic which is commonly used in books, newspapers and magazines. There is a wide variety of Arabic printed styles, and in this and succeeding Units the models from the reading and writing practice sections will be shown again on the drill page at the end of the Unit in a typical style of print. Certain other items will also appear in print within the Units. These examples of printed Arabic are intended for reading practice *only*. Don't attempt to use the typeset forms for writing practice – they contain certain features which are rarely used in handwriting.

There are differences between the typeset and handwritten forms of some letters, but they should not pose any problems. This chart shows the isolated forms of the letters you have learned so far, in both handwriting and print:

| handwritten | printed | handwritten | printed |
|---|---|---|---|
| د | د | ب | ب |
| ذ | ذ | ت | ت |
| ر | ر | ث | ث |
| ز | ز | ن | ن |
| س | س | ي | ي |
| ش | ش | ا | ا |
| | | و | و |

Notice that of the thirteen letters you have learned only ـس and ـش appear significantly different in their printed form. The portion of these two letters which appears as a straight line in handwriting, appears in print as three upright strokes, or 'teeth'. Look at these examples from the writing practice in both handwriting and print:

| | **handwritten** | **printed** |
|---|---|---|
| *shaba:b* | شَباب | شباب |
| *busta:n* | بُسْتان | بستان |
| *ba:ri:s* | باريس | باريس |
| *washwash* | وَشْوَش | وشوش |

The first printing presses in Europe were in operation well before the end of the fifteenth century. Though the first known Arabic press was installed in the Vatican in the early sixteenth century, the process was not introduced into the Arab world until some two hundred years later, probably in Aleppo in 1702. High standards in calligraphy, resistance from professional scribes and restrictions imposed on publishing in some areas are among the reasons for the long period of incubation which followed. By the middle of the ninteenth century, however, printing presses were at last available in many parts of the Arab world, and the dissemination of printed matter increased rapidly, particularly in Egypt (where Napoleon Bonaparte had established a press at the beginning of his 1798 expedition):

'Printed works became easily accessible to a large number of people and the editing and publication of Arabic manuscripts by Western orientalists in Rome, London, Leipzig, Leiden, Copenhagen, Paris and other European cities was extended to Constantinople, Bulaq (Cairo), Beirut, Damascus and other Near Eastern centres. While the publishing industry was restricted in much of the Arab world, it received great encouragement from official circles in Egypt which were independent of the other Arab states. Newspapers and magazines in great numbers were – and still are – the means for disseminating knowledge of current events and historical topics, and also a forum where important social issues have been discussed by the intelligentsia. Many Syrians and Lebanese flocked to Egypt . . . and founded several publications, some of which are flourishing today. Books of all sorts were also on the increase as was the number of publishing houses.' (A. Chejne, *The Arabic language – its role in history*, page 67)

Given below are the examples from Unit 6 printed in a common typeset style without the short vowels indicated. Remember that short vowels are rarely indicated in Arabic; the printed examples throughout this book will give you an opportunity to become familiar with the look of unvowelled printed Arabic. Use them for reading practice, with reference to the tape. You should eventually be able to pronounce the unvowelled printed examples, supplying the short vowels from memory, without reference to either transliteration or the vowelled handwritten examples. Don't be discouraged by the apparent difficulty of this task. You will be surprised how quickly you begin to associate an unvowelled word shape with the full sound of the word. For those who go on to study the language proper, reading unvowelled Arabic will cease to be a problem once you have an appreciation of certain basic structural features of the language.

## *Printed forms of examples from writing practice*

**For reading and pronunciation practice only**

| Final | | Medial | | Initial |
|---|---|---|---|---|
| نبس | 1 | نسب | 1 | سبت |
| نتش | 2 | بشر | 2 | شرب |
| سدس | 3 | دستور | 3 | شبر |
| ورش | 4 | رشيد | 4 | سرير |

| | | |
|---|---|---|
| درس 5 | أسد 5 | شباب 5 |
| وشوش 6 | بستان 6 | سوريا 6 |
| باريس 7 | أستاذ 7 | سودان 7 |
| برنس 8 | باشا 8 | شيراز 8 |

**Pronunciation drill** Ⓣ

**Contrast the long vowels and diphthongs**
**/i:/ and /ay/ /u:/ and /aw/**

| /aw/ | | /u:/ | | /ay/ | | /i:/ | |
|---|---|---|---|---|---|---|---|
| تَوْ ← | | توب | 5 | بَيْت ← | | بيت | 1 |
| ذَوْ ← | | ذوب | 6 | دَيْن ← | | دين | 2 |
| سَـ ← | | سود | 7 | رَيْب ← | | ريب | 3 |
| ثَوْ ← | | ثور | 8 | سَيْر ← | | سير | 4 |

# Unit 7

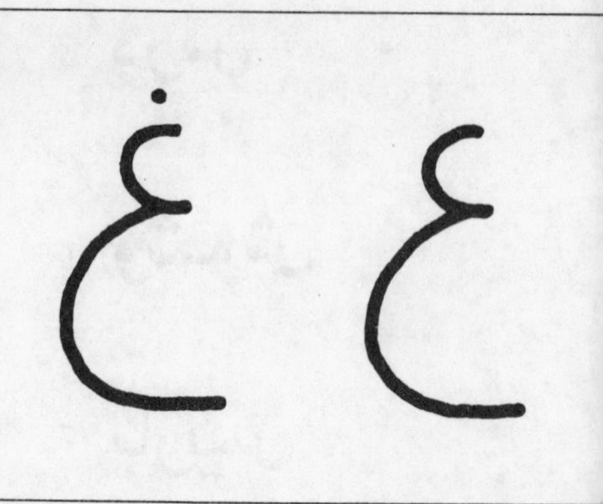

The basic shape shared by the isolated form of these two letters is: ع

The basic shape alone is *$^{c}$ayn.*

ع /*$^{c}$ayn*/ is made by tensing the gagging muscles of the pharynx and producing a strangled vibrating sound deep in the throat. There is no equivalent sound in English, and the only way to achieve an acceptable pronunciation is to make extensive use of the tape drills, or to follow the guidance of your teacher.

ع is transliterated as /$^{c}$/.

Since it would be impossible to transliterate this letter in a way suggestive of its pronunciation, we have chosen to use a symbol which is at least reminiscent of part of the shape of the Arabic letter.

The basic shape with one dot above is *ghayn.* غ

It is transliterated as /gh/.

There is no equivalent sound in English, though 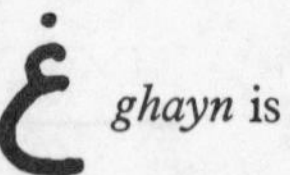 *ghayn* is very similar to the sound you make if you try to gargle without water. In fact, the onomatopoeic Arabic word for 'gargling' or 'gurgling' is pronounced *gharghar*.

These two sounds seem inextricably bound up, in the minds of certain European Arabists, with the camel. 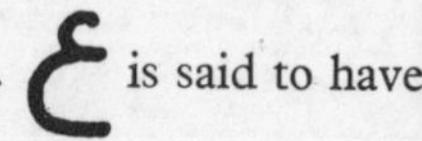 is said to have first entered the language when a bedouin made his camel kneel on a sharp stone. He was so taken by the sound it made in protest that he incorporated it into his speech.

غ is said by some to be the noise made by a camel growling at being loaded, by others to be the sound uttered in certain parts of the Arab world to make a camel kneel. The latter interpretation is clearly ideal for the auto-didact having trouble with this sound – simply acquire a camel and keep practising the غ until you succeed in making the camel kneel!

*solated form*

**Writing instructions** The ع / غ shape has two elements – a 'head' sitting on the line, and a 'tail' extending below the line.

□ First write a shallow letter 'c', with somewhat shortened 'arms' sitting on the line.

□ Retrace your pen back over the lower 'arm' of the head to lead into the tail. Finish by bringing your pen round and to the right in a controlled flourish to form the characteristic bulge of the tail.

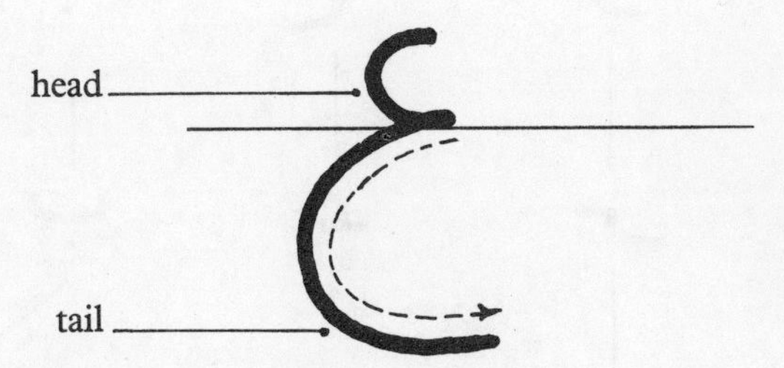


□ The two letters are distinguished from each other by a single dot above the head.

**Reading and writing practice** Trace and copy the models on page 92, saying the name of each letter as you write it – don't worry if you feel that you are unable to produce immediately an exact imitation of the tape models or your teacher's pronunciation. These are difficult sounds and require particular attention, but with practice and patience neither is beyond the capacity of a native English speaker.

Practise writing these letters until you can consistently produce examples which fall within the range of variation illustrated by the models.

**Proportion guide** You have now seen more than half the letters of the Arabic alphabet.

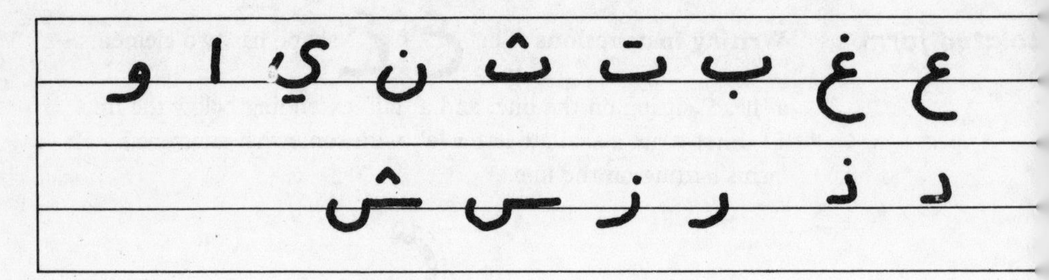

### *Initial position*

When these letters occur at the beginning of a word, they lose their tail and join to the following letter.

OBSERVE

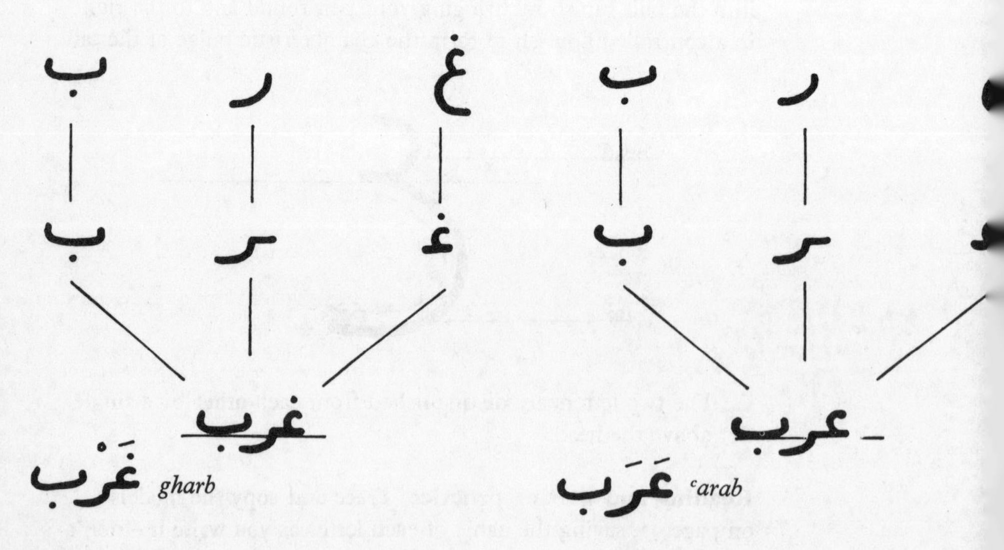

**Writing instructions** Initial ع / غ is a 'c' shape sitting on the line with a horizontal stroke extending from the lower arm of the 'c' shape to provide the connecting line to the next letter. It is written in one movement without taking the pen off the paper.

You have seen this shape before. The glottal stop sign ء *hamza* is in fact a miniature initial ع *ᶜayn*, though it represents a completely different sound.

**Reading and writing practice**

Ⓣ ☐ Read and pronounce each of the words below with reference to the tape.

☐ Trace and copy the models – pronounce each one both before and after you write it, and check your pronunciation frequently with the tape and/or your teacher.

☐ Keep your examples in constant relation to the line. Don't squash your examples together, give yourself plenty of space when you are writing. Monitor your own progress regularly by comparing your examples with the models in the book after every two or three attempts.

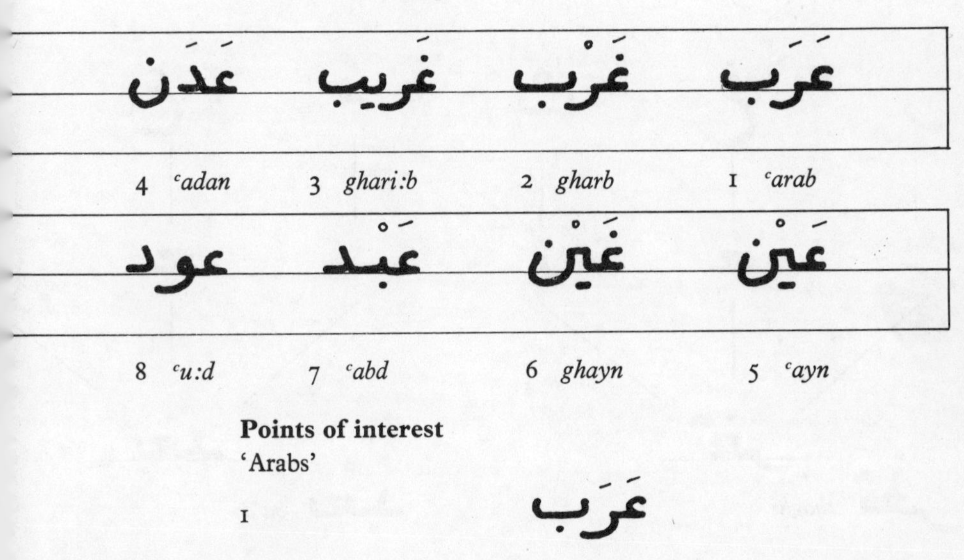


**Points of interest**

'Arabs'

1 عَرَب

'The earliest account that has come down to us of Arabia and the Arabs is that of the tenth chapter of Genesis, where many of the peoples and districts are mentioned by name. The world Arab, however, does not occur in this text, and makes its first appearance in an Assyrian inscription of 853 B.C. . . . The earliest classical reference is in Aeschylus, who in "Prometheus" mentions Arabia as a remote land whence came warriors with sharp pointed spears . . . It is in Greek writings that we find for the first time the place name Arabia, formed on the analogy of Italia, etc. . . . Herodotus and after him most Greek and Latin writers extend the terms Arabia and Arab to the entire peninsula and all its inhabitants.' (B. Lewis, *The Arabs in history*, pages 11-12.)

4 عَدَن

'Aden'. Capital of the People's Democratic Republic of Yemen. Often identified as the site of biblical 'Eden'.

5 عين

Name of the letter.

6 غين

Name of the letter.

***Medial position***

When these letters occur in the middle of a word they have a distinctive medial form and join to both the preceding and following letters.

OBSERVE

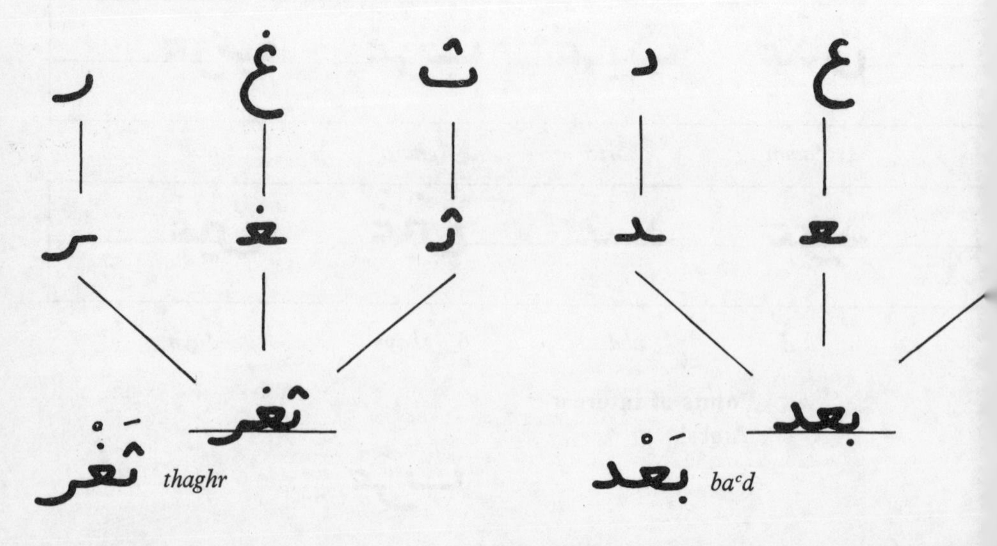

**Writing instructions** When these letters are joined on both sides in the middle of a word, they have a very distinctive inverted triangular shape. Make the shape in three continuous strokes.

1 A curved up stroke which is a continuation of the connecting line from the preceding letter and cuts back at a sharp angle leading into
2 a straight left to right stroke which forms the flat top of the shape and cuts back at a sharp angle to lead into
3 a curved down stroke which completes the triangle by bisecting the up stroke and provides the connecting line into the next letter.

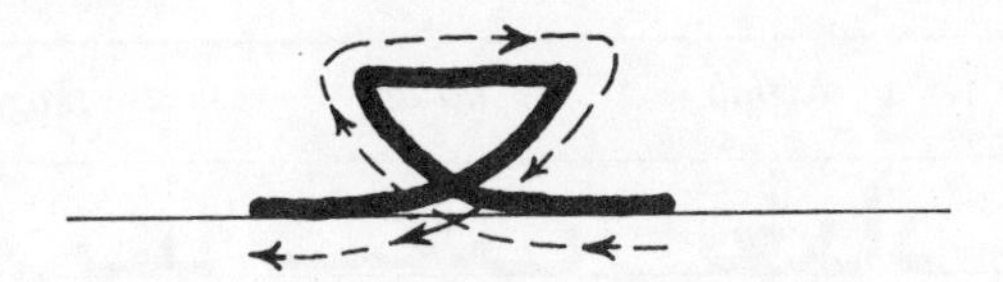

When preceded by one of the non-connectors medial ع and غ appears in their initial form and join to the following letter only:

*dacab* دَعَب ← ب + ع + د

*raghib* رَغِب ← ب + غ + ر

**Reading and writing practice**

(T) ☐ Read and pronounce each word on page 96 with reference to the tape.

☐ Trace and copy the model, making sure that you can identify both new letters. Pronounce each word several times both before and after writing it, and refer frequently to the tape.

☐ Medial ـعـ / ـغـ is one of the few angular shapes in the Arabic alphabet. Be sure to maintain this angularity – it is an important feature in distinguishing the medial shape of these letters from that of two you have yet to learn.

☐ Remember to write each word in three stages: first complete the basic shape of the word, then go back and put in the dots from *right to left*, and finally go back again to put in the short vowels and other signs, also from *right to left*.

If you have not yet found a size of writing with which you feel comfortable, continue to experiment. Take the size of the writing in this book as a rough guide, and always try to keep the letters within any one word in proportion to one another and in constant relation to the line.

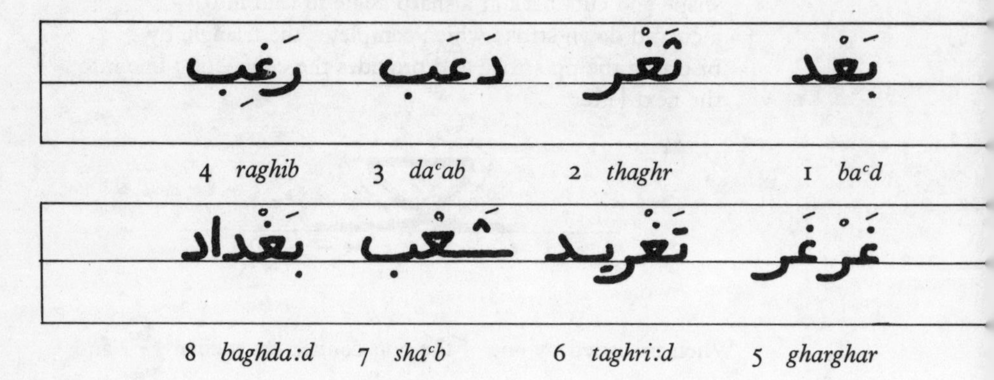


**Points of interest**

8 بَغْداد 'Baghdad' – the capital of Iraq.

***Final position***

When these letters occur at the end of a word they retain the shape of their medial form, regaining their tail and joining to the preceding letter.

OBSERVE

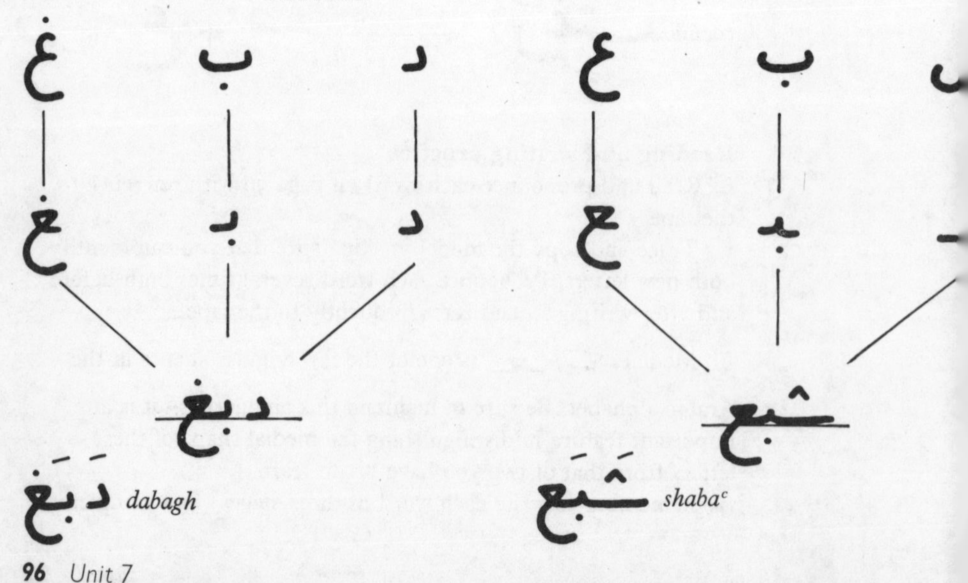

**Writing instructions** The joined final form of these letters is the distinctive triangular shape of the medial form, but with the curved right to left down stroke leading into the characteristic bulging tail of the isolated form. The medial form of these letters and the head of the final form are the only angular shapes you have encountered so far. While it is important to retain this angularity, don't forget that sharp angles and absolutely straight lines are unusual in handwritten Arabic. Your pen strokes should generally be smooth and fluid in order to reproduce the graceful curves, lines and loops that characterise the Arabic script.

All Arabic letters with a tail in their isolated form (except the non-connectors ز ر و) lose it in their initial and medial forms, and regain it in the final form. Compare with ش / س.

When preceded by one of the non-connectors final ع and غ stand alone in their isolated form.

*sa:$^c$* ساع ⟵ ع + ا + س

*sa:gh* ساغ ⟵ غ + ا + س

**Reading and writing practice**

Ⓣ ☐ Read and pronounce the words below with reference to the tape.

☐ Trace and copy the models – make sure that you can identify the names of the individual letters and the sounds they represent.

☐ Don't forget:

line – Keep all your examples in constant relation to the horizontal line, real or imaginary.

size – Keep all letters in proportion to one another.

dots – Number and position.

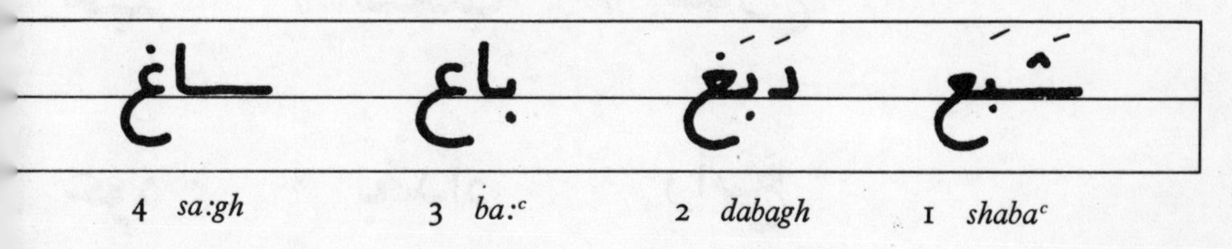


4 *sa:gh* 3 *ba:$^c$* 2 *dabagh* 1 *shaba$^c$*

| رابِغ | شارِع | بزوغ | سَريع |
|---|---|---|---|
| 8 *ra:bigh* | 7 *sha:ri$^c$* | 6 *buzu:gh* | 5 *sari:$^c$* |

***Printed forms of examples from writing practice***

**For reading and pronunciation practice only**

| Final | | Medial | | Initial |
|---|---|---|---|---|
| شبع | 1 | بعد | 1 | عرب |
| دبغ | 2 | ثغر | 2 | غرب |
| باع | 3 | رعب | 3 | غريب |
| ساغ | 4 | دغب | 4 | عدن |
| سريع | 5 | غرغر | 5 | عين |
| بزوغ | 6 | تغريد | 6 | غين |
| شارع | 7 | شعب | 7 | عبد |
| رابغ | 8 | بغداد | 8 | عود |

*Pronunciation drill* Ⓣ

**Contrast the following pairs:**

**(a)**

1 أَبَد ← عَبَد

2 أَنَب ← عَنَب

3 أُذْر ← عُذْر

4 أُسْر ← عُسْر

5 إِرْس ← عِرْس

6 إِتاب ← عِتاب

**(b)**

1 باد ← بَعَد

2 شاب ← شَعَب

3 روب ← رُعْب

4 دور ← دُعْر

5 شير ← شِعِر

6 ثيب ← ثِعِب

**(c)**

1 شي ← شيع

2 بي ← بيع

3 ذو ← ذوع

4 نو ← نوع

5 با ← باع

6 شا ← شاع

# Unit 8

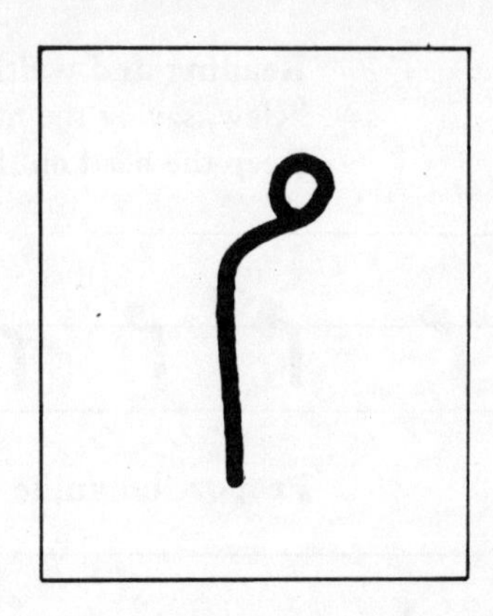

The name of this letter is *mi:m*. It is pronounced like the 'm' in '*m*outh' and transliterated as /m/.

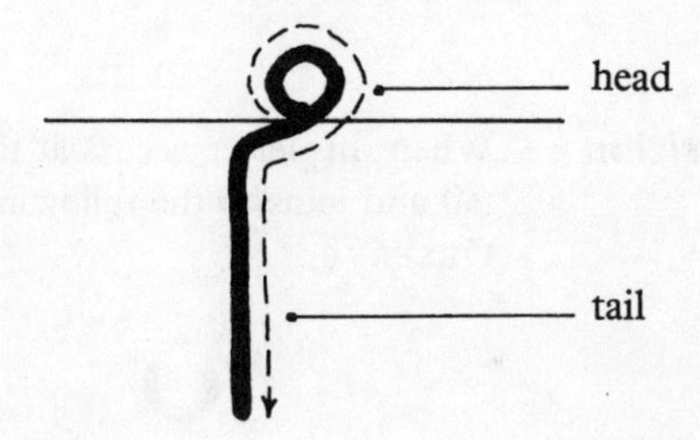


**'solated form**

**Writing instructions** This is another letter with a 'head' and a 'tail'. Write the head by drawing a very small clockwise loop sitting on the line. Extend the base of the loop a little to the left, then add the tail which should hang perpendicularly down from the line. The head is so small that it often gets filled in – especially when a fountain pen or felt tip is used – and appears as little more than a 'blob' on the line:

The tail is roughly the same length below the line as ا *alif* is above the line.

**Reading and writing practice** Trace and copy the models below, saying the name of the letter aloud each time you write it. Keep the head on the line and the length of the tail constant.

**Proportion guide**

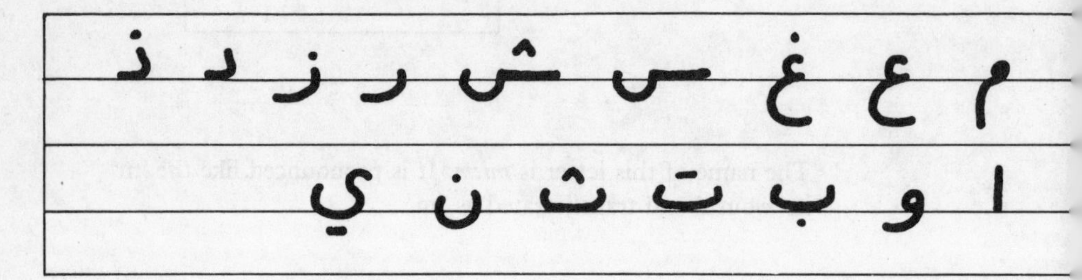

***Initial position***

When this letter occurs at the beginning of a word it loses its tail and joins to the following letter.

OBSERVE

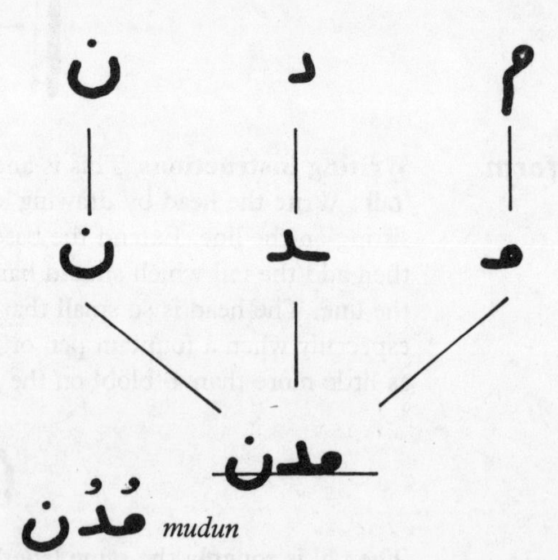

مُدُن *mudun*

**Writing instructions** Notice that the head is so small that it often appears simply as a blob on the line with a connecting line to join it to the following letter:

**Reading and writing practice**

Ⓣ ☐ Read and pronounce the words below with reference to the tape.

☐ Trace and copy the models. Monitor your progress frequently by checking your examples with the book.

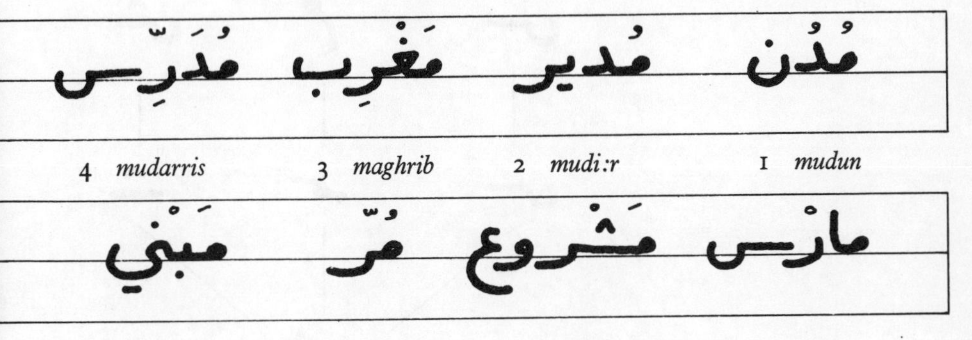


**Points of interest**

3

'Morocco'. Literally 'the place where the sun sets' (i.e. 'the West'). Morocco is the westernmost point of the Islamic world, with the Atlantic Ocean having formed a natural barrier to further expansion in the days of the Arab conquests.

5 مَارْس

'March' (the month). Passed into Arabic from French.

**Medial position** When this letter occurs in the middle of a word it has a distinctive looped medial form which sits on the line and joins to both the preceding and following letters.

OBSERVE

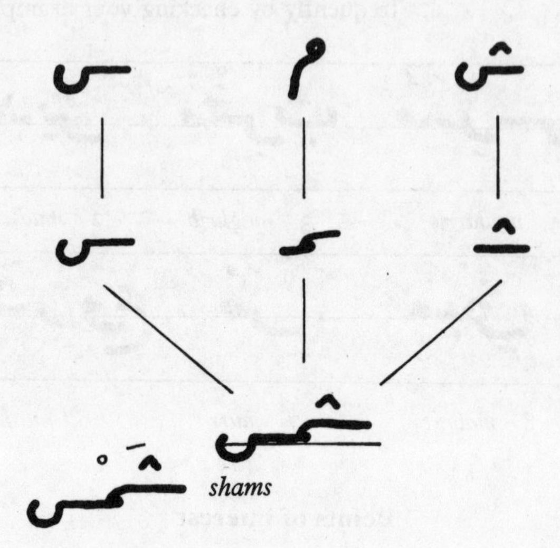


**Writing instructions** Notice that medial م sits on the line and joins to preceding letters from above. It is therefore necessary to start a preceding initial letter from a slightly higher position in relation to the line than usual. Lead into the *anti-clockwise* loop with the connecting line from the preceding letter, and then out to provide the connecting line to the following letter:

When preceded by one of the non-connectors, medial م appears in its initial form and joins to the following letter only:

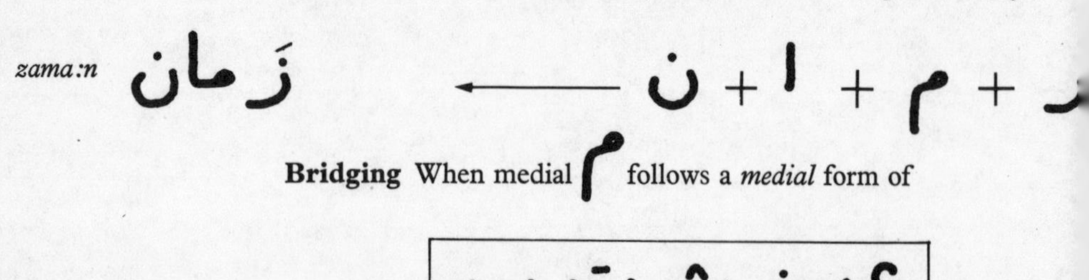


**Bridging** When medial م follows a *medial* form of

| ي ن ث ت ب |
|---|

(i.e. in a word of four letters or more), the modification called bridging occurs:

*yanmu:*

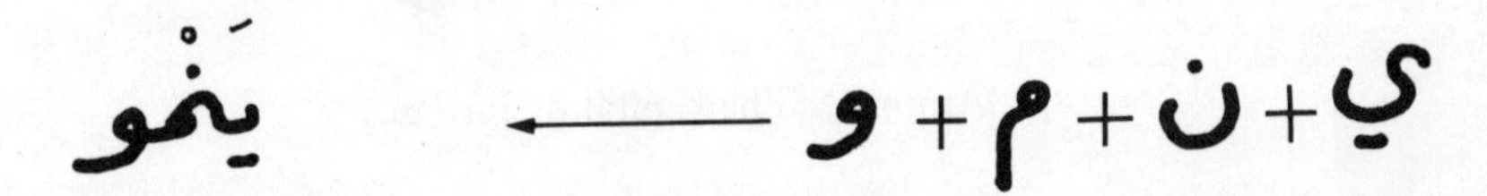

**Reading and writing practice**

Ⓣ ☐ Read and pronounce the words below with reference to the tape.

☐ Trace and copy the models. Notice that the loop of medial is so small that it often gets filled in and appears as a blob on the line.

☐ Don't forget to start initial letters a little higher than you normally would. This 'stacking' of certain letters one on top of the other is a common feature of handwritten Arabic and, like bridging, is a short cut towards the development of a natural and cursive hand.

☐ Remember to complete the basic shape of a word before going back to put in first the dots, and then the short vowels and other signs, all from *right to left*.

☐ Pronounce each word several times as soon as you have completed it.

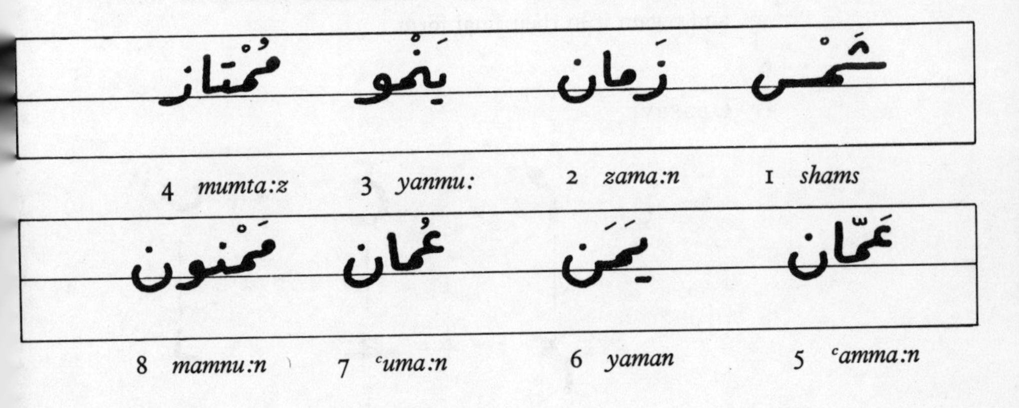


**Points of interest**

1

'Sun'. An old semitic word which has remained virtually unchanged since the time of the Akkadians (c. 2000 B.C.).

5

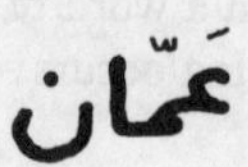

'Amman'. The capital of Jordan.

6

'Yemen'. Derived from a root meaning 'prosperity, good fortune' – hence the Latin name 'Arabia Felix', which was for a long time applied to the south-western area of the Arabian Peninsular, the modern 'Yemen Arab Republic' and 'People's Democratic Republic of Yemen'.

7

'Oman'. Same basic word shape as (5) above, but different pronunciation.

***Final position***

When this letter occurs at the end of a word it retains the shape of its medial form, regaining its tail and joining to the preceding letter from above. Remember that all letters with a tail in their isolated forms lose the tail in their initial and medial forms, and regain it in their final form.

OBSERVE

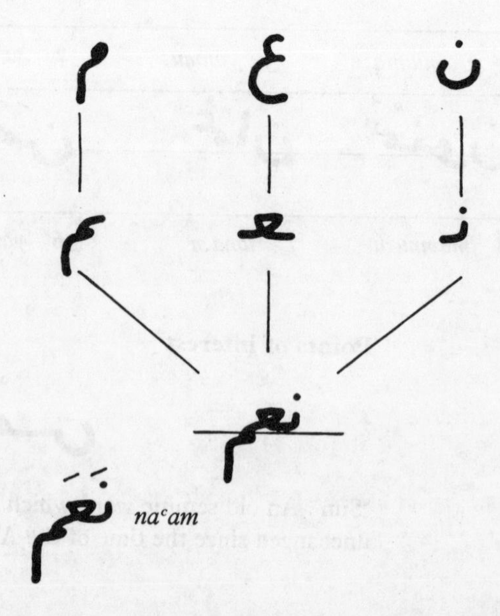

**Writing instructions** Same as for medial form, except for the re-appearance of the tail. If final م is preceded by a non-connector it stands alone in its isolated form:

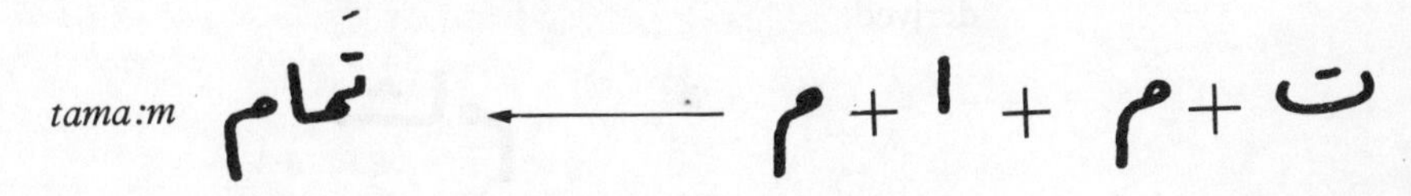


**Bridging** If final م is preceded by a *medial*

you should use the bridging technique to join the two letters:

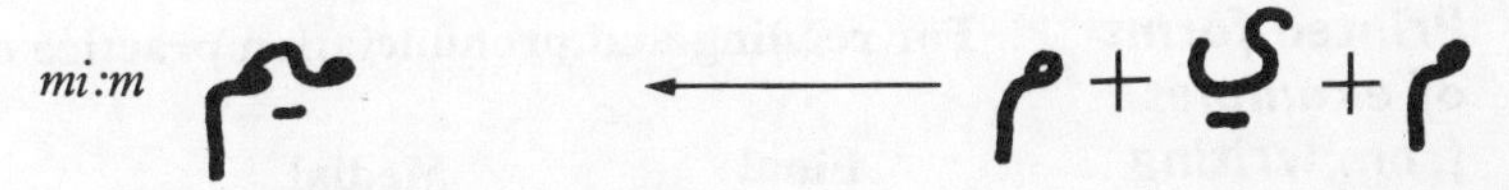


**Reading and writing practice**

Ⓣ □ Read and pronounce the words below with reference to the tape.

□ Trace and copy the models.

□ Look out for:

line – Are your letters in constant relation to it?

size – Do you feel comfortable with it? Is it roughly the same as the size of the writing in the book?

dots – Have you put the right number in the right places?

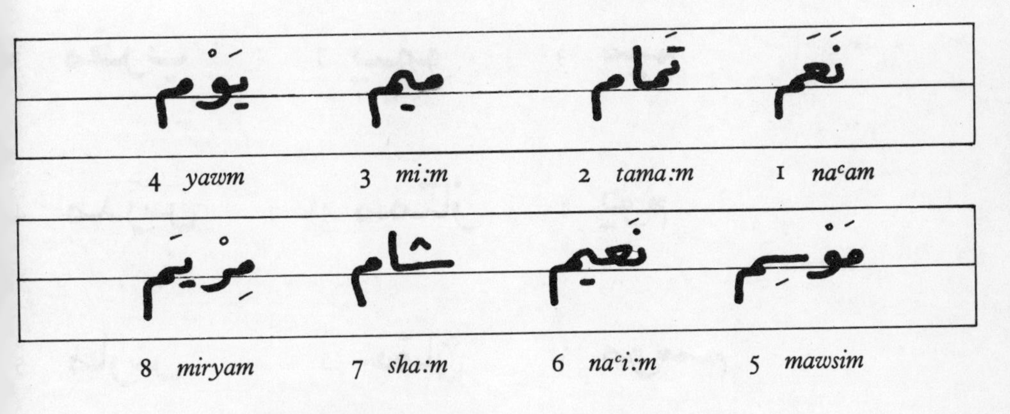


**Points of interest**

3

Name of the letter.

5

'season'. From which the English 'monsoon' is ultimately derived.

7

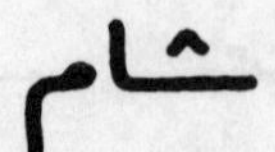

The common Arabic name for Damascus, the capital of Syria.

8

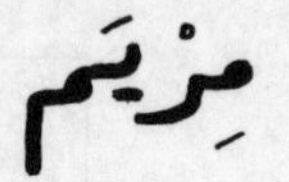

A woman's name. The Arabic equivalent to 'Mary'.

### *Printed forms of examples from writing practice*

**For reading and pronunciation practice only**

| | **Final** | | **Medial** | | **Initial** |
|---|---|---|---|---|---|
| 1 | نعم | 1 | شمس | 1 | مدن |
| 2 | تمام | 2 | زمان | 2 | مدير |
| 3 | ميم | 3 | ينمو | 3 | مغرب |
| 4 | يوم | 4 | ممتاز | 4 | مدرّس |
| 5 | موسم | 5 | عمّان | 5 | مارس |
| 6 | نعيم | 6 | يمن | 6 | مشروع |

7 مرّ　　7 عمان　　7 شام

8 مبني　　8 ممنوع　　8 مريم

# Unit 9

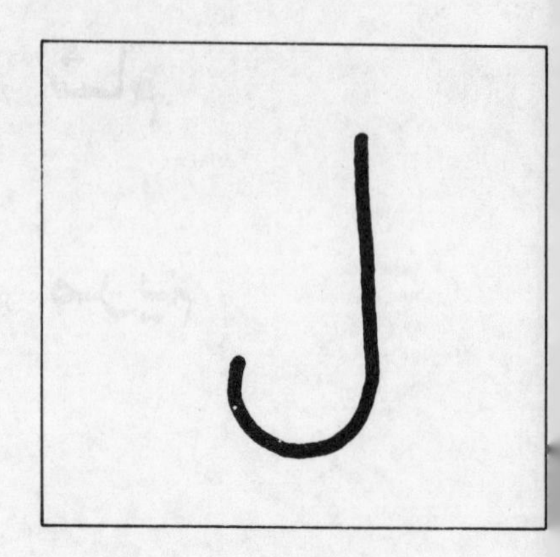

The name of this letter is *la:m*. It is pronounced like the 'l' in '*l*ick' and is transliterated as /l/. ل

## *Isolated form*

**Writing instructions** This letter has two elements:

A down stroke above the line, the same height as ا *alif*, leading into a tail which descends below the line and resembles the tail of س / ش .

First draw the down stroke and then complete the letter by adding the tail in a controlled flourish to the left.

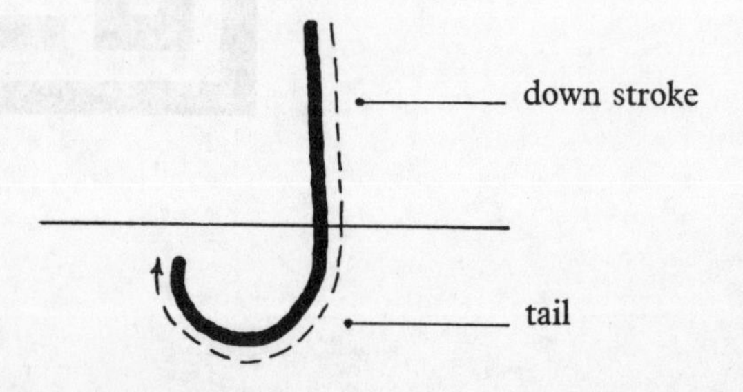


**Reading and writing practice** Trace a few of these models onto a blank sheet of paper in order to get a feel for the letter before making any freehand attempts. Don't press too firmly on the paper when writing the tail – try and complete the letter from the base of the down stroke in a single controlled flourish. Say the name of the letter each time you write it.

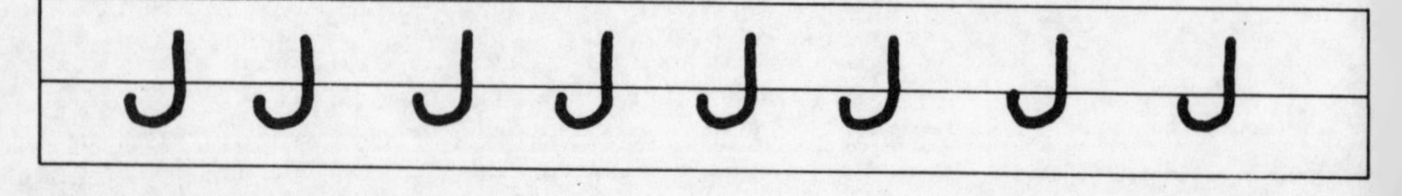

**Proportion guide** Look at this new letter in proportion to the isolated forms of the letters from the previous Units. Use the models for further writing practice.

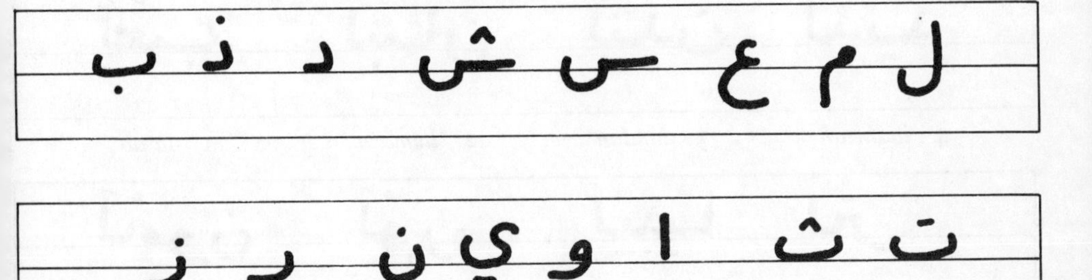


***Initial position*** When this letter occurs at the beginning of a word it loses its tail, and joins to the following letter.

OBSERVE

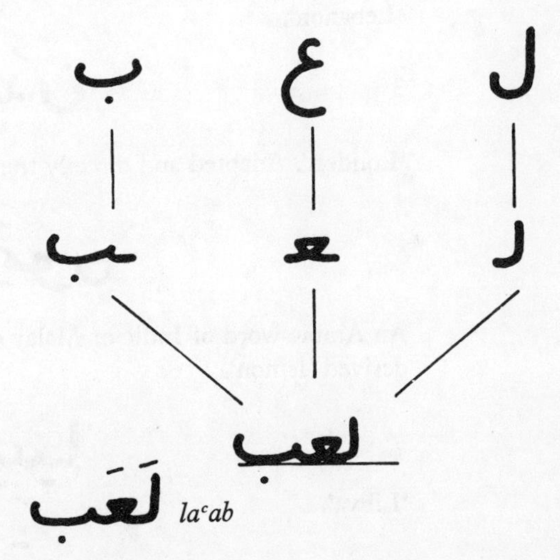


**Writing instructions** The down stroke of the initial form is about the same height as ا *alif*, and joins to a following letter by a connecting line from its base.

**Reading and writing practice**

Ⓣ ☐ Read and pronounce the words on page 112 with reference to the tape.

☐ Trace and copy the models, pronouncing each word several times before and after writing it. Check your examples for dots, proportion of letters to one another within any one word, and position of words in relation to the horizontal line.

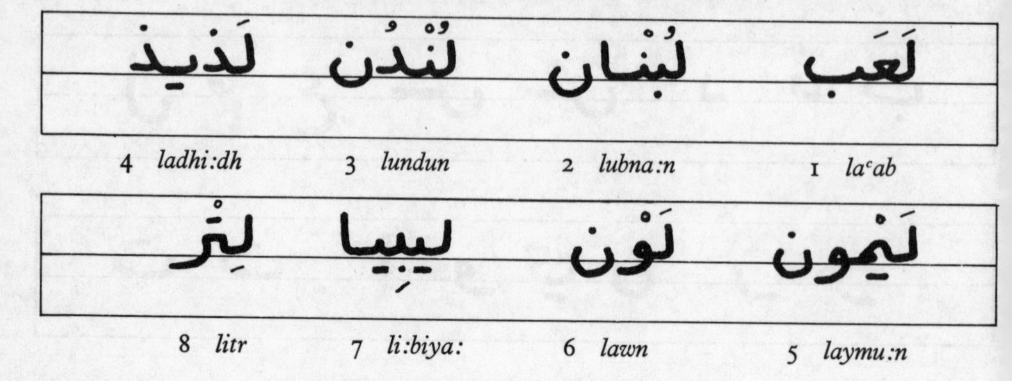


**Points of interest**

2 لُبْنان

'Lebanon'.

3 لُنْدُن

'London'. Adapted and directly transliterated from the English.

5 لَيْمون

An Arabic word of Indic or Malay origin, from which we have derived 'lemon'.

7 ليبِيا

'Libya'.

8 لِتْر

'litre'. Adapted and directly transliterated from the French.

***Medial position*** When this letter occurs in the middle of a word, it retains the shape of its initial form but joins to both the preceding and following letters.

Observe

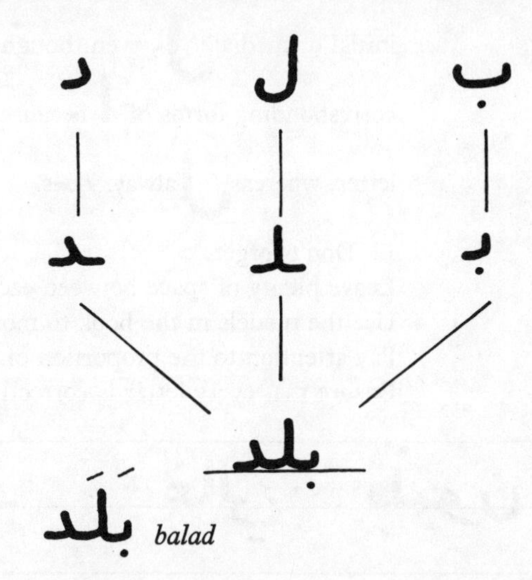


**Writing instructions** Lead into the medial form from the connecting line of the preceding letter. Make an up stroke the same height as ا *alif*, then retrace the down stroke over the up stroke almost to the horizontal line before veering away to provide the connecting line to the following letter. If you come right back down to the line before leading into the next letter, the resultant shape will be too angular and stylised:

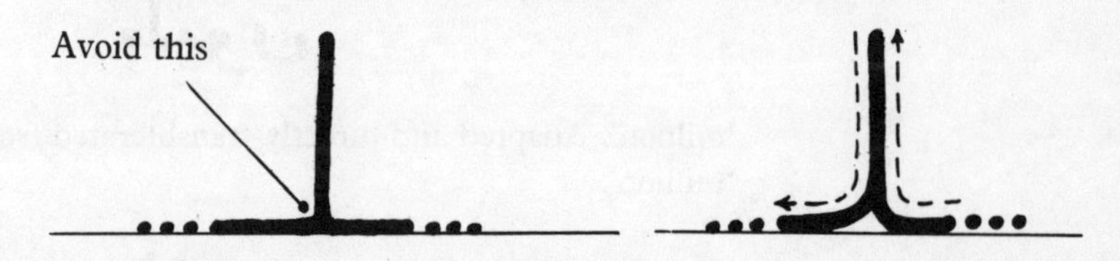


When preceded by one of the non-connectors, medial ل appears in its initial form and joins to the following letter only:

*walad* وَلَد ← د + ل + و

**Reading and writing practice**

Ⓣ ☐ Read and pronounce the words on page 114 with reference to the tape.

☐ Trace and copy the models. Notice that you can never confuse initial or medial ل, even though tailless, with the corresponding forms of ا because ا never joins to a following letter, whereas ل always does.

□ Don't forget:
Leave plenty of space between each of your examples
Use the models in the book to monitor the size of your writing
Pay attention to the proportion of letters within a word
Ensure that every letter is correctly dotted

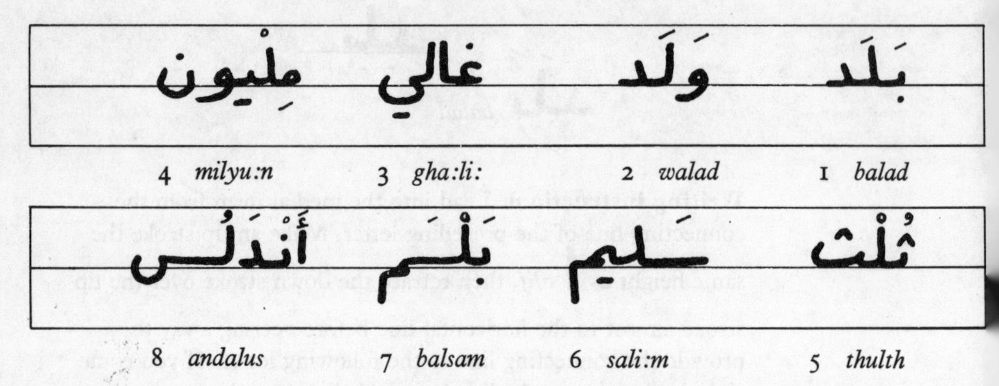


**Points of interest**

4 

'million'. Adapted and directly transliterated from the French 'million'.

5 

The name of a style of Arabic script commonly used for headings and titles in books and newspapers, and for other decorative purposes.

6 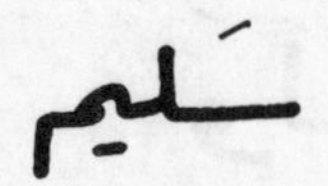


'Salim'. A common man's name.

7

'An aromatic preparation for preserving the dead; a fragrant oil or ointment used for soothing pain or healing wounds' – whence English 'balm; balsam; enbalm; balmy.'

8

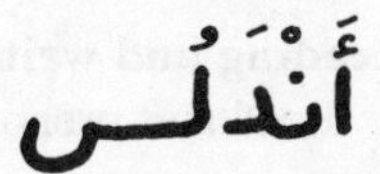

The old Arab name for the Iberian peninsular, from which 'Andalucia' (the name of the southern region of Spain) is derived.

***Final position***

When this letter occurs at the end of a word, it retains the shape of its isolated form and joins to the preceding letter.

OBSERVE

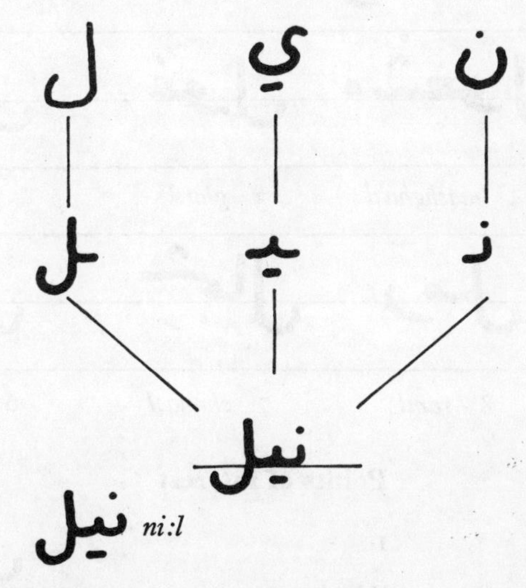


**Writing instructions** Lead into the up stroke from the connecting line of the preceding letter then retrace the down stroke over the up stroke, continuing down below the line to add the tail in a controlled flourish to the left:

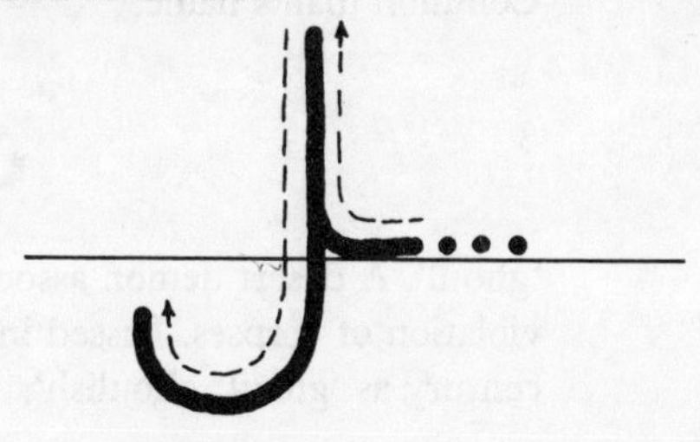

When preceded by one of the non-connectors, final ل stands alone in its isolated form:

*shima:l* شِمال ← ل + ا + م + ش

**Reading and writing practice**

Ⓣ ☐ Read and pronounce the words below with reference to the tape.

☐ Trace and copy the models. Check your examples by frequent reference to the book and practise as long as it takes for you to produce consistent copies of the models. Make particularly sure you aren't joining non-connectors to following letters, and take care to distinguish between the various forms of ل and ا.

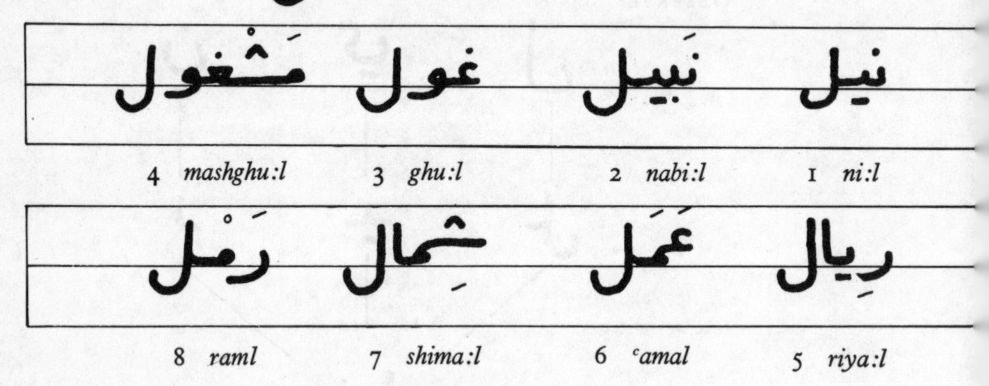


**Points of interest**

1 نيل

'Nile'.

2 نَبيل

Common man's name.

3 غول

'ghoul'. A desert demon associated with grave robbing and violation of corpses. Passed into English in the late eighteenth century as 'ghoul; ghoulish'.

5 ريال

'riyal'. A unit of currency commonly used in the Arabian Peninsular. Perhaps passed into Arabic from Spanish or Portuguese, whence English also derived 'rial' – the name of a gold coin originally worth 10 shillings and first minted in 1465 in the reign of Edward IV.

**Special shapes for combinations of ل with م 'mi:m' and ا 'alif'**

**A** The combination of ل followed by ا *alif* is so frequent that it has both its own name – *la:m alif* – and its own special shape:

i) initial ل *la:m* followed by ا *alif*.

First make a down stroke like a large ر *ra:'*, but with the tip of the tail just touching the line rather than descending down below it. This is the modified part of the *la:m alif*. Then add a slightly shortened ا *alif* standing vertically on the tail of the modified ل *la:m*:

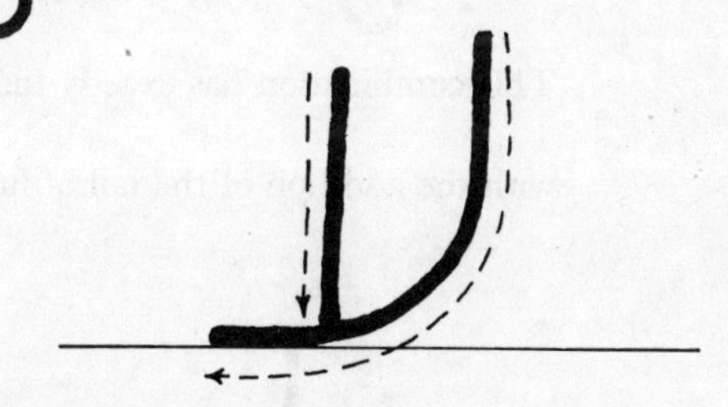

ii) medial ل *la:m* followed by ا *alif*.

Lead into the up stroke of the medial ل, as usual, with the connecting line from the preceding letter, but make the down stroke, as in (i) above, like an enlarged ر *ra:'*. Then add the slightly shortened ا *alif*, again standing vertically on the tail of the modified ل *la:m*:

*sala:m* سَلام ← م + ا + ل + س

**B** The combination of ل *la:m* followed by م *mi:m* also has its own special shape:

i) initial ل *la:m* followed by medial م *mi:m*.

The medial form of م *mi:m* is looped around the base of initial ل *la:m*:

*lamma:* لمّا ← ا + م + ل

ii) initial ل *la:m* followed by final م *mi:m*.

This combination has exactly the same shape as (i) above, but with the addition of the tail of final م *mi:m*:

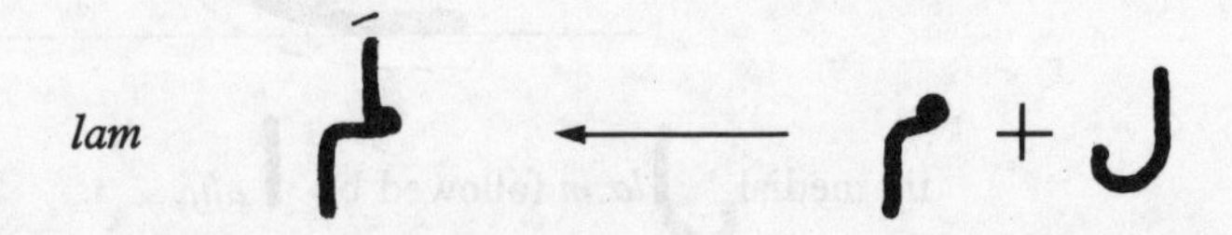

iii) medial ل *la:m* followed by medial or final م *mi:m*.

The connecting line from medial ل *la:m* to medial or final م *mi:m* starts about half way down the down stroke of the ل *la:m*

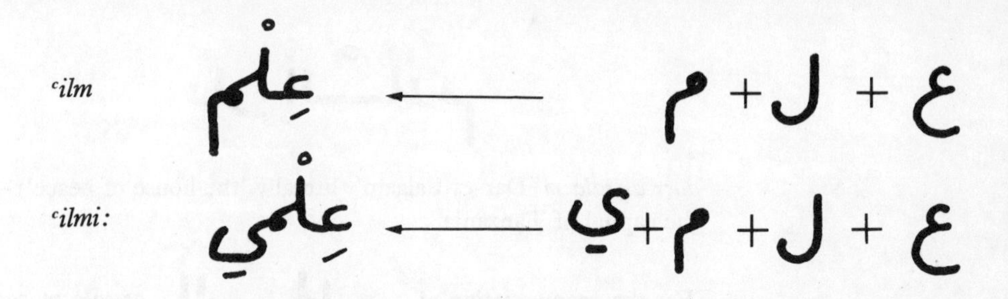


These special shapes for combinations of certain letters are commonly known as 'ligatures'. They occur frequently and an ability to use them with ease will give your handwriting a more natural and cursive appearance.

**Reading and writing practice**

Ⓣ □ Read and pronounce the models below with reference to the tape.

□ Trace and copy the models. Make sure you can recognise and reproduce the various ligatures without difficulty before you go on.

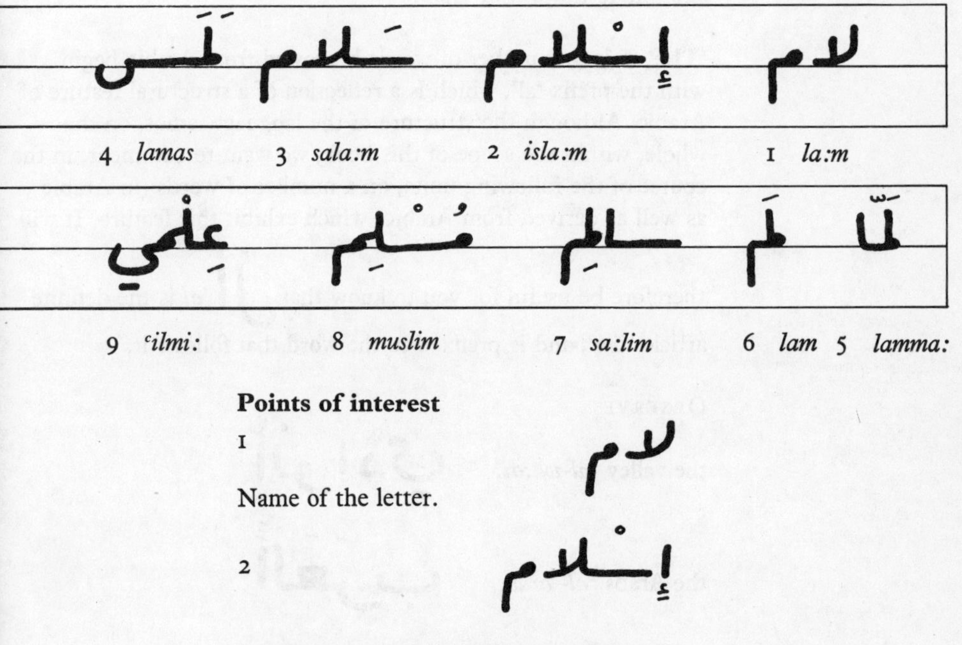


**Points of interest**

1

Name of the letter.

2

'Islam' (literally submission to God's will), derived from the same root as the following words:

3

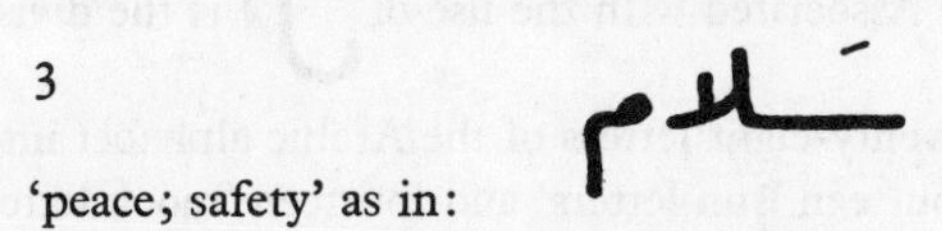

'peace; safety' as in:

دار أَلسَّلام

*da:r as-sala:m* 'Dar-es-Salaam' (literally 'the house of peace') – the capital of Tanzania.

(For the pronunciation of أَلسَّلام *as-sala:m*, see under 'the' below.)

7 سالم

A common man's name.

8 مُسْلِم

'Muslim' (often spelt 'Moslem' in English), literally 'one who submits to the will of God'.

**'The'** A large number of words borrowed from Arabic begin with the prefix 'al', which is a reflection of a structural feature of Arabic. Although the structure of the language is not, on the whole, within the scope of this book, we want to comment, in the course of the following units, on a number of words (in Arabic as well as derived from Arabic) which exhibit this feature. It will therefore be useful for you to know that أَلْ *'al* is the definite article 'the', and is prefixed to the word that follows it.

OBSERVE

the valley *'al-wa:di:* أَلْوادي

the Arabs *'al-'arab* أَلْعَرَب

Associated with the use of أَلْ is the division of the twenty-eight letters of the Arabic alphabet into two groups – fourteen 'sun letters' and fourteen 'moon letters'. The definite article أَلْ is pronounced *'al* when prefixed to a word beginning with a 'moon letter', such as و and ع in the examples on page 120.

The seven moon letters you have seen so far are

However, when prefixed to a word beginning with a 'sun letter', the ل of the article, though written, is not pronounced. It is in fact assimilated to the following letter, which is consequently pronounced double. In these circumstances, the ل loses its ْ *suku:n* and the 'sun letter' is written with ّ *shadda* to show that it is doubled in pronunciation.

OBSERVE

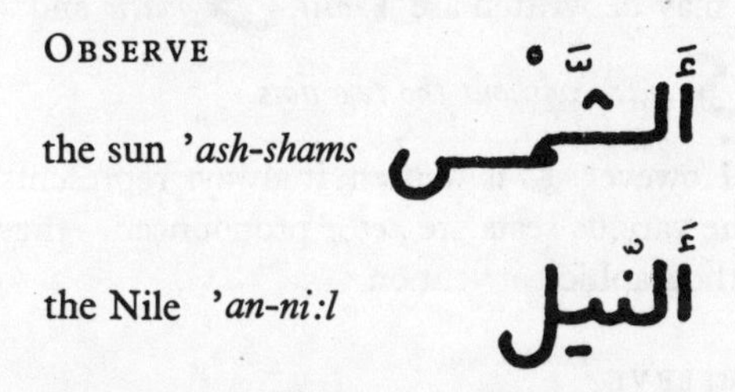

the sun *'ash-shams*

the Nile *'an-ni:l*

The name 'sun letters' derives from the Arabic word for sun,

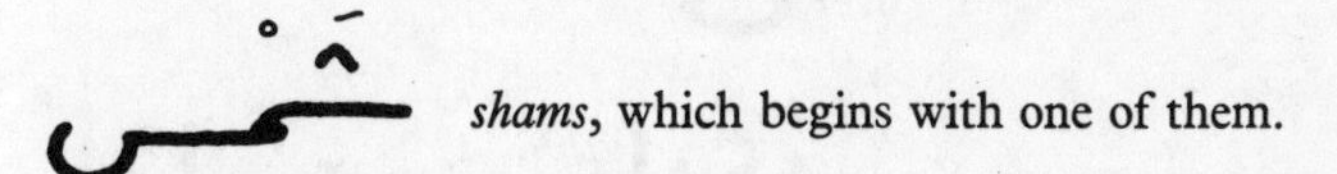

*shams*, which begins with one of them.

Similarly, the Arabic word for 'moon', which you will see in due course, provides the name for the second group of fourteen letters.

Of the seventeen letters you have seen so far, the following ten are 'sun letters':

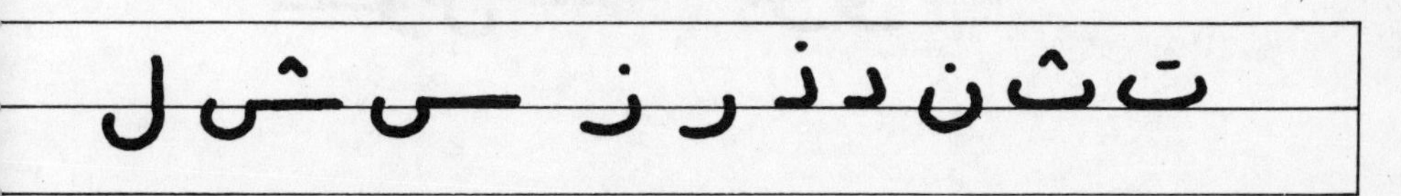

A complete list appears with the alphabet table at the end of the book.

### ء 'hamza' in the middle and at the end of a word

In Unit 3 you saw that when ء *hamza*, the symbol for the glottal stop sound, occurs at the beginning of a word, it cannot be written alone. It always sits either above or below a silent ا, depending on the short vowel accompanying it.

OBSERVE

Similarly, when ء occurs in the middle or at the end of a word it is usually written above a silent 'seat', but sometimes stands alone on the line. Choosing a seat for medial and final ء is complicated. There are rules, but all you really need to know at this stage is that the three seats over which medial and final ء may be written are ا *alif*, و *wa:w* and ى, which is ي *ya:' without the two dots.*

However ء is written, it always represents the same sound. The various seats are *never* pronounced – they are merely an orthographic convention.

OBSERVE

Examples of words with medial and final ء *hamza*.

1 over ى

*ba:di'* بادئ *su'il* سُئِل

2 over و

*maru'* مَرُؤ *su'a:l* سُؤال

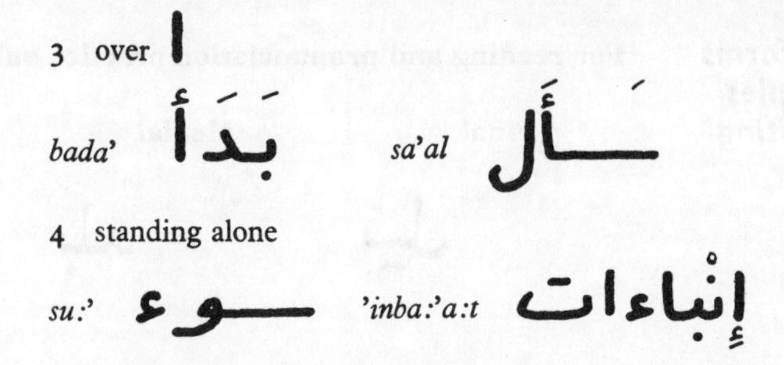


**Reading and writing practice**

Ⓣ □ Read and pronounce the words below with reference to the tape.

□ Trace and copy the models. Always complete the basic shape of a word before going back to put in first the dots, and then the short vowels and ء , all from *right to left*. When ء stands alone on the line write it as part of the basic shape. Pronounce each word several times as soon as you have completed it.

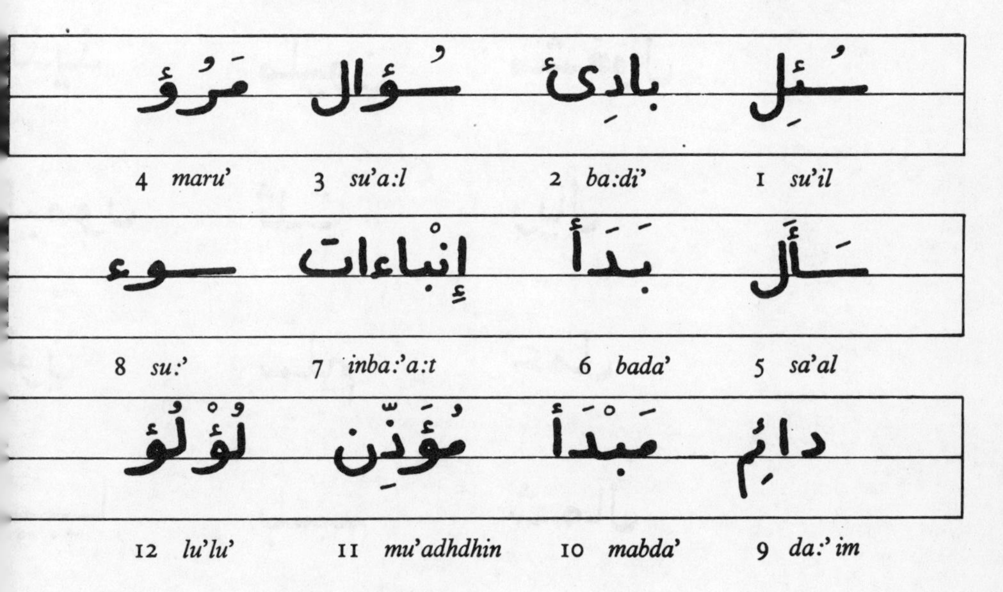


**Points of interest**

11 

The man who announces the call to prayer from the minaret of the mosque, usually spelt 'muezzin' in English.

***Printed forms of examples from writing practice***

**For reading and pronunciation practice only**

| Final | Medial | Initial |
| --- | --- | --- |
| نيل | بلد | لعب |
| نبيل | ولد | لبنان |
| غول | غالي | لندن |
| مشغول | مليون | لذيذ |
| ريال | ثلث | ليمون |
| عمل | سليم | لون |
| شمال | بلسم | ليبيا |
| رمل | اندلس | تر |

# Unit 10

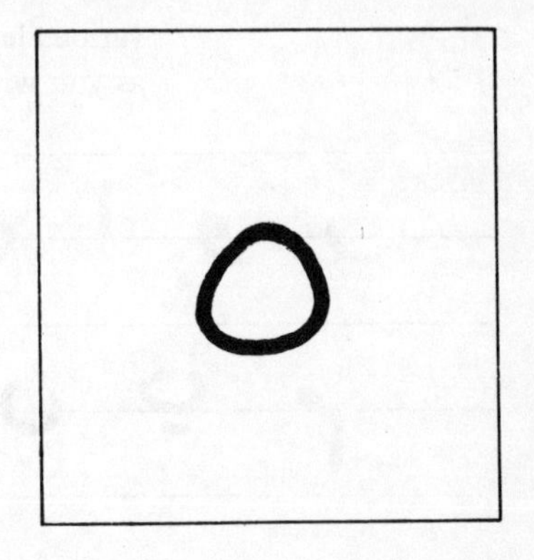

The name of this letter is *ha:'*. ه
It is pronounced like the 'h' in '*h*ot' and transliterated as /h/.

***'solated form***

**Writing instructions** This letter is made in one clock-wise movement of the pen. Begin at the point above the line from which you would start the د / ذ shape, and draw a circle meeting at the top:

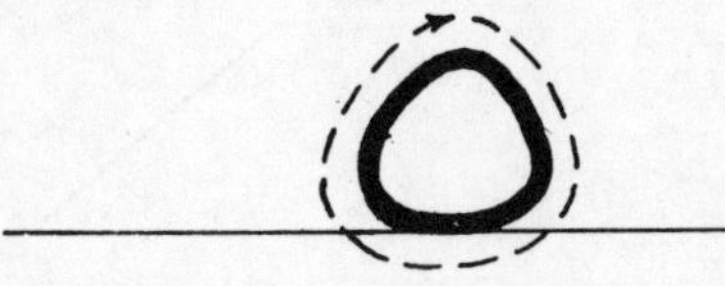

It is not always a true circle – it tends to be slightly flattened out at the bottom.

Because of the similarity between this letter, our own letter 'o' and our symbol for zero, it will at first feel more natural for you to write this letter anti-clockwise. Resist the temptation. Be consistent in your *right to left* habits.

**Reading and writing practice** Trace and copy the models below – they will give you an idea of the degree of variation you can allow yourself when making this isolated shape for the first time. Say the name of the letter each time you write it.

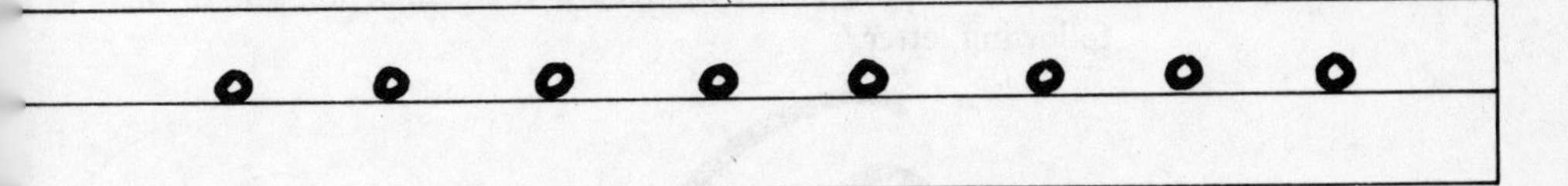

Use the proportion guide for extra writing practice of isolated forms, and pay particular attention to the positions of the various letters in relation to the line. Say the name of each letter as you write it.

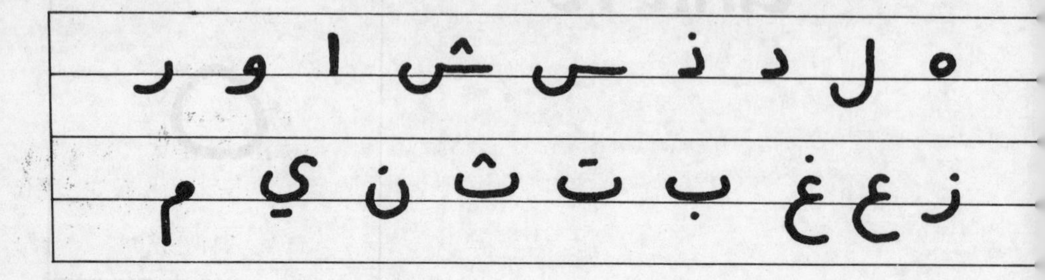

***Initial position*** When this letter occurs at the beginning of a word it has a distinctive initial form and joins to the following letter.
OBSERVE

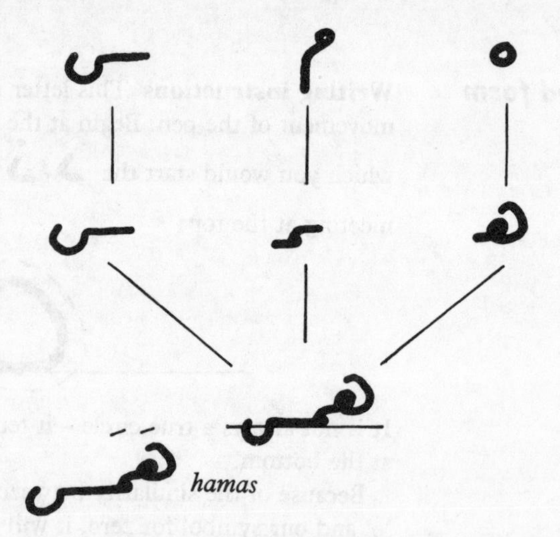

*hamas*

**Writing instructions** Of all the letters in the Arabic alphabet this is the least uniform in shape from form to form. For the initial form draw a clockwise semi-circle (like a backwards 'c') beginning at the point above the line from which you would start the ذ / د shape. The lower arm of the semi-circle leads into a small clockwise loop which sits on the line under the upper arm. The line leading out of the loop is the connecting line to the following letter.

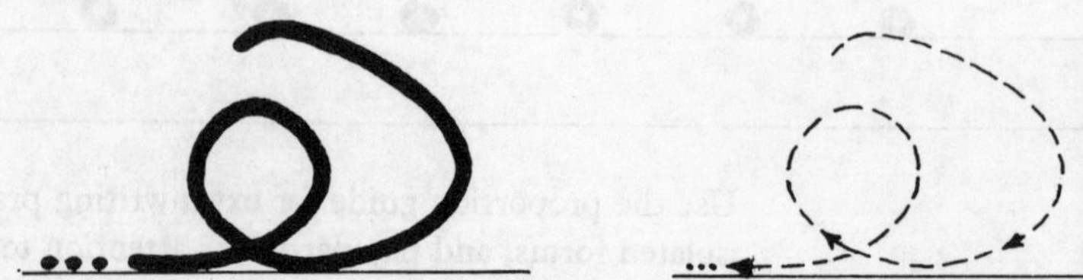

**Reading and writing practice**

Ⓣ □ Read and pronounce the words below with reference to the tape.

□ Trace and copy the models below. Notice that there is a tendency for the eye of the small loop of initial ھـ to get filled in, depending on size of writing and thickness of pen used.

□ Pronounce each word as soon as you complete it – pay particular attention to dots, short vowels, *shadda*, and *suku:n*.

| هِلال | هِبْر | هِنْد | هَمَس |
|---|---|---|---|
| 4 *hila:l* | 3 *hibr* | 2 *hind* | 1 *hamas* |

| هُدُب | هَرَس | هُروب | هامِش |
|---|---|---|---|
| 8 *hudub* | 7 *haras* | 6 *huru:b* | 5 *ha:mish* |

**Points of interest**

2 هِنْد 'India'

4 هِلال 'crescent moon' – the universal symbol of Islam.

**Medial position** When this letter occurs in the middle of a word it has a distinctive medial form and joins to both the preceding and following letters.

OBSERVE

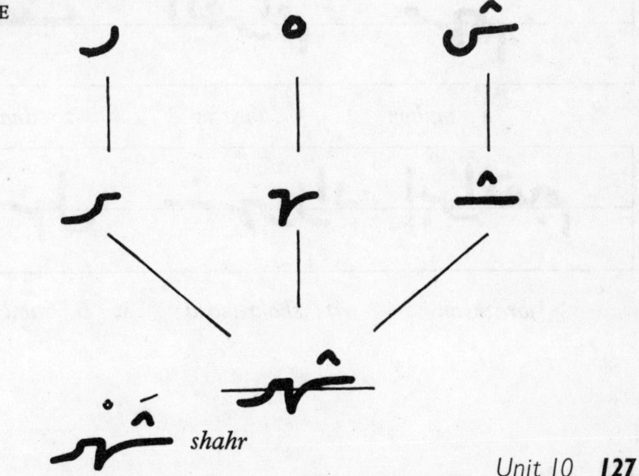

**Writing instructions** The medial form of ه *ha:'* bears absolutely no resemblance to either its isolated or initial forms. Avoid confusion by paying particular attention to this letter and making sure you can confidently recognise and reproduce it in its various guises.

Lead into the down stroke of the medial form with the connecting line from the preceding letter and make an elongated 'v' shape below the line. The down stroke slopes to the right and the up stroke is more or less vertical, leading at a right angle into the connecting line to the following letter.

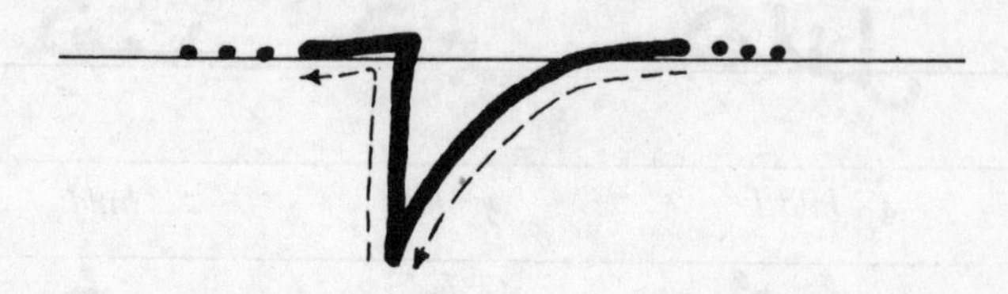

When preceded by one of the non-connectors, medial ه *ha:'* appears in its initial form and joins to the following letter only:

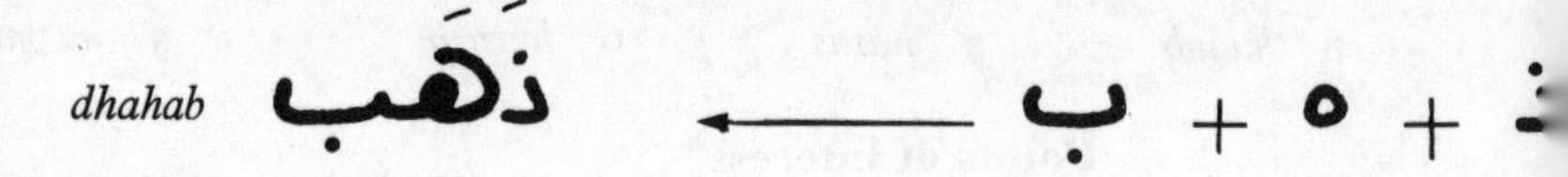


**Reading and writing practice**

Ⓣ □ Read and pronounce the words below with reference to the tape.

□ Trace and copy the models. Check that your examples are correctly positioned in relation to the horizontal line, and that all letters are in proportion to one another. By now the size of your writing should be fairly constant.

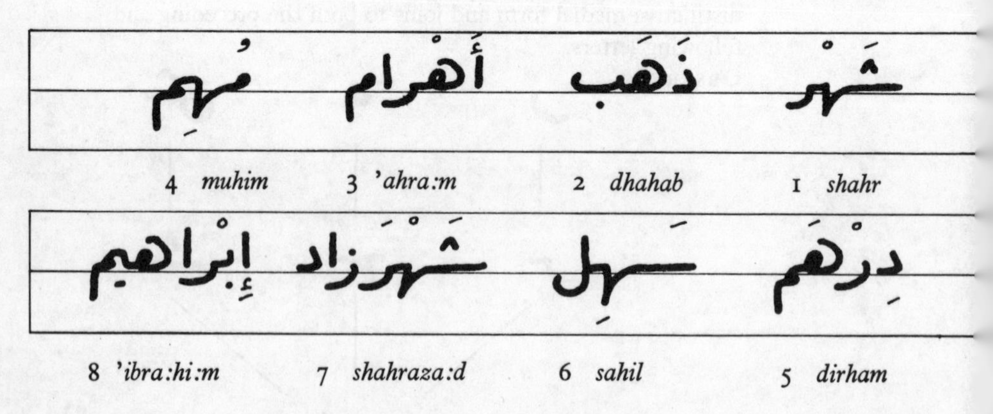

**Points of interest**

3

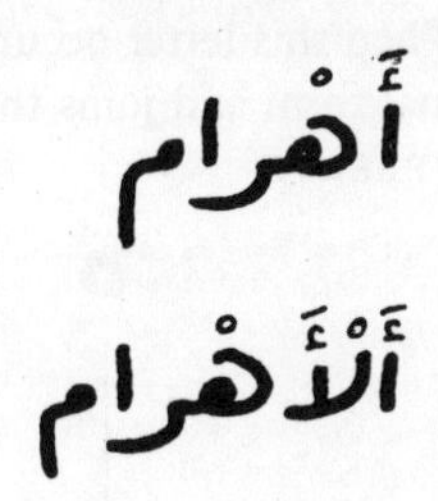

'pyramids' as in:

*'al-'ahra:m* – name of a leading Cairo newspaper (literally 'The Pyramids').

5

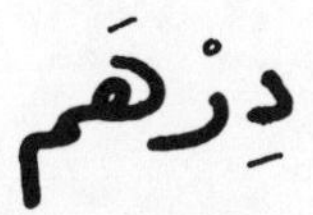

A unit of currency used in parts of the Arab world. Usually spelt 'dirhem' in English, it is derived from the same source as the modern Greek 'drachma'.

7

'Shahrazad' – the story teller who entertained King Shahriyar for 1001 nights.

8

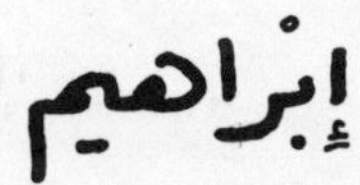

Common man's name, equivalent to English Abraham.

**Final position** When this letter occurs at the end of a word it has a distinctive final form and joins to the preceding letter.

OBSERVE

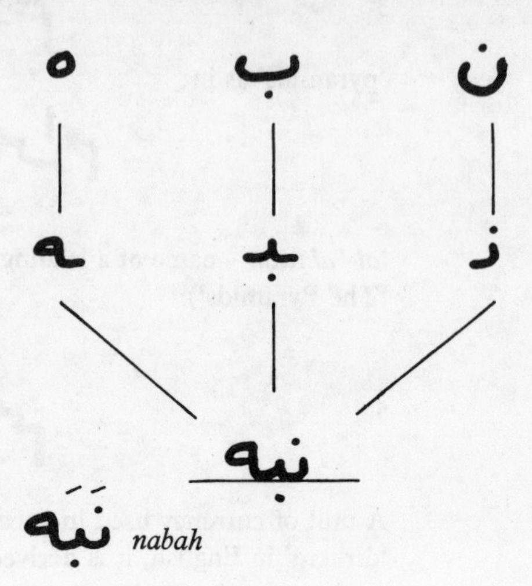

**Writing instructions** With the connecting line from the preceding letter lead into a vertical up stroke about the same height as the ـد / ـذ shape, then make a 'c' shaped loop that joins the up stroke about half way down:

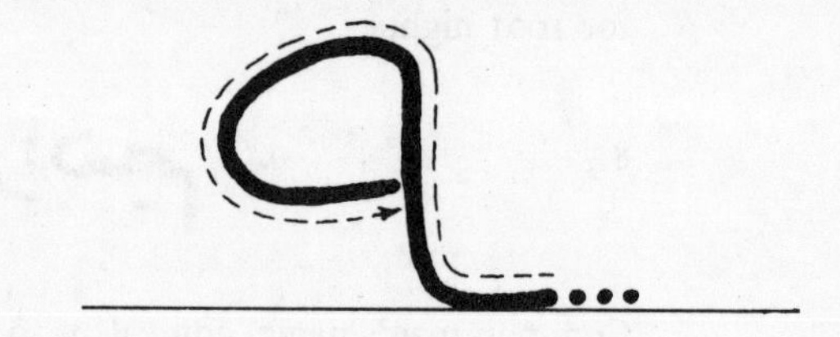

When preceded by one of the non-connectors, final ه *ha:'* stands alone in its isolated form:

*mashbu:h*

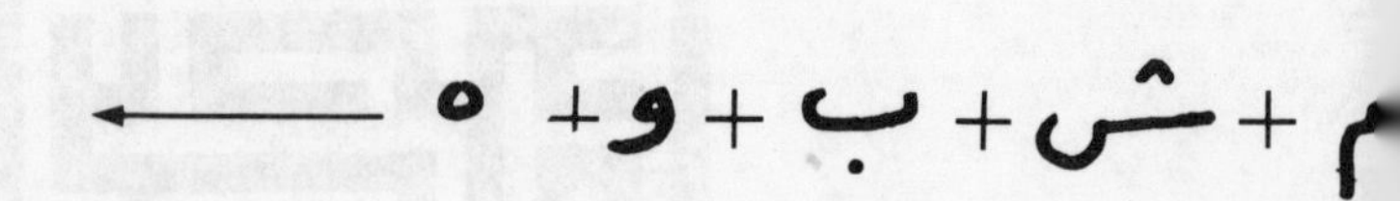

**Reading and writing practice**

Ⓣ □ Read and pronounce the words on page 131 with reference to the tape.

□ Trace and copy the models. This letter is unique in the degree of dissimilarity between its four forms. Make sure you can write and recognise each form confidently before going on.

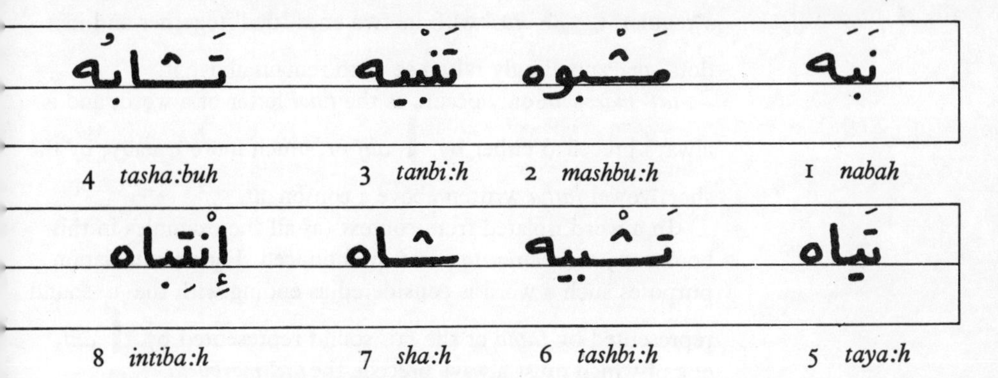


**Points of interest**

7 شاه

'Shah'. The hereditary title of the ex-ruler of Persia. Notice also: *sha:h ma:t*

شاه مات

'. . . chess was invented by the Indians, and the Arabs first came across it in Persia. The English (and still more the French) name as well as the expression which announces the end of the game, 'check-mate', came through the Arabs from the Persian 'shah' and 'shah mat', meaning 'the king' and 'the king is dead'. '(Edward Atiyah, *The Arabs*, page 52.)

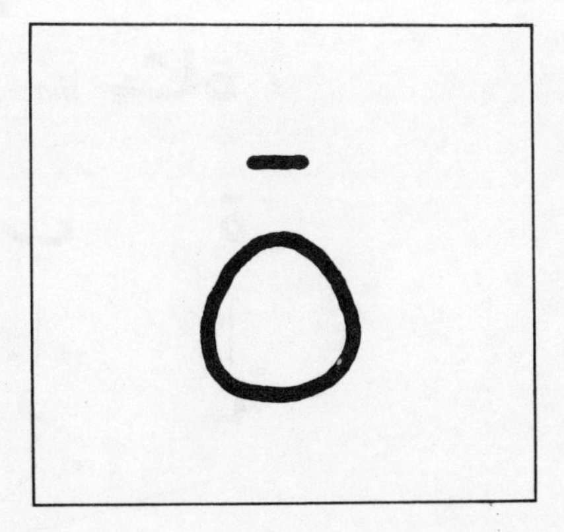

The shape of ه *ha:'* is shared by another letter, called *ta:' marbu:ta*. The literal meaning of *ta:' marbu:ta* is 'tied' *ta:'*. This reflects the common view that *ta:' marbu:ta* is in fact a regular ت ta:' with its two ends 'tied' together and its dots correspondingly raised so as to remain above it.

□ ta:' marbu:ta only occurs as the *final* letter of a word, and is always preceded either by ا *alif* or, much more usually, by the short vowel *fatha* written above a consonant.

□ In a word isolated from context (as all the examples in this book are), *ta:' marbu:ta* is not pronounced. For pronunciation purposes such a word is considered as ending with the /a/ sound represented by *fatha* or the /a:/ sound represented by ا *alif*, one of which must always precede the *ta:' marbu:ta*.

OBSERVE

ة *ta:' marbu:ta* occurs *only* as the final letter in a word and shares the shape of final ه *ha:'*, but with two dots above. Like final ه *ha:'* it either:

*a* joins to the preceding letter, or

*b* appears in its isolated form if the preceding letter is one of the non-connectors.

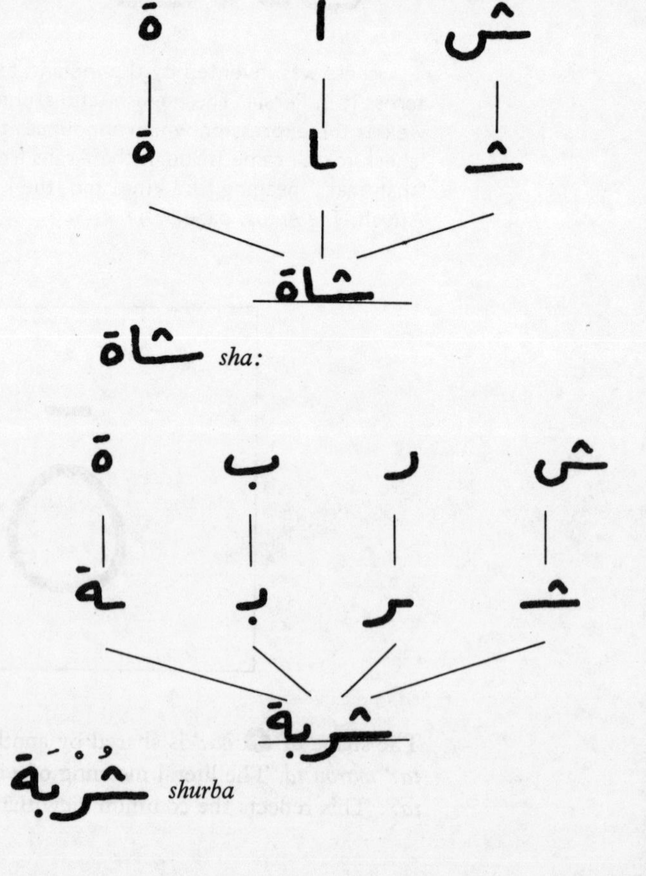

Ⓣ **Reading and writing practice** Read and pronounce the words below with reference to the tape.

Remember that ة *ta:' marbu:ṭa* itself is not pronounced in a word isolated from context.

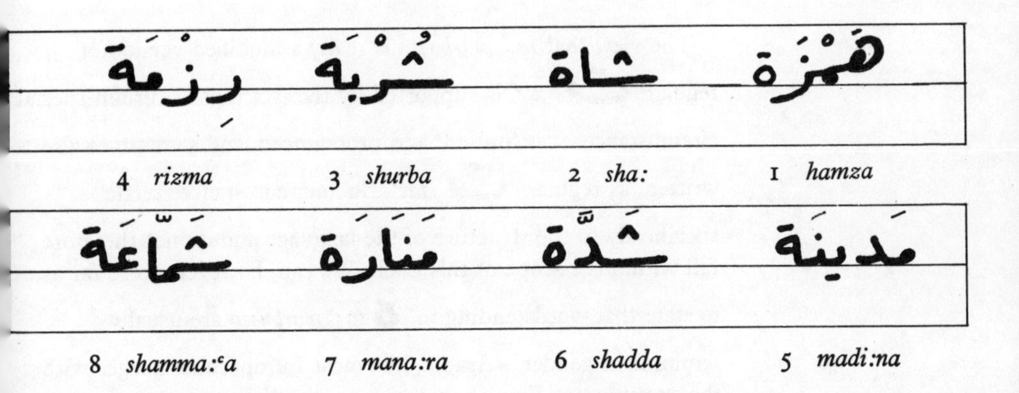


**Points of interest**

3 شُرْبَة

'drink', from which English 'sherbet' is derived.

4 رِزْمَة

'bundle; bale (of paper, etc.)', from which English 'ream' is derived.

5 مَدِينَة

The name of the second holiest city of Islam, in western Saudi Arabia. Commonly spelt 'Medinah' in English.

6 شَدَّة

The name of the sign signifying the doubling of a consonant.

7 مَنارَة

'minaret' is the English adaptation of the Arabic word for the tower of a mosque from which the call to prayer is made.

The view that *ta:' marbu:ta* is really a modified version of regular ت *ta:'* is supported by the fact that in certain special circumstances it is 'untied' and pronounced, and sometimes also written, as regular ت *ta:'*. Such circumstances relate specifically to the structure of the language and do not therefore fall within the scope of this book. We can, however, go so far as to state that words ending in ة *ta:' marbu:ta* are usually feminine in gender – Arabic, like most European languages with the exception of English, makes a formal distinction between masculine and feminine nouns. The words in the two columns below are in fact common Arabic personal names – those on the right, ending in ة *ta:' marbu:ta*, are women's names, and those on the left are the corresponding men's names.

| | | | |
|---|---|---|---|
| *nabi:l* | نَبيل | *nabi:la* | نَبِيلَة |
| *sami:r* | سَمير | *sami:ra* | سَمِيرَة |
| *sali:m* | سَليم | *sali:ma* | سَلِيمَة |
| *ᶜazi:z* | عَزيز | *ᶜazi:za* | عَزِيزَة |
| *saᶜi:d* | سَعيد | *saᶜi:da* | سَعِيدَة |

***Printed forms of examples from writing practice***

**For reading and pronunciation practice only**

| | **Final** | | **Medial** | | **Initial** |
|---|---|---|---|---|---|
| 1 | نبه | 1 | شهر | 1 | همس |
| 2 | مشبوه | 2 | ذهب | 2 | هند |
| 3 | تنبيه | 3 | أهرام | 3 | هبر |
| 4 | تشابه | 4 | مهم | 4 | هلال |
| 5 | تياه | 5 | درهم | 5 | هامش |
| 6 | تشبيه | 6 | سهل | 6 | هروب |
| 7 | شاه | 7 | شهرزاد | 7 | هرس |
| 8 | إنتباه | 8 | إبراهيم | 8 | هدب |

ة ta:' marbu:ta

| | | | |
|---|---|---|---|
| 1 | همزة | 2 | شاة |
| 3 | شربة | 4 | رزمة |
| 5 | مدينة | 6 | شدة |
| 7 | منارة | 8 | شماعة |

The printed initial, medial and final shapes of *ha:'* ه are slightly different from their corresponding handwritten forms. Make sure you can recognise the printed medial form in particular as it is so different from the handwritten form you have learned.

handwritten printed

ههه ههه

# Unit 11

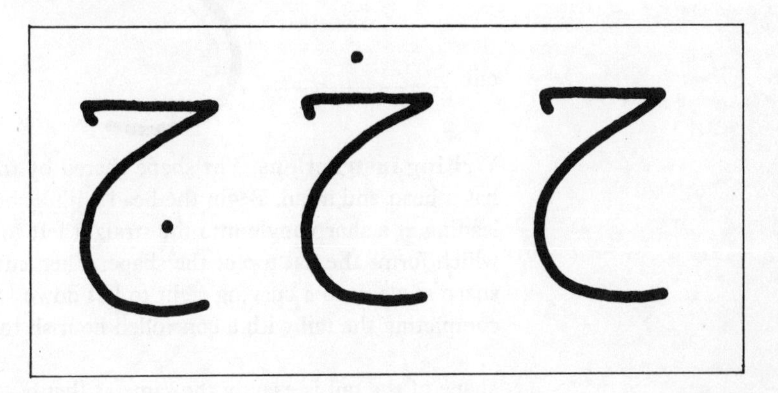


The basic shape shared by the isolated forms of these three letters is: ح

The basic shape alone is *h̲a:’*.

There is no equivalent sound in English. ح *h̲a:’* is an ‘h’ sound articulated with more force than ه *ha:’* or English ‘h’. It also comes from further back in the throat, with the gagging muscles in the pharynx tensed. One way to approximate this sound is to whisper ‘Hey you!’ as loud as you can, trying to get the ‘h’ as far back in the throat as possible, and at the same time tensing the gagging muscles.

ح is transliterated as /h̲/.

The basic shape with one dot above is *kha:’* خ

Although there is no equivalent sound in English, similar sounds do occur in many other languages, such as ‘ch’ in German ‘a*ch*tung’ (and in the Scottish pronunciation of ‘lo*ch*’), and ‘j’ in Castilian Spanish ‘trabajo’.

خ is transliterated as /kh/.

The basic shape with one dot inside the tail is *ji:m* ج
It is pronounced like the ‘j’ in ‘*j*uice’ and transliterated as /j/.

**Isolated form**

**Writing instructions** The shape shared by these three letters has a head and a tail. Begin the head with a short up stroke leading at a sharp angle into the straight left to right stroke which forms the flat top of the shape. Then cut back, again at a sharp angle, into a curving right to left down stroke before completing the tail with a controlled flourish to the right. The shape of the tail is exactly the same as that of 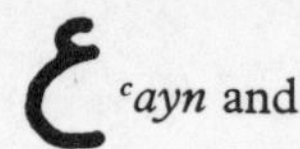 *ʿayn* and

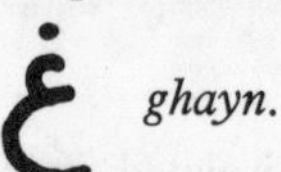 *ghayn.*

**Reading and writing practice** Trace and copy the models below. Concentrate on getting a consistent tail shape, and notice the variation in angle and length of the short initial up stroke of the head. In some models it is actually touching the upper part of the tail, and the head appears as a triangle. Say the name of each letter as you write it.

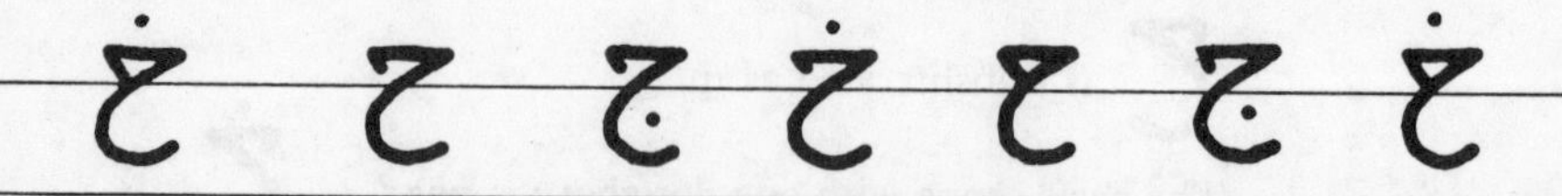

**Proportion guide**

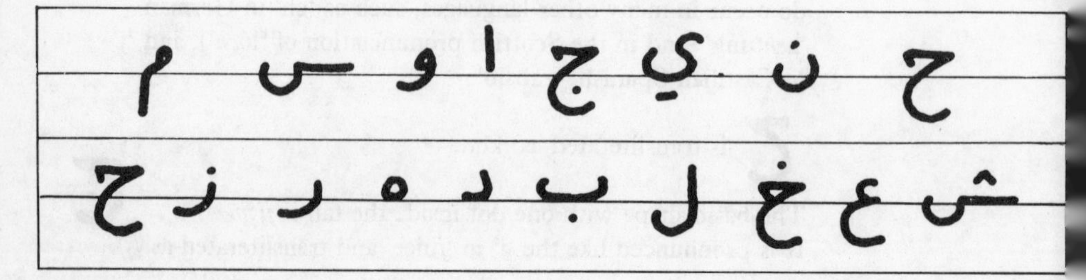

**Initial position** When these letters occur at the beginning of a word they lose their tails and have a distinctive initial form which joins to the following letter.

OBSERVE

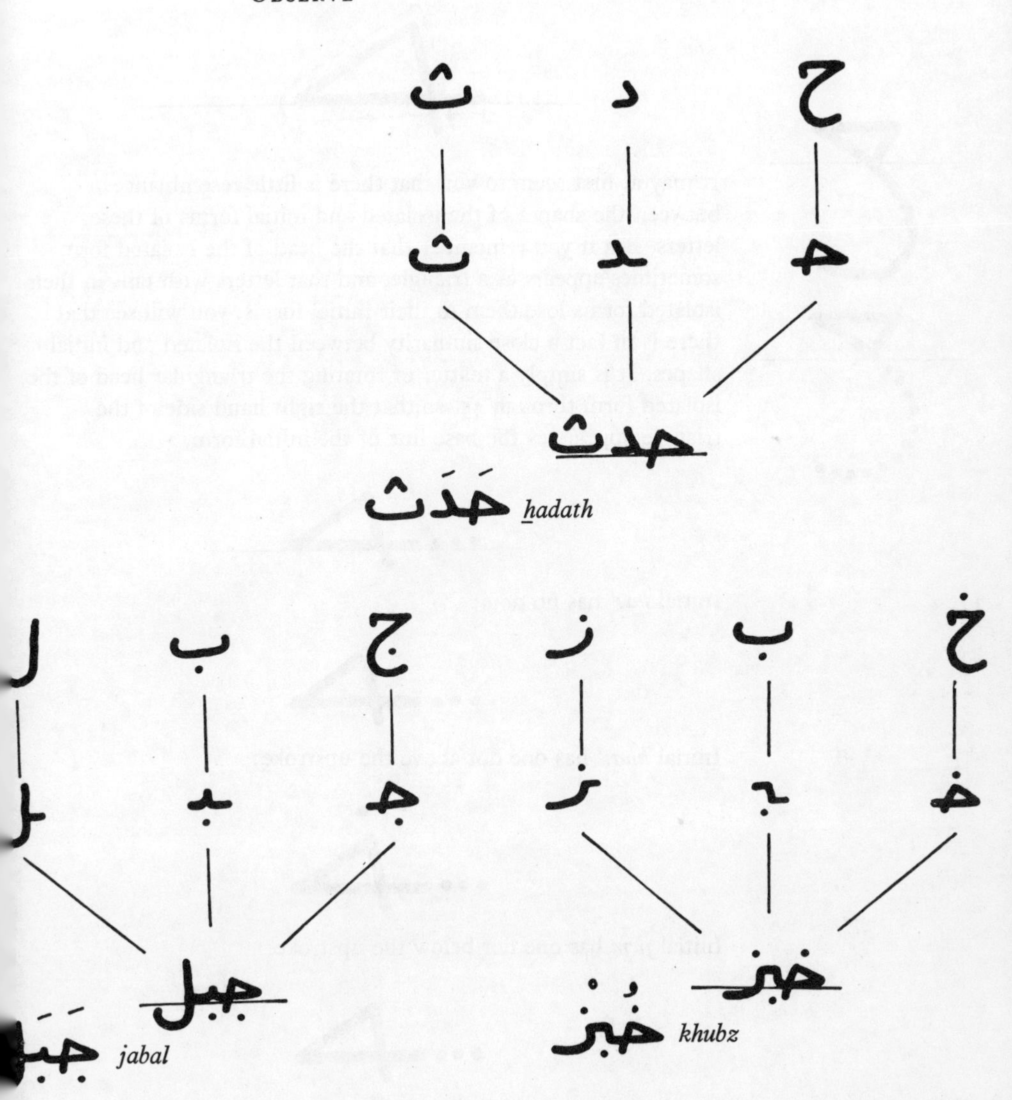


**Writing instructions** The triangular initial form shared by these letters is written in three strokes:

1. An initial up stroke sloping slightly to the right of vertical, and about the same height as the ر / ز shape.
2. A straight left to right stroke leading back down to the line.

3 A right to left base stroke which sits on the line and crosses the initial up stroke to provide the connecting line into the next letter:

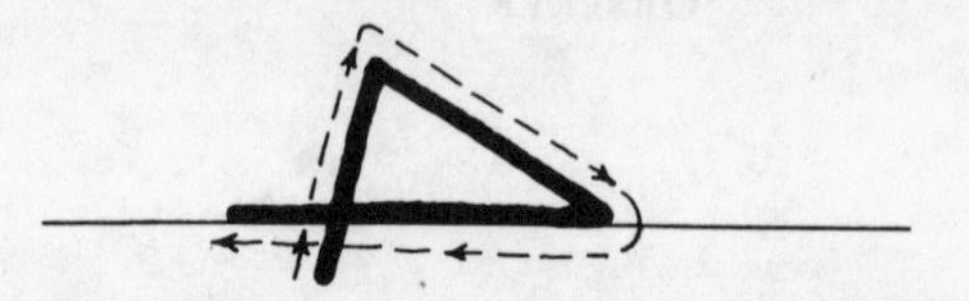

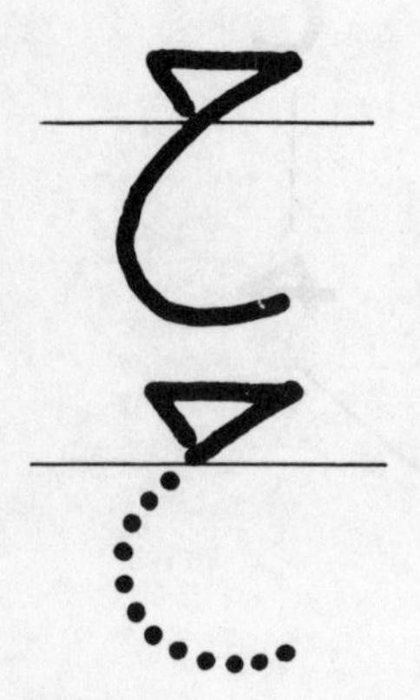

It may at first seem to you that there is little resemblance between the shapes of the isolated and initial forms of these letters. But if you remember that the head of the isolated form sometimes appears as a triangle, and that letters with tails in their isolated forms lose them in their initial forms, you will see that there is in fact a close similarity between the isolated and initial shapes. It is simply a matter of rotating the triangular head of the isolated form through 45° so that the right hand side of the triangle appears as the base line of the initial form.

Initial *h̲a:'* has no dots:

Initial *kha:'* has one dot above the upstroke:

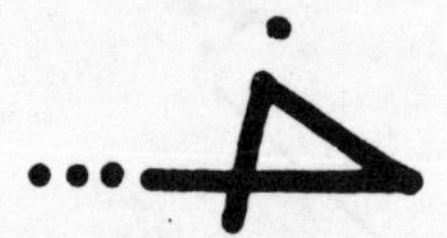

Initial *ji:m* has one dot below the upstroke:

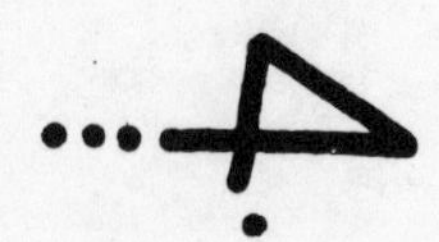

**Reading and writing practice**

Ⓣ □ Read and pronounce the words on page 141 with reference to the tape.

□ Trace and copy the models. Pay particular attention to the dots since they are the only feature distinguishing between the three new letters in all their forms. Pronounce each word several times as soon as you have completed it.

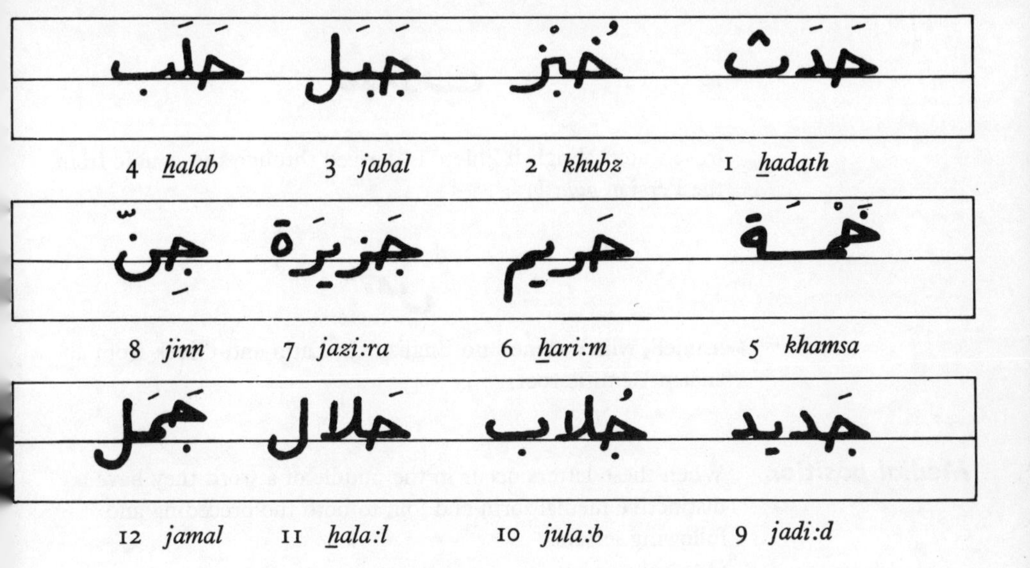


**Points of interest**

4 حَلَب

The Arabic name for Aleppo in northern Syria.

6 حَرِيم

'a sacred inviolable place; the part of a house where women live; women', from which is derived English 'harem'.

7 جَزِيرَة

'island', from which the Spanish place name 'Algeciras' is derived.

8 جِنّ

An order of spirits commonly mentioned in popular folklore and literature. Said to have the power of assuming human and animal forms, and to exercise supernatural influence over mortals – hence English 'genie'.

10 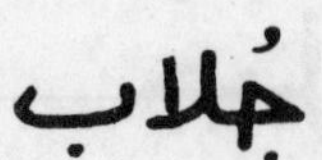

'rose water'. English 'julep' is derived through the Arabic from the Persian *gula:b*.

11 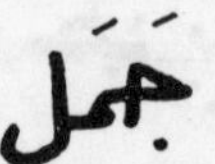

'camel', which came into English via Latin and Greek from an ancient semitic root.

**Medial position** When these letters occur in the middle of a word they have a distinctive medial form and join to both the preceding and following letters.

OBSERVE

ب ح ر

بـ ـحـ ـر

بحر

بَحْر *bahr*

ب خ ت ن ج د

بـ ـخـ ـتـ نـ ـجـ ـد

بخت نجد

بَخْت *bakht*

نَجْد *najd*

**Writing instructions** Notice that the medial form of these three letters, like medial م *mi:m*, joins to preceding letters from above. You must therefore start preceding letters from a higher position in relation to the line than usual.
The shape shared by the medial form of these three letters is written in three strokes:

1 A connecting line from the preceding letter, sloping down to the left.
2 A second stroke which cuts back down.
3 A base stroke which is more or less parallel to the first stroke and provides the connecting line to the next letter:

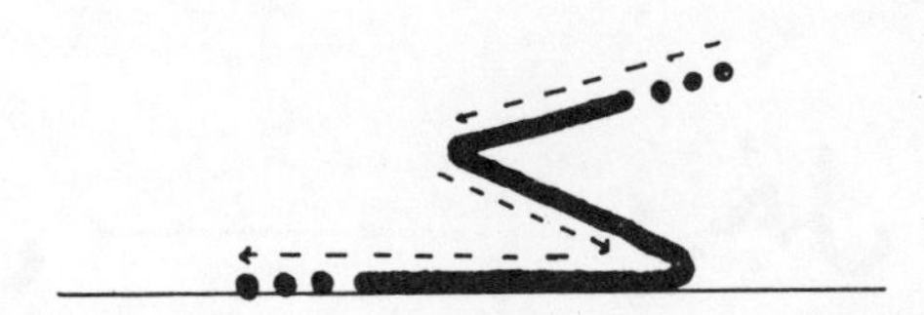

At first glance the resemblance between the medial and initial forms seems as remote as that between the initial and isolated forms. However, imagine the initial form without the initial upstroke:

Add the sloping connecting line from the preceding letter:

You will see that the shapes of the two forms are in fact very similar.

**Bridging** When the medial form of these letters follows a *medial* form of

(i.e. in a word of four letters or more), the bridging modification occurs:

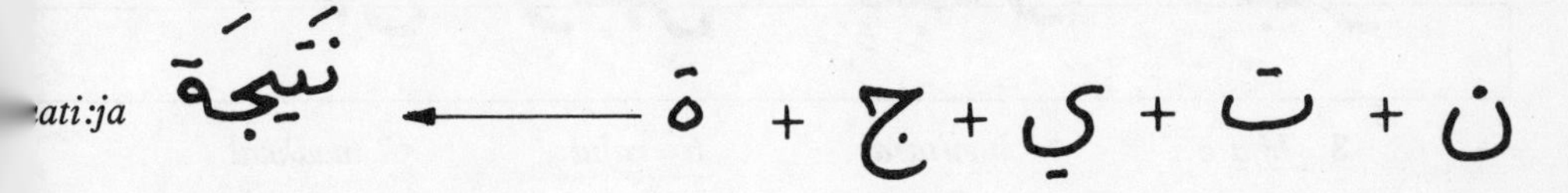

When preceded by one of the non-connectors, medial ح خ and ج appear in their initial form and join to the following letter only:

*wa:ḫid* واحِد ⟵ د + ح + ا + و

*madkhal* مَدْخَل ⟵ ل + خ + د + م

*rajul* رَجُل ⟵ ل + ج + ر

**Reading and writing practice**

Ⓣ □ Read and pronounce the words below with reference to the tape. Don't worry if you feel you are unable to produce an exact imitation of the tape models or your teacher's pronunciation immediately. Two of these new letters represent difficult sounds which require practice and patience.

□ Trace and copy the models. Remember to start letters preceding medial ح خ and ج higher than usual.

This will produce the 'stacking' effect which we have already noted in connection with م *mi:m.*

12 *masjid* 11 *zanjabi:l* 10 *muhammad* 9 *makhzan*

**Points of interest**

1

'sea'. Notice also

*al-bahrain* – 'Bahrain' (literally 'the two seas').

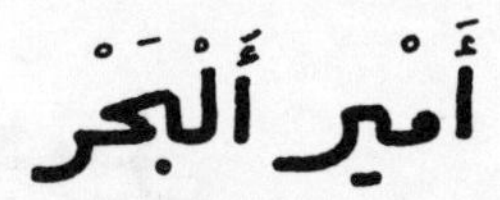

*'amir al-bahr* (literally 'prince of the sea'), from which are derived English 'admiral', French 'amiral', Spanish 'almirante', etc.

3

'Nejd' – the central region of Saudi Arabia.

7 إِنْجِلْتَرا

'England'. Adopted and transliterated directly from the Italian 'Inghilterra'.

9 مَخْزَن

'store room', from which English 'magazine' and French 'magasin' ('shop') are derived.

10

The name of the Prophet. Also reckoned to be the commonest man's name in the world today. Other names derived from the same root are:

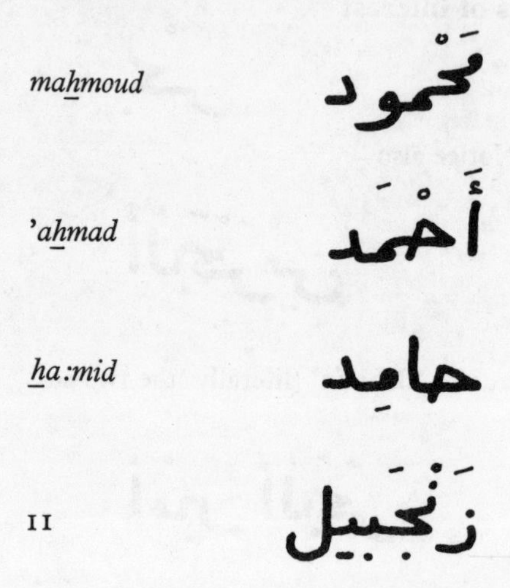


The word from which English 'ginger' is derived.

12

'mosque'. The English is derived from Arabic via French and Italian.

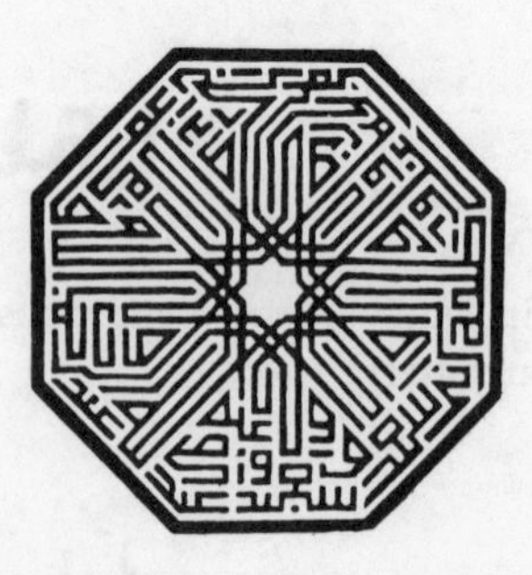

**Final position**

When these letters occur at the end of a word they retain the shape of their medial form, regaining their tail and joining to the preceding letter.

Observe

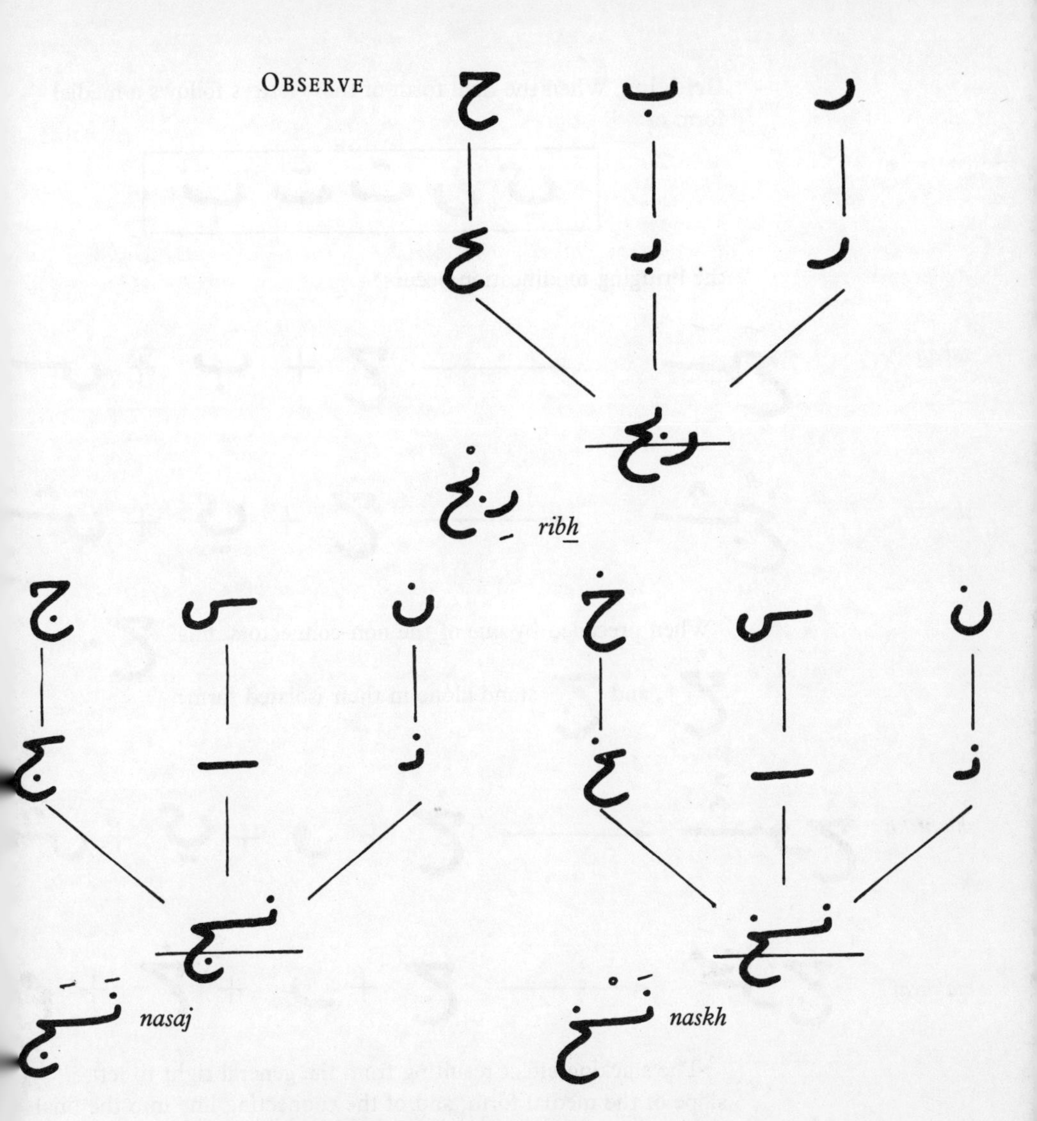


**Writing instructions** The joined final form of these letters is the distinctive 'zig-zag' shape of the medial form, but with the re-appearance of the bulging tail of the isolated form:

**Bridging** When the final form of these letters follows a medial form of

the bridging modification occurs:

*sabah* سَبَح ← ح + ب + س

*shaykh* شَيْخ ← خ + ي + ش

When preceded by one of the non-connectors, final ح, خ, and ج stand alone in their isolated form:

*shuyu:kh* شُيوخ ← خ + و + ي + ش

*makhraj* مَخْرَج ← ج + ر + خ + م

The stacking effect resulting from the general right to left slope of the medial form, and of the connecting line into the final form, together with the fact that both medial and final forms of these letters join to preceding letters from above, can be well illustrated by joining together an initial, a medial and a final form of the ح خ ج shape:

حخج

## Reading and writing practice

Ⓣ ☐ Read and pronounce the words below. Pay particular attention to the two new sounds.

☐ Trace and copy the models. Check the dots, short vowels and other signs carefully. Try to keep your examples in constant relation to the line, and all letters in proportion to one another within any one word. Pronounce each word several times as soon as you have completed it.

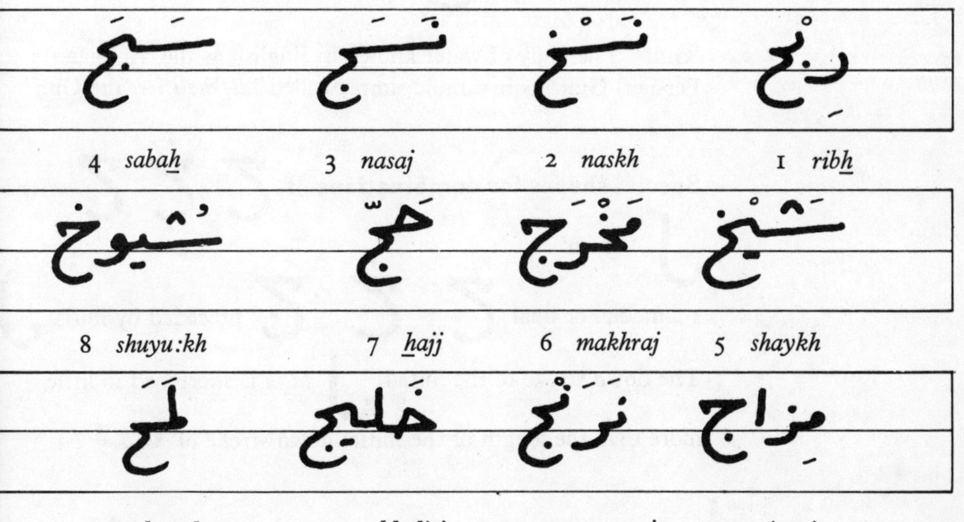


## Points of interest

2

Name of a style of Arabic script which has been widely used since the tenth century. In its typeset form it is still commonly used in books and other printed material.

5

'old man; tribal chief'. Usually spelt as 'sheikh' in English.

7

Name of the annual Muslim pilgrimage to Makkah.

10 

'orange', from which the English word is ultimately derived.

11 خَلِيج

'Gulf'. The body of water known in English as the 'Arabian (or Persian) Gulf', is in Arabic simply called *'al-khali:j* – 'the Gulf'.

**Special shapes for combinations of** ح خ ج **with** ل **'la:m'**

1 medial or final ح خ ج preceded by initial ل

The down stroke of the initial ل *la:m* is shortened to little more than the length of the initial down stroke of ب *ba:'*:

*lahm* لَحْم ⟵ م + ح + ل

*ma:lih* مالِح ⟵ ح + ل + ا + م

2 medial or final ح خ ج preceded by medial ل *la:m*

Lead into the up stroke of medial ل, as usual, with the connecting line from the preceding letter, but retrace the down stroke less than half way down the up stroke before veering away into the connecting line to the following letter:

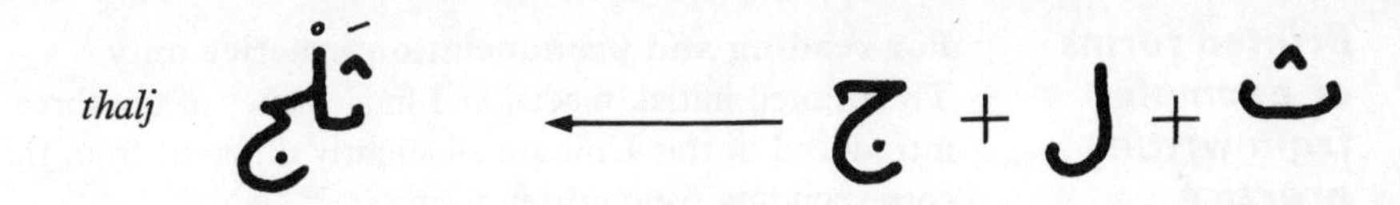


**Reading and writing practice**

Ⓣ □ Read and pronounce the words below with reference to the tape.

□ Trace and copy the models. These ligatures are a common feature of hand-written Arabic – practise until you can write and recognise them with ease.

**_Printed forms of examples from writing practice_**

**For reading and pronunciation practice only**
The printed initial, medial and final shapes of the three letters introduced in this Unit are all slightly different from the corresponding handwritten forms.
OBSERVE

| handwritten | | printed | |
|---|---|---|---|
| ححح | ح | ححح | ح |

Notice particularly that the 'stacking' effect produced by the medial and final handwritten forms does not occur in print. Like bridging, the stacking of letters one above the other is a vertical feature of handwriting which does not suit the essentially linear process of print.

| Final | | Medial | | Initial |
|---|---|---|---|---|
| ربح | 1 | بحر | 1 | حدث |
| نسخ | 2 | بخت | 2 | خبز |
| نسج | 3 | نجد | 3 | جبل |
| سبح | 4 | واحد | 4 | حلب |
| شيخ | 5 | مدخل | 5 | خمسة |
| مخرج | 6 | رجل | 6 | حريم |

7 جزيرة 7 انجلترا 7 حج

8 جن 8 حجاز 8 شيوخ

9 جديد 9 مخزن 9 مزاج

10 جلاب 10 محمد 10 نرنج

11 حلال 11 زنجبيل 11 خليج

12 جمل 12 مسجد 12 لمح

**Ligatures**

1 لحم 5 الجزيرة

2 مالح 6 بلح

3 ثلج 7 زلج

4 لحن 8 الخبز

**Pronunciation drill** Ⓣ    **Contrast ه and ح**

| | /h/ | | /ḥ/ |
|---|---|---|---|
| 1 | هَبّ | ← | حَبّ |
| 2 | شَبَه | ← | شَبَح |
| 3 | هَمّام | ← | حَمّام |
| 4 | تَهْديد | ← | تَحْديد |
| 5 | مَهْسوس | ← | مَحْسوس |
| 6 | مُشْهور | ← | مَشْحور |

**Contrast** خ **and** غ

| | /kh/ | | /gh/ |
|---|---|---|---|
| 1 | خاب | ← | غاب |
| 2 | خَيْر | ← | غَيْر |
| 3 | خَيْمة | ← | غَيْمة |
| 4 | يَخْبُر | ← | يَغْبُر |
| 5 | يُخَرِّب | ← | يُغَرِّب |
| 6 | ساخ | ← | ساغ |

# Unit 12

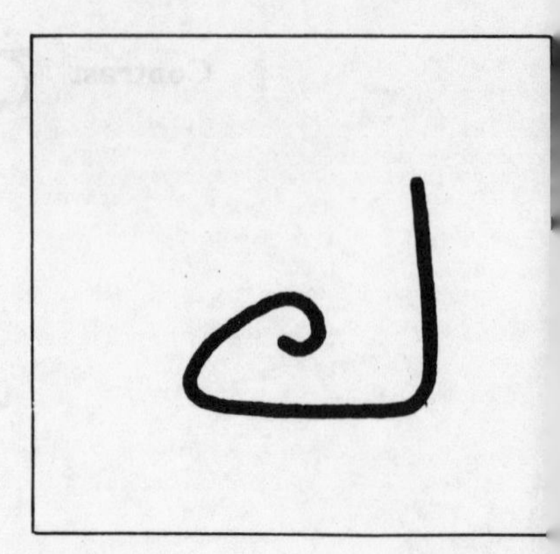

The name of this letter is *ka:f*. ك

It is pronounced like the 'k' in '*k*iss' and transliterated as /k/.

***Isolated form***

**Writing instructions** The down stroke and the base of ك *ka:f* are both more or less the same length as ا *alif*. They meet at a rounded right angle, with the base stroke sitting on the line. The small flourish at the end of the base stroke is reminiscent of the turned-up toe of a Turkish slipper.

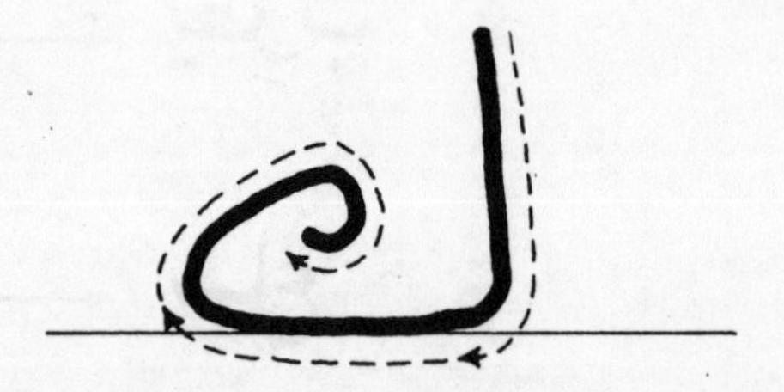

**Reading and writing practice** Trace over the models below before making any freehand attempts, then practise until you can write the letter in one fluid movement. Check your examples with the book to make sure they fall within the range indicated by the slight degree of variation between each of the models. Say the name of the letter each time you write it.

Use the proportion guide below for further writing practice. Say the name of each letter as you write it.

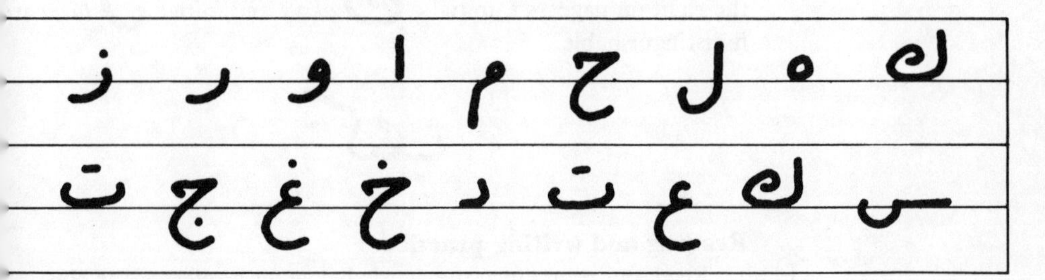

**initial position** When this letter occurs at the beginning of a word it has a distinctive initial form and joins to the following letter.
OBSERVE

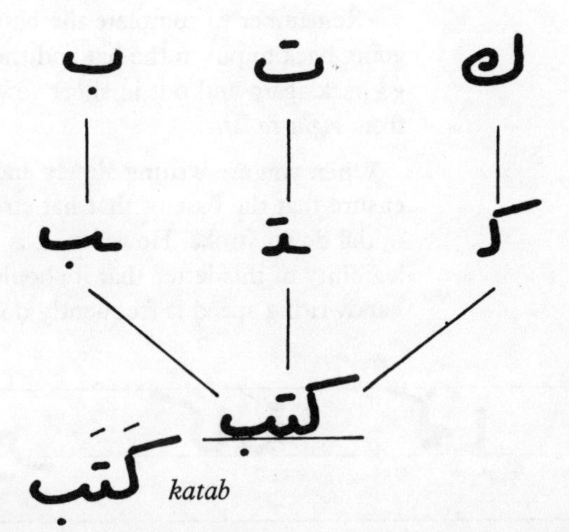


**Writing instructions** This initial form is made in two stages.

First make a down stroke as for initial ﻟ *la:m*, join it to the next letter and complete the basic word shape. Then, when you come back to the beginning of the word to put in the dots from *right to left*, add the oblique 'hat' stroke to the initial down stroke:

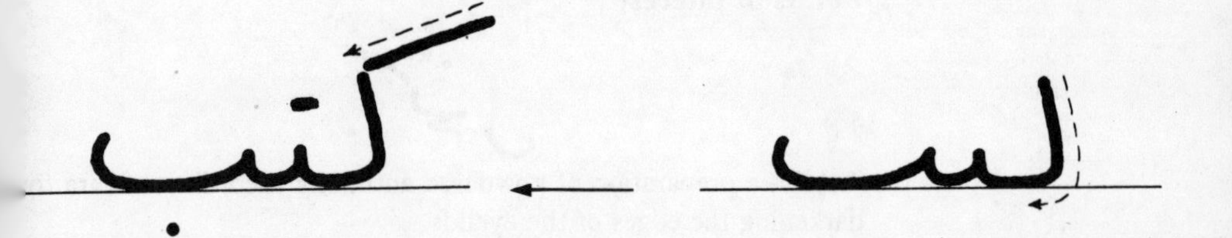

Without the hat, as you can see from the incomplete example on the right on page 157, initial ك *ka:f* and initial ل *la:m* a indistinguishable.

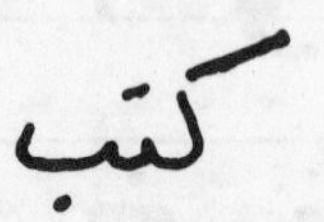

### Reading and writing practice

Ⓣ ☐ Read and pronounce the words below with reference to the tape.

☐ Trace and copy the models. Notice that the down stroke of initial ک *ka:f* sometimes slopes slightly to the left of upright.

☐ Remember to complete the basic shape of each word before going back to put in the hat and the dots from *right to left*. Then go back again and put in short vowels, *shadda*, and *suku:n*, also from *right to left*.

When you are writing slowly and carefully it is easy to always ensure that the base of that hat stroke just touches the top of the initial down stroke. However, it is in no way vital to the legibility of this letter that it should do so, and at normal handwriting speed it frequently does not.

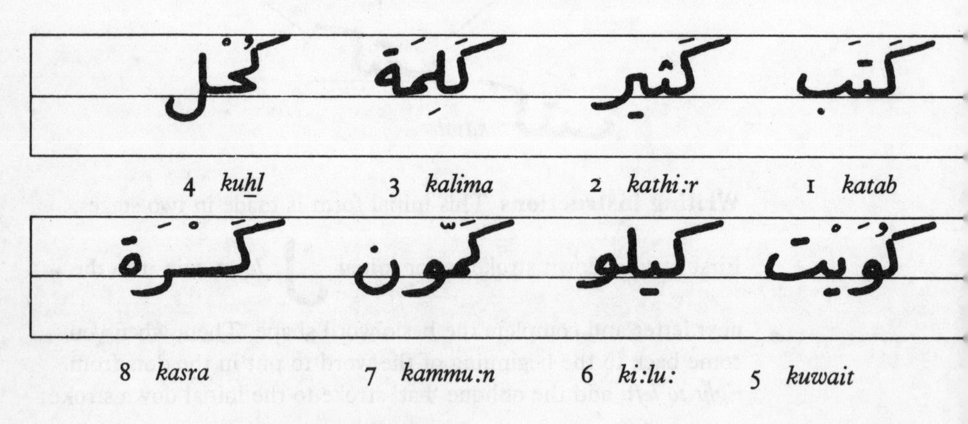


### Points of interest

4 كُحْل

'kohl' – a preparation of powdered antimony used like mascara fo darkening the edges of the eyelids.

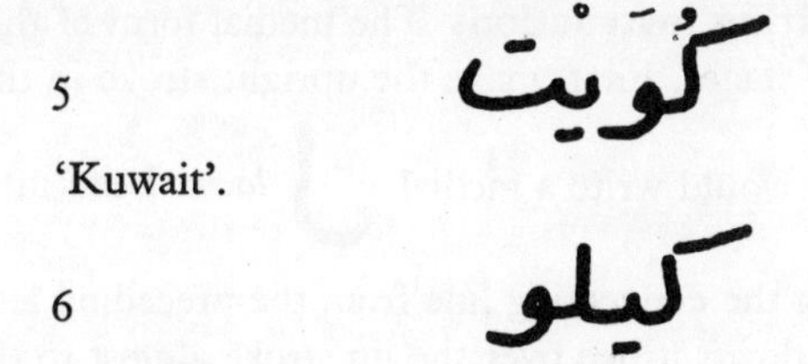


The Arabic word for 'kilogram', transliterated directly from the French.

'cumin', the name of this spice passed into English from Arabic via Greek and Latin.

The name of the short vowel.

**Medial position** When this letter occurs in the middle of a word it has the same shape as its initial form, but joins to both the preceding and following letters.

OBSERVE

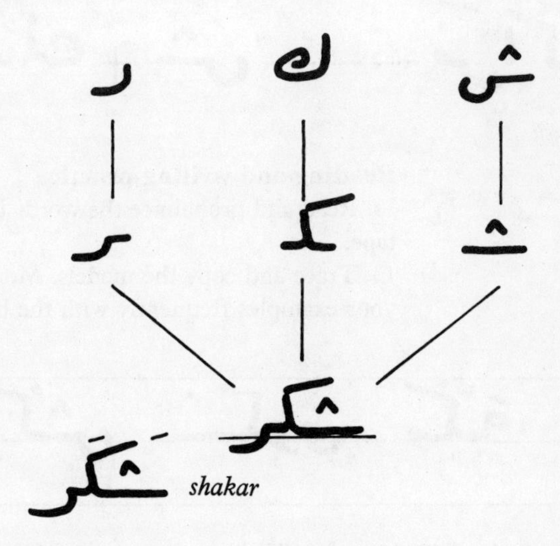

**Writing instructions** The medial form of this letter is made in two stages. First, make the upright stroke in the same way as

you would write a medial ل *la:m*. Lead into the up stroke

with the connecting line from the preceding letter, then retrace the down stroke over the up stroke almost to the horizontal line before veering away to provide the connecting line to the next letter. Then, when you have completed the basic word shape, come back to the beginning of the word and put in the dots and the oblique hat stroke from *right to left:*

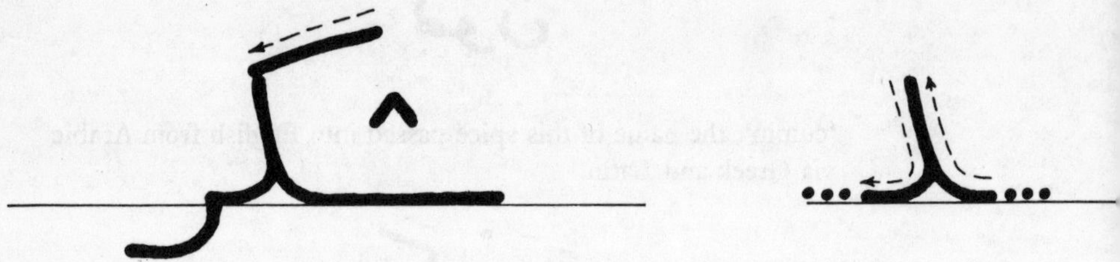

Without the hat, as you can see from the incomplete example on

the right, medial ك *ka:f* and medial ل *la:m* are

indistinguishable.

When preceded by one of the non-connectors, medial ك appears in its initial form and joins to the following letter only:

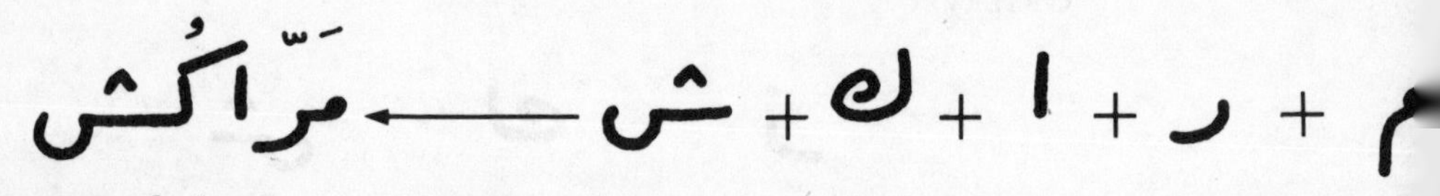

*marra:kush*

**Reading and writing practice**

Ⓣ ☐ Read and pronounce the words below with reference to the tape.

☐ Trace and copy the models. Monitor your progress by checkin[g] your examples frequently with the book.

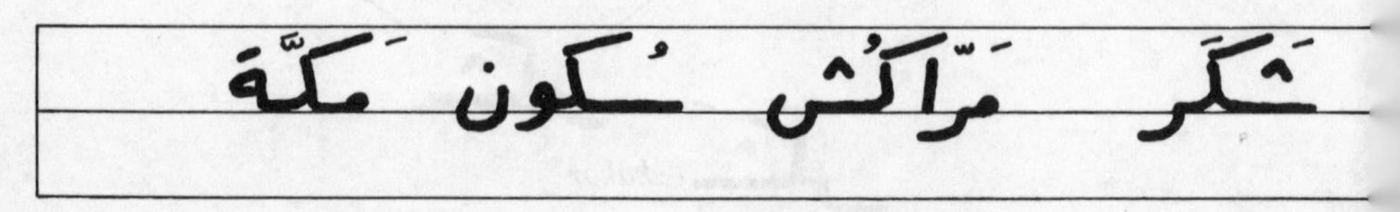


4 *makka* 3 *suku:n* 2 *marra:kush* 1 *shakar*

8 *'iskandariya* 7 *duktu:r* 6 *sukkar* 5 *'amri:ka:*

**Points of interest**

2

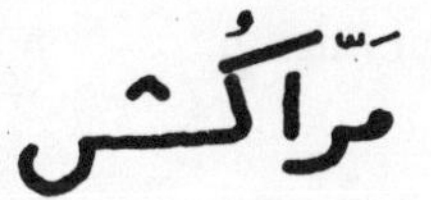

'Marrakech' – a city in western Morocco, and the old Arabic name for Morocco.

3

The name of the 'zero vowel' sign.

4

'Makkah' – the holiest city of Islam, in western Saudi Arabia. The birth place of the Prophet Muhammad (c. 570 A.D.).

5

The Arabic name for America, transliterated directly from English.

6

'sugar' is the English adaptation of the Arabic word. Discussing the delicacies brought back from the Arab world by the Crusaders, Hitti says:

> 'More important than all the others is sugar, the Arabic "sukkar". Europeans had hitherto used honey for sweetening their foods. On the martime plain of Syria-Lebanon, where children can still be seen sucking sugar cane, the Franks became acquainted with this plant which has since played such an important role in our domestic economy and medical prescriptions. Sugar was the first luxury introduced into the West and nothing else so delighted the Western palate. With it went soft drinks, waters tinctured by distillation with roses, violets or other flowers, and all varieties of

candy (of Arabic etymology) and sweetmeats.' (Philip K. Hitti, *The Arabs: a short history*, pages 182-3)

7 

One of several Arabic words for 'doctor', directly transliterated from English.

8 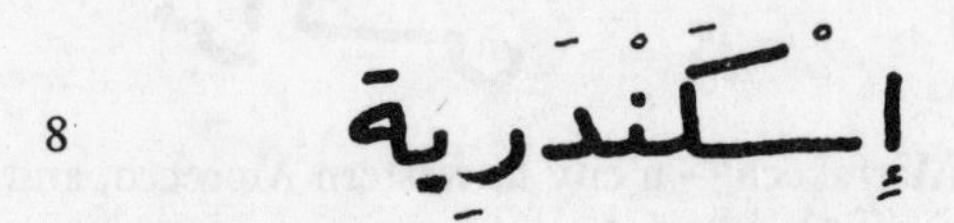

'Alexandria', the second city and main port of Egypt.

***Final position***

When this letter occurs at the end of a word it retains the shape of its isolated form, but joins to the preceding letter.

OBSERVE

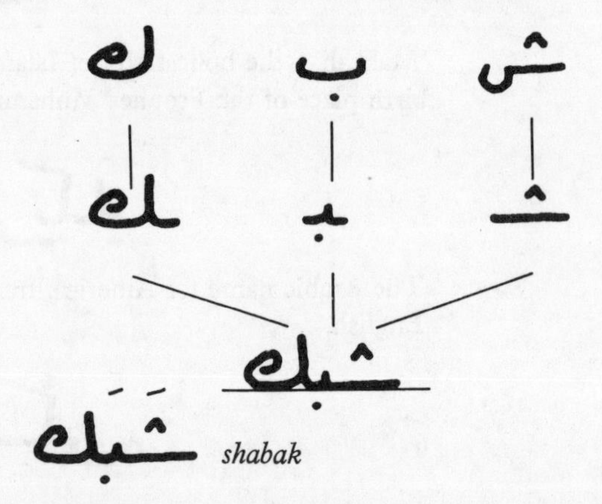

*shabak*

**Writing instructions** Lead into the up stroke of the final form with the connecting line from the preceding letter, then retrace th down stroke over the up stroke, make the base stroke on the line and complete the letter with its distinctive inward curling final flourish:

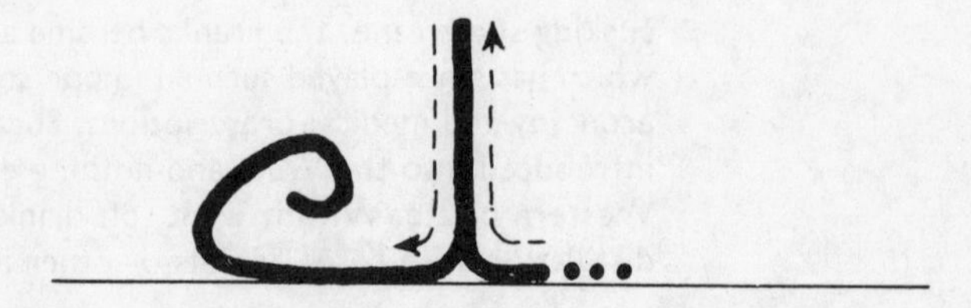

When preceded by one of the non-connectors, final ك *ka:f* stands alone in its isolated form:

م + م + ل + و + ك ← مَمْلوك *mamlu:k*

**Reading and writing practice**

Ⓣ ☐ Read and pronounce the words below with reference to the tape.

☐ Trace and copy the models.

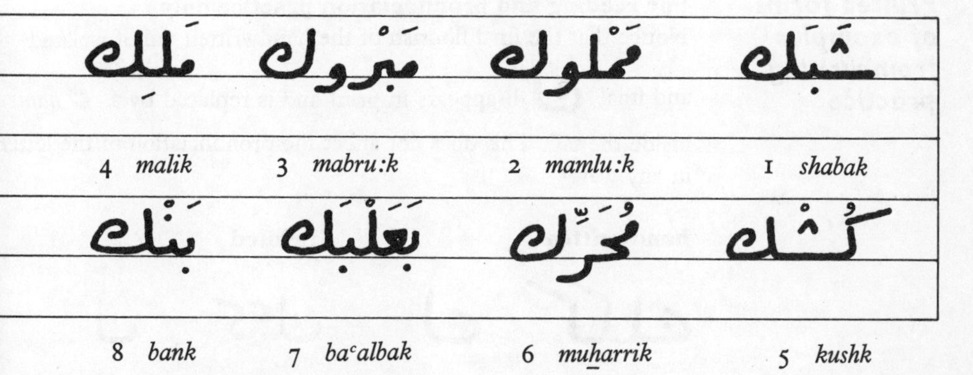


**Points of interest**

2 مَمْلوك

'Mamluk' – literal meaning is 'owned'. The name of the dynasty of former slaves which ruled Egypt from 1250–1517 A.D.

5 كُشْك

A Persian word, also used in Arabic, from which the English 'kiosk' derives.

7 بَعَلْبَك

A small town in central Lebanon, noted, among other things, for its fine Roman ruins.

Always monitor your progress by constant reference to the book. Go back and re-do the reading and writing practice from previous

Units, especially those containing any letters you may still be having difficulty with. Don't go on to the next Unit unless you are quite confident that you have assimilated everything so far.

The writing should be coming much more easily now, and you should be developing a fair degree of control over its size. Practise regularly, and always refer back to the book in case of difficulty.

Experiment with different pens – you will find that it can be very aesthetically pleasing to vary the thickness of your strokes.

***Printed forms of examples from writing practice***

**For reading and pronunciation practice only**

Notice that the final flourish of the handwritten tail of isolated and final ك disappears in print and is replaced by a ء *hamza* inside the tail. This does not affect the pronunciation of the letter in any way.

| handwritten | | printed | |
|---|---|---|---|
| ككك | ك | ككك | ك |

| Final | | Medial | | Initial |
|---|---|---|---|---|
| شبك | 1 | شكر | 1 | كتب |
| مملوك | 2 | مراكش | 2 | كثير |
| مبروك | 3 | سكون | 3 | كلمة |
| ملك | 4 | مكّة | 4 | كحل |
| كشك | 5 | أمريكا | 5 | كويت |

| | | | | | |
|---|---|---|---|---|---|
| 6 | كيلو | 6 | سكر | 6 | محرك |
| 7 | كمون | 7 | دكتور | 7 | بعلبك |
| 8 | كسرة | 8 | إسكندرية | 8 | بنك |

**Pronunciation drill** Ⓣ

**Contrast** ك **and** خ    ح **and** ع

| | /k/ | /kh/ | | /h̲/ | /c/ |
|---|---|---|---|---|---|
| 1 | كَبير | خَبير | 1 | حام | عام |
| 2 | شَكَر | شَخَر | 2 | حاد | عاد |
| 3 | شَرَك | شَرَخ | 3 | بَحْث | بَعْث |
| 4 | مُبَكِّر | مُبَخِّر | 4 | نَبَح | نَبَع |
| 5 | بَكَّر | بَخَّر | 5 | روح | روع |
| 6 | كَد | خَد | 6 | شَبَح | شَبِع |

# Unit 13

This is the letter *fa:'*. ف
It is pronounced like the 'f' in '*f*inger', and transliterated as /f/.

**Isolated form**

**Writing instructions** This is another letter with a head and a tail. The head is roughly the same size as the head of و *wa:w* and sits just above the line. It has a short neck leading into a flat bottomed tail like the shape of isolated ب *ba:'*, lying on the line. The single dot is placed centrally above the head of the letter.

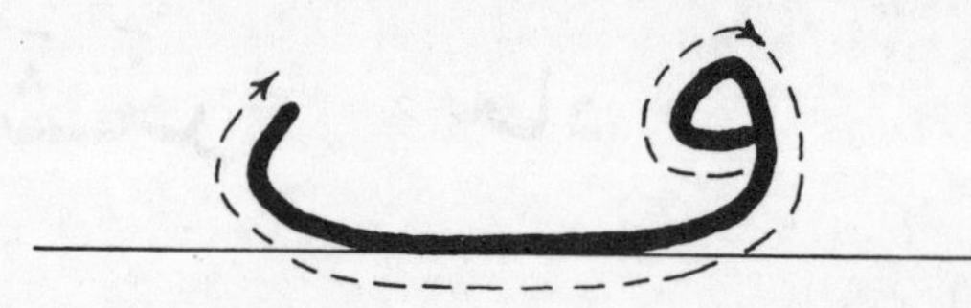

**Reading and writing practice** Trace and copy these models, saying the name of the letter each time you write it.

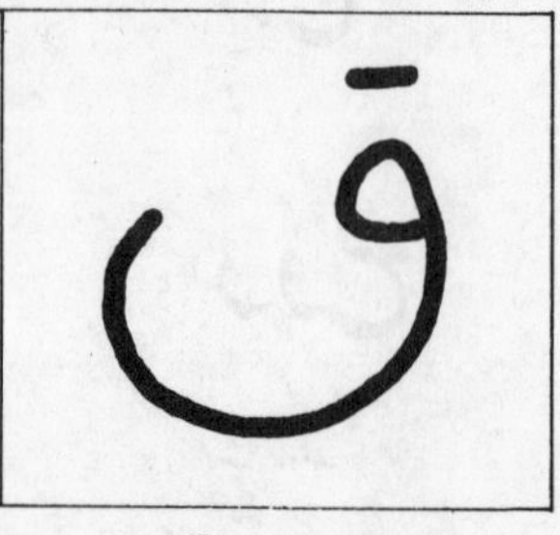

This is the letter *qa:f*. 

There is no equivalent sound in English. ق *qa:f* is a 'k' sound made further back in the mouth than ك *ka:f* and English 'k'. To pronounce ق *qa:f* say the work 'fork' and hold the mouth and tongue position which you make in preparation for the final 'k', but don't actually articulate the sound. Feel where the back of your tongue makes contact with the roof of your mouth, then slide it even further back so that it is touching the rearmost part of the roof of the mouth. If you now release the 'k' sound, you will be pronouncing ق *qa:f*. Practise this sound extensively with the aid of the tape drills and/or your teacher's own pronunciation – it should come fairly quickly.

ق *qa:f* is transliterated as /q/.

***Isolated form***

**Writing instructions** Like ف *fa:'*, ق *qa:f* also has a head and a tail. The heads of the two letters are identical, but the tail of ق *qa:f* is like the bulbous shape of ن *nu:n*, sinking below the line. The two dot stroke / ـ / is placed above the head of the letter.

**Reading and writing practice** Trace and copy the models on page 168. Say the name of the letter each time you write it. Notice that, as with و *wa:w*, م *mi:m* and the initial form of هـ *ha:'*, there is sometimes a tendency for the head of these two letters to get filled in, depending on size of writing and thickness of pen used. Don't make a deliberate effort to fill the head in, but if it happens don't worry – it's a common feature of cursive handwriting.

**Proportion guide**

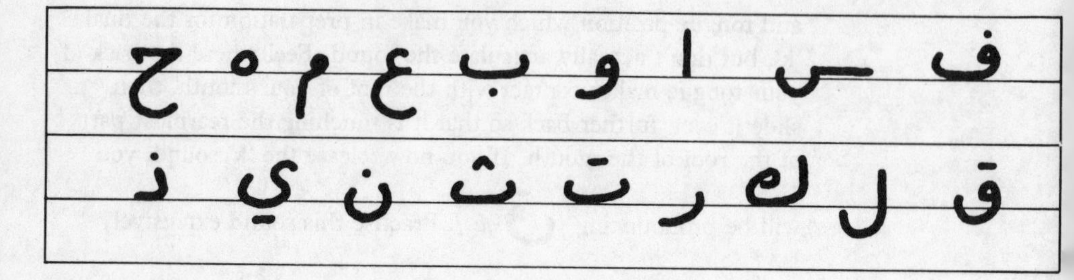

***Initial position*** When these letters occur at the beginning of a word they lose their tail and join to the following letter.

OBSERVE

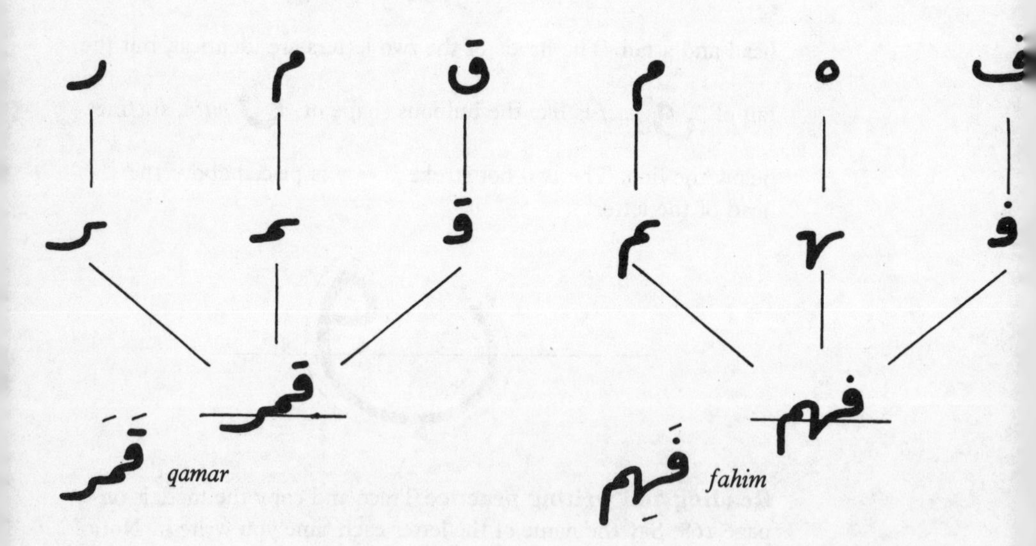


**Writing instructions** In their initial forms ف *fa:'* and ق *qa:f* are distinguished from one another only by their dots.

The head is a small clockwise circle sitting a little above the line on a short neck which provides the connecting line to the next letter.

**Reading and writing practice**

Ⓣ □ Read and pronounce the words below with reference to the tape. Don't worry if you feel that you are unable to make the sound of ق *qa:f* immediately. It is a new sound and one which requires special attention.

□ Trace and copy the models. Remember to write each word in three stages: first complete the basic word shape, then go back and put in the dots from *right to left*, and finally go back again and put in the short vowels and other signs, also from *right to left*.

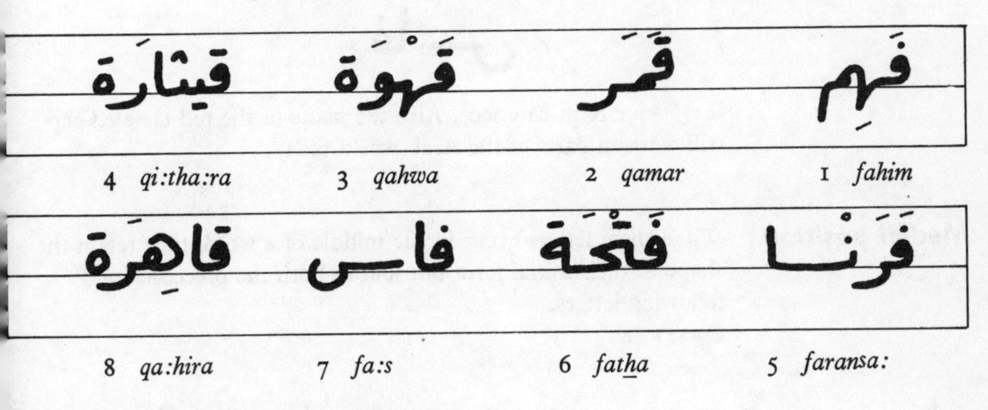


4 *qi:tha:ra* 3 *qahwa* 2 *qamar* 1 *fahim*

8 *qa:hira* 7 *fa:s* 6 *fatha* 5 *faransa:*

**Points of interest**

2 قَمَر

'moon' – the word which gives the 'moon letters' their name.

3 قَهْوَة

The word from which English 'coffee' derives. First recorded use in English c. 1598.

4 قيثارَة

'guitar' derived from Greek.

5 

The Arabic name for 'France', transliterated from the French.

6 

Name of the short vowel.

7 

'Fez' – a city in Morocco. Also the name of the red tasseled cap still worn in parts of the Arab world today.

***Medial position*** When these letters occur in the middle of a word, they retain the shape of their initial form but join to both the preceding and following letters.

OBSERVE

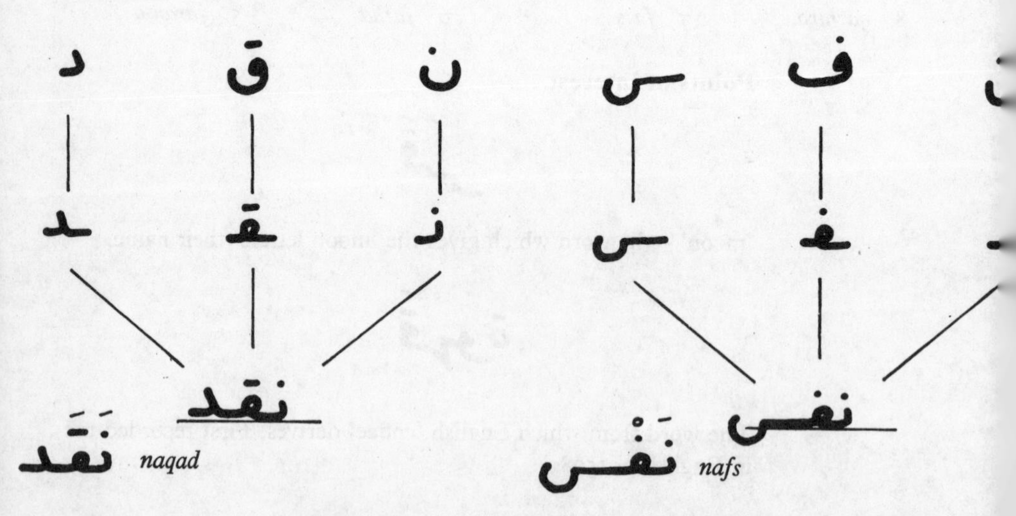


**Writing instructions** The medial form of both these letters is a small clockwise loop sitting on the line. Lead into the loop with the connecting line from the preceding letter, make the loop and then extend the stroke leading out of it to provide the connecting line to the next letter.

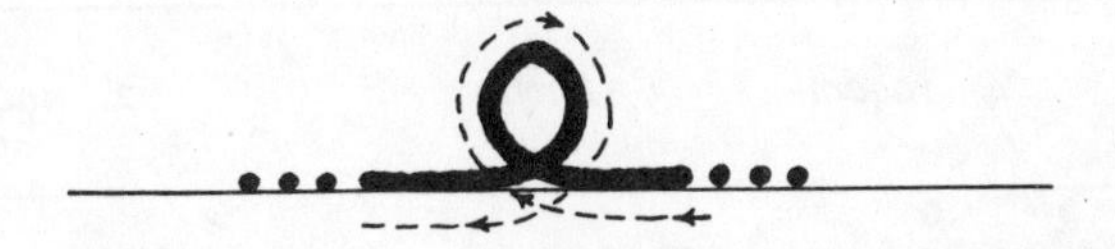

When preceded by one of the non-connectors, medial ف *fa:'* and ق *qa:f* appear in their initial form and join to the following letter.

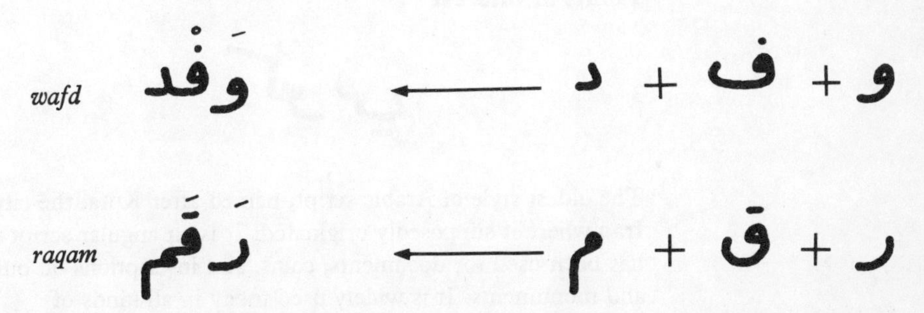


**Reading and writing practice**

Ⓣ ☐ Read and pronounce the words on page 172 with reference to the tape.

☐ Pay attention to the dots – they are the only feature distinguishing between the otherwise identical medial forms of

ف *fa:'* and ق *qa:f*.

☐ Monitor your own progress – go back and check your examples with the models in the book. Your writing should be fairly consistent by now. Don't slip into careless habits.

☐ Check for: line – size – dots.

☐ Note the similarity between the medial forms of ـفـ *fa:'* and ـغـ *ghayn*. The only distinguishing feature is the roundness of the one compared with the angularity of the other. Make sure you preserve this contrast whenever you write the medial forms of these two letters.

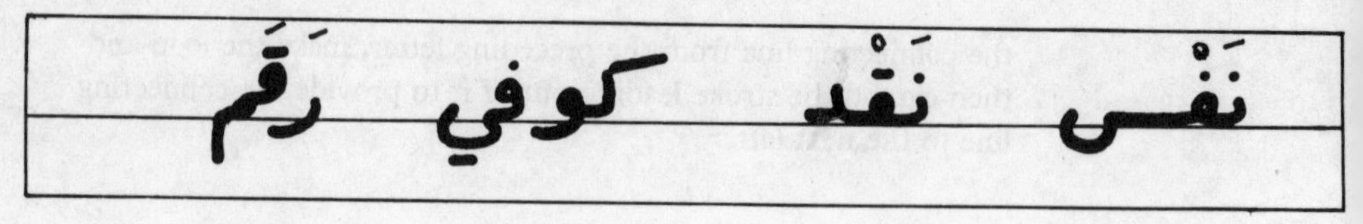


4 *raqam* 3 *ku:fi:* 2 *naqd* 1 *nafs*

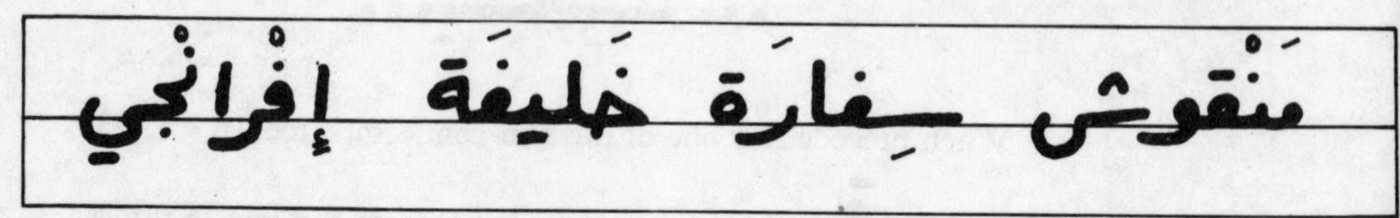


8 *'ifra:nji:* 7 *khali:fa* 6 *sifa:ra* 5 *manqu:sh*

**Points of interest**

3 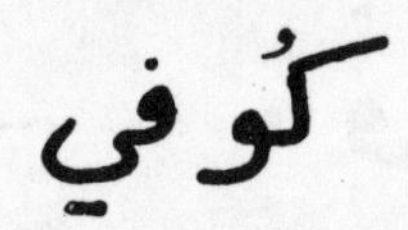

The oldest style of Arabic script, named after Kufa, the city in Iraq where it supposedly originated. It is an angular script which has been used for documents, coins, and inscriptions on buildings and monuments. It is widely used today in all kinds of advertising and commercial design.

The word كُوفِي *ku:fi:* written in Kufic script.

5 

'Apparently the earliest Arabic loan-word in English is the Old English "mancus", the name of a coin of gold equal to the Latin "solidus"; this represents the Arabic *man-kus* – "stamped (with a dye)", and may have reached England from France or from Spain; at this time the Moors had the upper hand in Spain and southern France, and evidence that England was influenced by Moorish finance is afforded by the existence of a gold coin, minted in England at the time of Offa, which besides the title "Offa rex" bears also an Arabic inscription. "Mancus" is found in English documents, chiefly charters, from the year 799 onwards; it does not however survive the Conquest.' (Mary S. Serjeantson, *A history of foreign words in English*, page 213)

This word is still current in Arabic meaning 'engraved; inscribed'.

6 

In modern Arabic, 'Embassy'. The word from which 'safari' is ultimately derived. Passed into English via Swahili.

7 

'Caliph' – the title of the head of the Islamic state. The Caliphate was abolished in 1924.

8 

Ultimately derived from the word 'Frank'. Used by the Arabs to describe the Crusaders, many of whom were the eponymous settlers of France. Today used with the general meaning of 'European'.

***Final position***

When these letters occur at the end of a word they retain the shape of their isolated form, but join to the preceding letter.

OBSERVE

ق ل ح ف ل س

حلق سلف

حَلْق *halq* سَلَف *salaf*

**Writing instructions** ف *fa:'* and ق *qa:f*, like all tailed letters (the only exceptions are the non-connectors ر و ز ) lose their tails in their initial and medial forms, and regain them in their final form.

Lead into the small clockwise circle of the head with the connecting line from the preceding letter. Then, having drawn the head, continue the line leading out of it to form the tail in a final controlled flourish. Remember that the flat-bottomed tail of ف *fa:'* lies on the line, while the deeper tail of ق *qa:f* sinks below it.

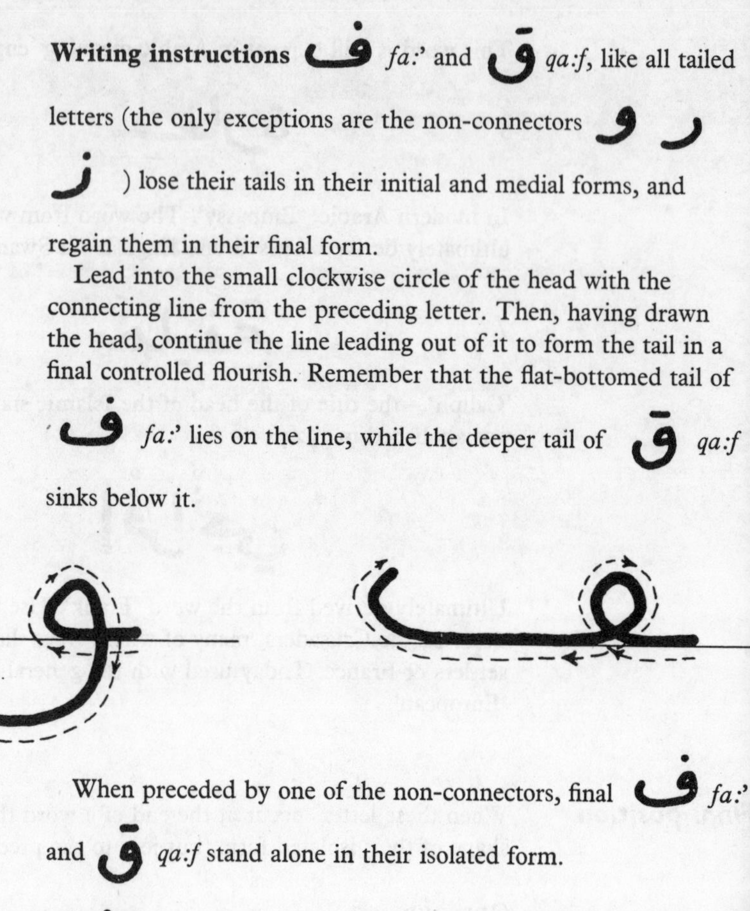

When preceded by one of the non-connectors, final ف *fa:'* and ق *qa:f* stand alone in their isolated form.

*qa:f* قاف ← ف + ا + ق

*su:q* سوق ← ق + و + س

**Reading and writing practice**

Ⓣ ☐ Read and pronounce the words on page 175 with reference to the tape.

☐ Trace and copy the models. Make sure to maintain the contrast between the tails of these two letters, and don't forget to check the dots –

one for ف *fa:'*

two for ق *qa:f*

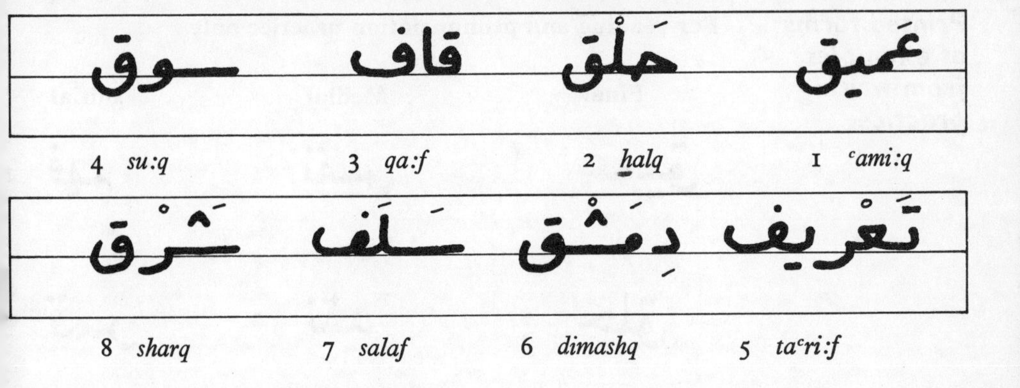


**Points of interest**

3 قاف

Name of the letter.

5 تَعْريف

'announcement; notification', from which English 'tariff' is derived.

6 دِمَشْق

'Damascus'. The English adjective 'Damask' is derived from the Arabic, and has been applied to a wide variety of products originating in Syria – from roses (cultivated in the east for their essential oil) to richly embroidered silk fabrics.

8 شَرْق

'East'. From the Arabic word are derived 'Saracen' (the name given by the Crusaders to the Arabs of the Levant) and 'sirroco' (a hot wind which blows over southern Europe from North Africa.)

*Printed forms of examples from writing practice*

**For reading and pronunciation practice only**

| Final | | Medial | | Initial |
|---|---|---|---|---|
| عميق | 1 | تفس | 1 | فهم |
| حلق | 2 | نقد | 2 | قمر |
| قاف | 3 | كوفي | 3 | قهوة |
| سوق | 4 | رقم | 4 | قيثارة |
| تعريف | 5 | منقوش | 5 | فرنسا |
| دمشق | 6 | سفارة | 6 | فتحة |
| سلف | 7 | خليفة | 7 | فاس |
| شرق | 8 | إفرانجي | 8 | قاهرة |

**Pronunciation drill** Ⓣ

**Contrast ك and ق**

| | /k/ | | /q/ | | /k/ | | /q/ |
|---|---|---|---|---|---|---|---|
| 1 | كاف | → | قاف | 6 | رُكوب | → | رُقوب |
| 2 | رِكاب | → | رِقاب | 7 | شُك | → | شُق |
| 3 | عَرَك | → | عَرَق | 8 | كيس | → | قيس |
| 4 | كُدْس | → | قُدْس | 9 | تَرْكيب | → | تَرْقيب |
| 5 | بَرَك | → | بَرَق | 10 | مُشْرِك | → | مُشْرِق |

# Unit 14

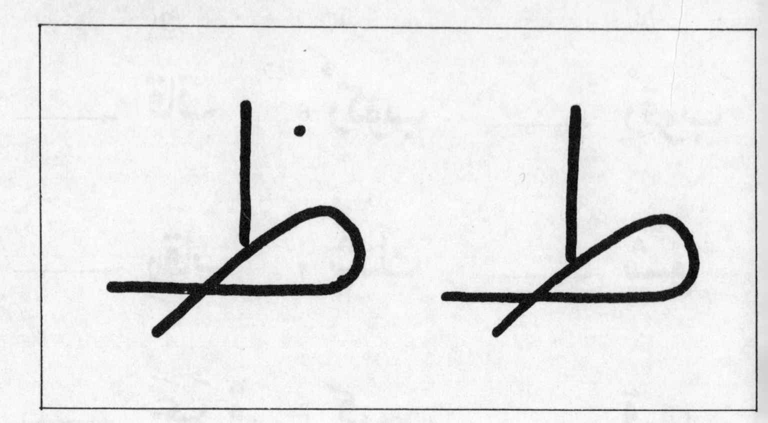

The basic shape shared by the isolated forms of these two letters is: ط

The basic shape alone is ṯa:'.

There is no equivalent sound in English. ط ṯa:' is a 't' sound but distinguished in several respects from Arabic ت ta:' and English 't'. In pronouncing ت ta:' the tip of the tongue touches the back of the upper teeth, while for ط ṯa:' a larger area of the front upper surface of the tongue makes contact with the gum ridge behind the upper teeth. The emphatic quality is achieved by tensing the back of the tongue and raising it towards the back of the roof of the mouth. ط is transliterated as /ṯ/.

The basic shape with one dot is d͟ha:' ظ

Again there is no equivalent sound in English. ظ d͟ha:' is a 'dh' sound, but distinguished in several respects from Arabic ذ *dha:l* and the English 'th' (as in '*th*ese'). As with the ذ *dha:l* the tip of the tongue is placed between the upper and lower teeth, but an added emphatic quality is achieved, as with ط *t̲a:'*, by tensing the back of the tongue and at the same time raising it towards the back of the roof of the mouth.

ظ is transliterated as /dh/.

Like ق *qa:f*, ط and ظ have a 'deepening' effect on the adjacent long and short vowels. Again it is the quality of surrounding vowels as much as the quality of the consonants themselves which distinguishes ط from ت , and ظ from ذ . Be sure to keep this in mind when listening to the tape drills.

## Isolated form

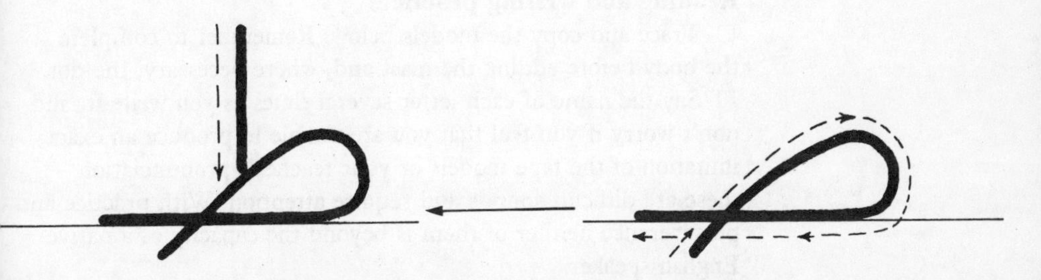

**Writing instructions** The ط / ظ shape consists of two elements, a 'body' and a 'mast'.
Draw the body first in one clockwise movement. The shape you should aim for is reminiscent of a tear drop lying on its side – tapering to a point at its left, swelling bulbously to the right, with its flattish base sitting on the line. To write the body start a little below the line and draw an up stroke climbing to the right at an angle of 45° until you reach the height from which you would begin a د . Then curve the stroke round and down until it reaches the line, at which point straighten it out to form the base stroke, and complete the body by crossing back over the initial up stroke. Finally add the mast in a single down stroke about

the same height as ا *alif*. In the case of ظ dha:' put in the single dot to the right of the mast and about half way down it.

When you are writing slowly and carefully it is easy to always make sure that the foot of the mast is just touching the body. However it is in no way vital to the legibility of these letters that it should do so, and at normal handwriting speed it frequently does not.

In this connection, compare the 'mast' of ط and ظ with the 'hat' stroke of initial and medial ك *ka:f*, Unit 12. This is similar to a very common feature of handwritten Latin script where 't's' and 'i's' are often inaccurately crossed at no cost to their legibility.

**Reading and writing practice**

☐ Trace and copy the models below. Remember to complete the body before adding the mast and, where necessary, the dot.

☐ Say the name of each letter several times as you write it, and don't worry if you feel that you are unable to produce an exact imitation of the tape models or your teacher's pronunciation – these are difficult sounds and require attention. With practice and perseverance neither of them is beyond the capacity of a native English speaker.

**Proportion guide**

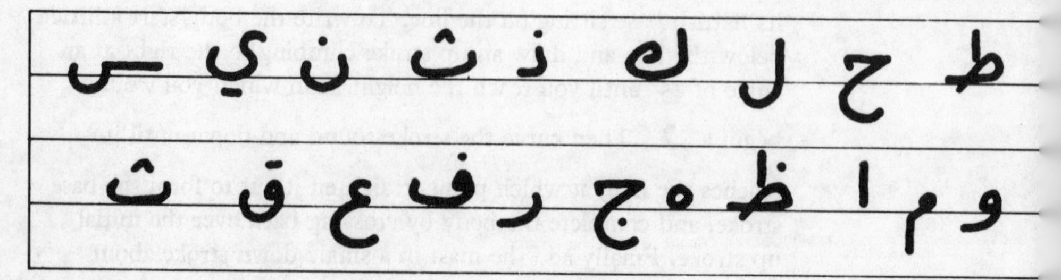

**Initial position**

When these letters occur at the beginning of a word they retain the shape of their isolated form and join to the following letter.
OBSERVE

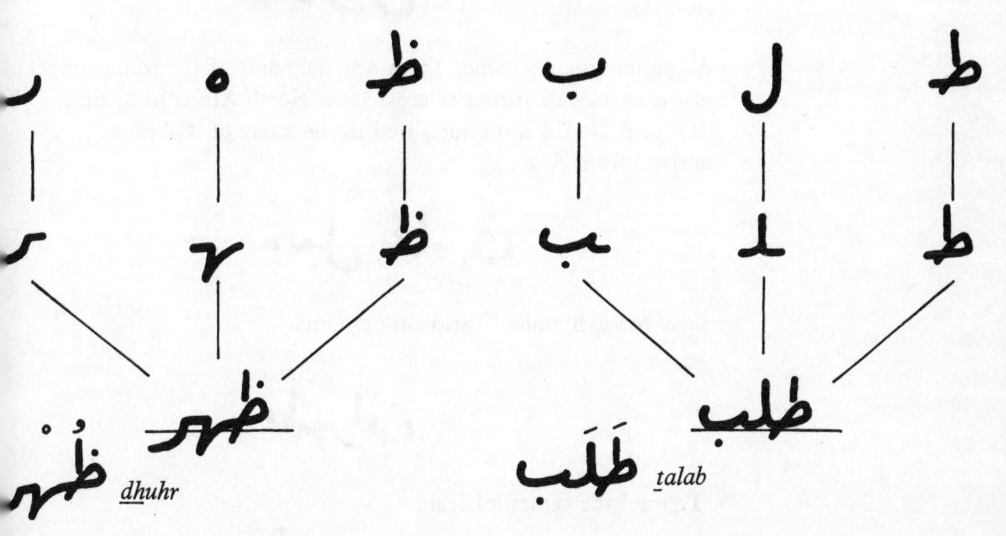


**Writing instructions** Same as for isolated form, but with the base stroke extended to provide the connecting line to the next letter.

**Reading and writing practice**

Ⓣ □ Read and pronounce the words below with reference to the tape.

□ Trace and copy the models. Try to keep your writing in constant relation to the horizontal line. Complete the basic shape of a word before going back to put in the mast and dots from *right to left*.

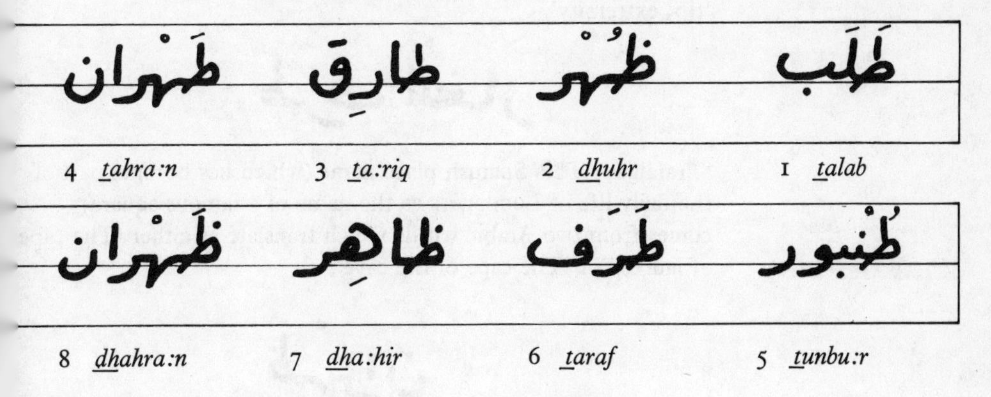

**Points of interest**

1 طارِق

A common man's name. Tariq was the name of the commander of the first Arab armies to cross from North Africa to Spain in 711-12 A.D. He is immortalised in the name of 'Gibraltar', derived from Arabic.

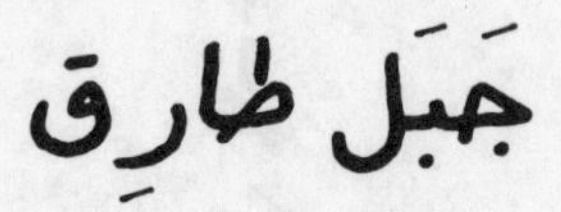

*jabal ta:riq* literally 'Tariq's mountain'.

4

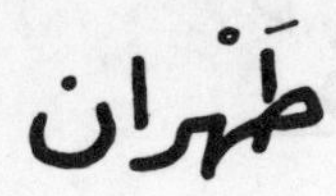

'Tehran' the capital of Iran.

5

'tabor'. The Arabic word describes a long necked stringed instrument resembling the mandolin. It was adopted by the Crusaders in Syria, but later the name 'tabor' was applied to a small drum, from which the word 'tambourine' is probably derived.

6

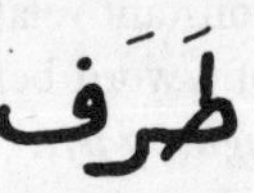

'tip; extremity'.

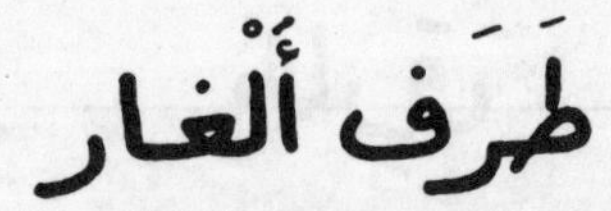

'Trafalgar'. This Spanish place name (which has become part of the daily life of Londoners as the name of a famous square) comes from two Arabic words which translate as either 'The cape of laurels' or 'The cape of the cave'.

8

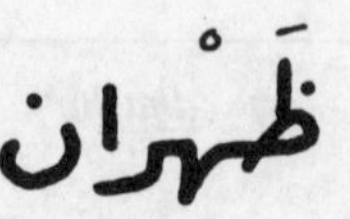

'Dhahran' – a city in the eastern province of Saudi Arabia.

**_Medial position_** When these letters occur in the middle of a word they retain the shape of their isolated form and join to both the preceding and following letters.

OBSERVE

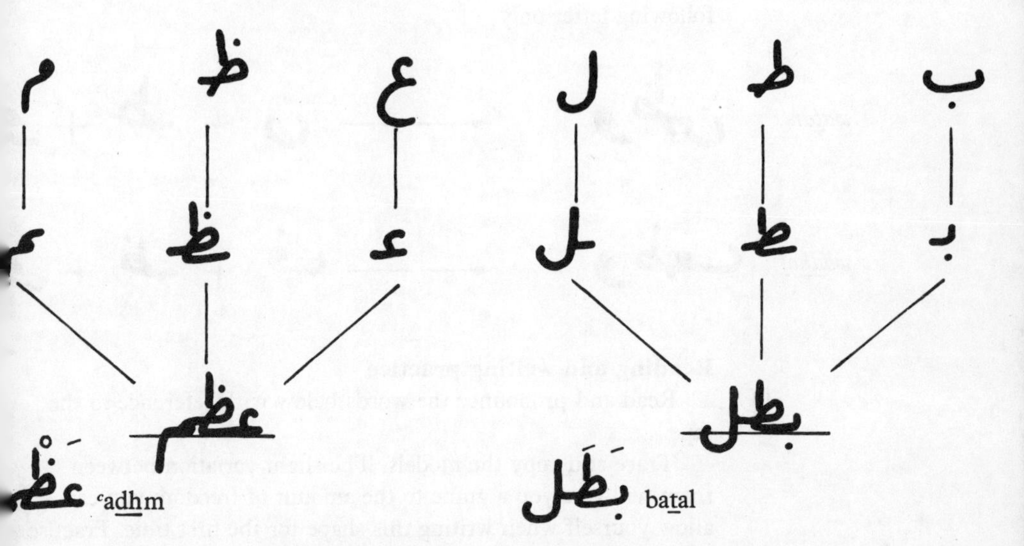


**Writing instructions** Extend the connecting line from the previous letter much further than you normally would and use its furthest point as the beginning of the initial up stroke of the body. Complete the body as described in the writing instructions for the isolated shape – notice that the body hovers above the extended connecting line, with the base stroke crossing the initial up stroke just above the connecting line, and more or less parallel to it.

It is important that the angle between the connecting stroke and the initial up stroke be sharp – this is the easiest way of producing the characteristic tapered shape of the body. Go back and add the mast after you have completed the basic shape of a word:

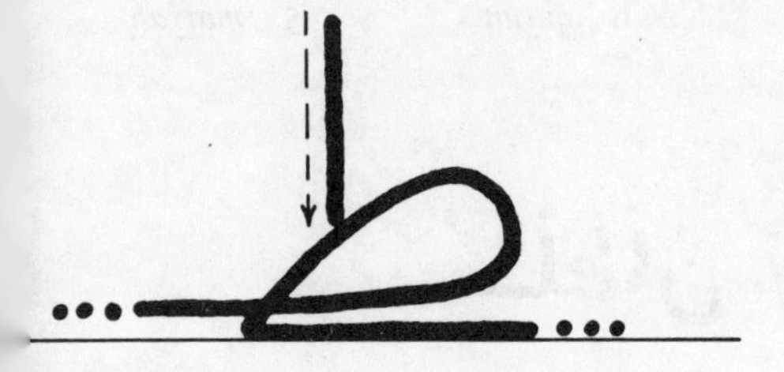

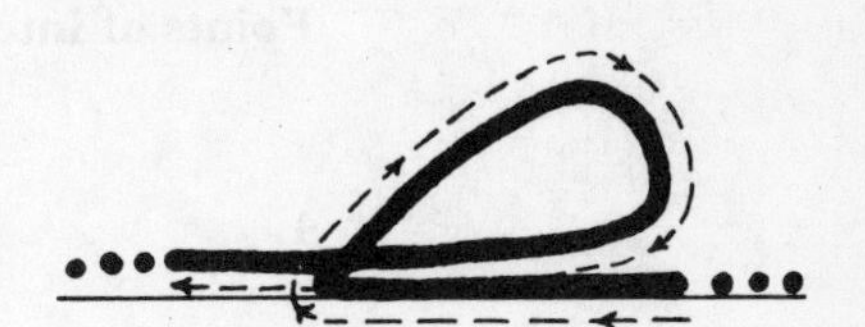

When preceded by one of the non-connectors, medial ط / ظ appear in their initial form and join to the following letter only.

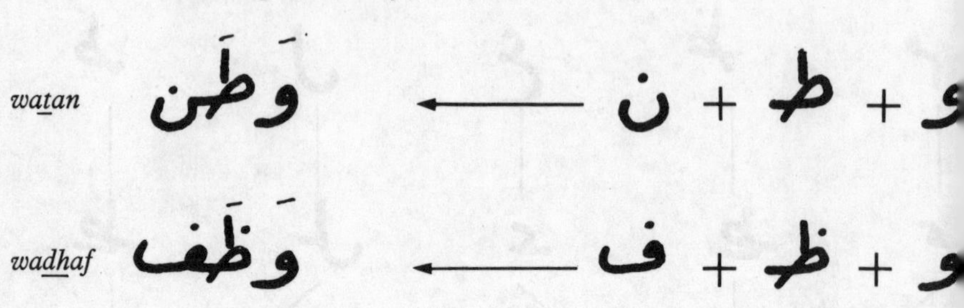


**Reading and writing practice**

Ⓣ □ Read and pronounce the words below with reference to the tape.

□ Trace and copy the models. The slight variation between them will give you a guide to the amount of freedom you can allow yourself when writing this shape for the first time. Practise until you can consistently produce examples which fall within the range of variation illustrated by the models. Complete the basic word shape before going back to put in the dots and masts from *right to left*.

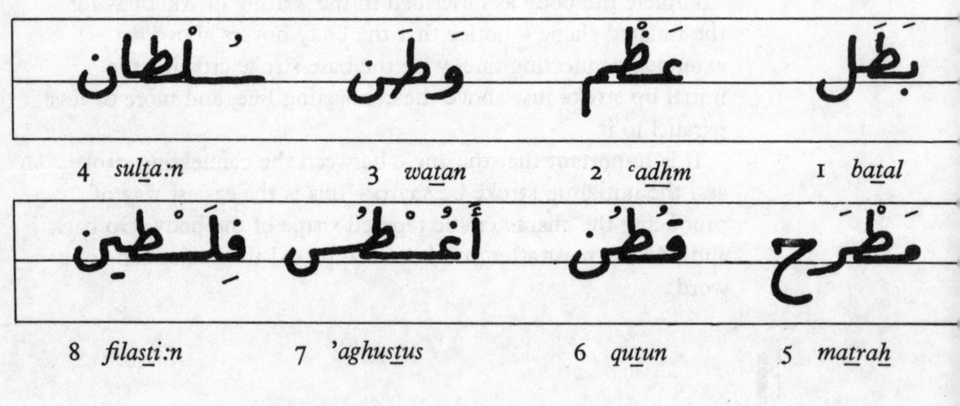


**Points of interest**

4 سُلْطَان

'Sultan' – a title often applied to a ruler in the Islamic world.

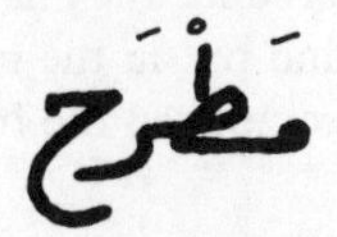

'sultana' – the name of a small seedless raisin first produced in Turkey is derived from this word.

5

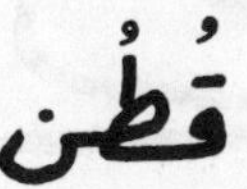

'place where something is put down', from which the English 'mattress', French 'matelas' and Spanish and Portuguese 'almadraque' are derived. Also the name of a town in Oman.

6

'cotton', passed into English from French in the mid-sixteenth century.

7

'August'.

8

فِلَسْطِين

'Palestine'.

**Final position**

When these letters occur at the end of a word they retain the shape of their isolated form but join to the preceding letter.
OBSERVE

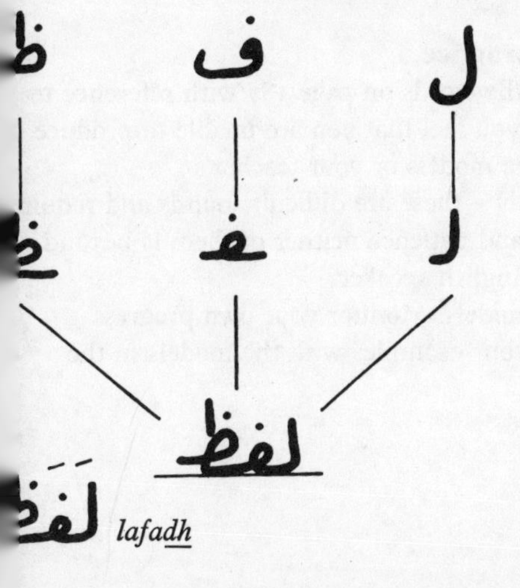


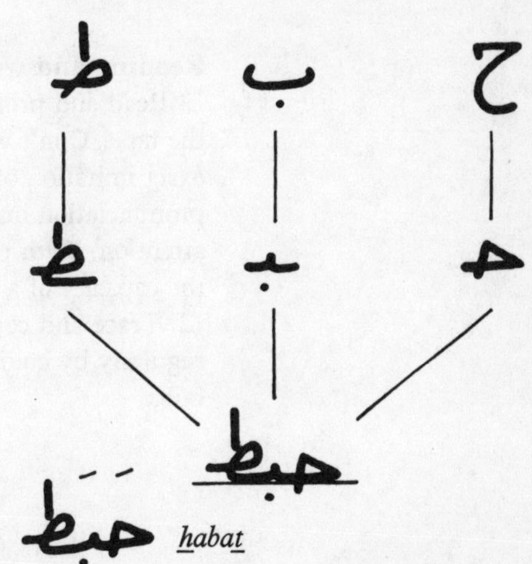

**Writing instructions** Same as for the medial form. Lead into the final form with an extended connecting line from the preceding letter and draw the body shape hovering above the connecting line. The base stroke crosses over the up stroke to produce the characteristic 'tie' of the isolated form. Go back and put in the mast and dots, from *right to left*, once you have completed the basic shape of a word:

When preceded by one of the non-connectors, final ط and ظ appear in their isolated form, standing alone at the end of the word.

*riba:t* رِباط ← ط + ا + ب + ر

*mahdhu:dh* مَحْظوظ ← ظ + و + ظ + ح + م

**Reading and writing practice**

Ⓣ □ Read and pronounce the words on page 187 with reference to the tape. Don't worry if you feel that you are unable to produce a exact imitation of the tape models or your teacher's pronunciation immediately – these are difficult sounds and require attention. With practice and patience neither of them is beyond the capacity of a native English speaker.

□ Trace and copy the models. Monitor your own progress regularly by comparing your examples with the models in the book.

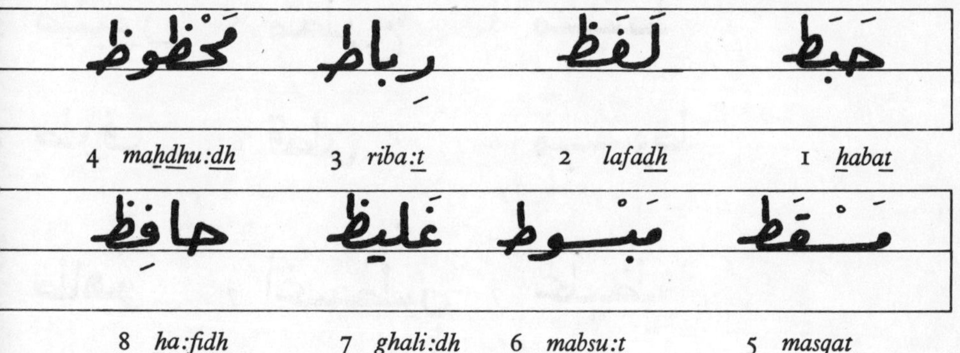


**Points of interest**

3 رِباط

'Rabat' – capital of Morocco.

5 مَسْقَط

'Musqat' – the capital of Oman.

**rinted forms f examples rom writing ractice**

**For reading and pronunciation practice only**

| | Final | | Medial | | Initial |
|---|---|---|---|---|---|
| 1 | حبط | 1 | بطل | 1 | طلب |
| 2 | لفظ | 2 | عظم | 2 | ظهر |
| 3 | رباط | 3 | وطن | 3 | طارق |
| 4 | محظوظ | 4 | سلطان | 4 | طهران |

| | | | | |
|---|---|---|---|---|
| مسقط | 5 | مطرح | 5 | طنبور |
| مبسوط | 6 | قطن | 6 | طرف |
| غليظ | 7 | أغسطس | 7 | ظاهر |
| حافظ | 8 | فلسطين | 8 | ظهران |

**Pronunciation drill** Ⓣ

**Contrast** ت **and** ط
ذ **and** ظ

| /d̲h̲/ | | /dh/ | | /t̲/ | | /t/ |
|---|---|---|---|---|---|---|
| ظال | ← | ذال | 1 | طابِع | ← | تابِع |
| ظَرْف | ← | ذَرْف | 2 | قطَر | ← | قَتَر |
| نَظير | ← | نَذير | 3 | طين | ← | تين |
| ناظِر | ← | ناذِر | 4 | راطِب | ← | راتِب |
| بُظور | ← | بُذور | 5 | طوب | ← | توب |
| يَحْظُر | ← | يَحْذُر | 6 | طُرْفَة | ← | تُرْفَة |

## Years and months – the Gregorian Calendar in Arabic

There are two calendar systems in use in the Arab world today – the Gregorian calendar which we ourselves use, and an older Muslim system based on a lunar year of about 354 days (see Unit 15).

Arabic has two sets of names for the months of the Gregorian calendar, both of which are in common use. One consists of Arabic names, and the other of names borrowed and more or less directly transliterated into Arabic from European languages.

OBSERVE

| | | | | |
|---|---|---|---|---|
| January | يَنايِر | *yana:yir* | كانون أَلثّاني | *ka:nu:n ath-tha:ni:* |
| February | فِبْرايِر | *fibra:yir* | شُباط | *shuba:t̲* |
| March | مارْس | *ma:rs* | آذار | *'a:dha:r** |
| April | أَبْريل | *'abri:l* | نيسان | *ni:sa:n* |
| May | مايو | *ma:yu:* | أَيّار | *'ayya:r* |
| June | يونِيو | *yu:niyu:* | حَزيران | *h̲azi:ra:n* |
| July | يولِيو | *yu:liyu:* | تَمّوز | *tammu:z* |
| August | أَغُسْطُس | *'aghus̲tus* | آب | *'a:b** |

| | | | | |
|---|---|---|---|---|
| September | سِبْتَمْبِر | *sibtambir* | أَيْلول | *'aylu:l* |
| October | أُكْتوبِر | *'uktu:bir* | تِشْرين ألأَوَّل | *tishri:n al-'awwal* |
| November | نوفِمْبِر | *nu:fimbir* | تِشْرين ألثّاني | *tishri:n ath-tha:ni:* |
| December | ديسِمْبِر | *di:simbir* | كانون ألأَوَّل | *ka:nu:n al-'awwal* |

*For the special symbol representing initial ء *hamza* followed by ا *alif*/ ( /'a:/ ), see pages 56 and 57.

# Unit 15

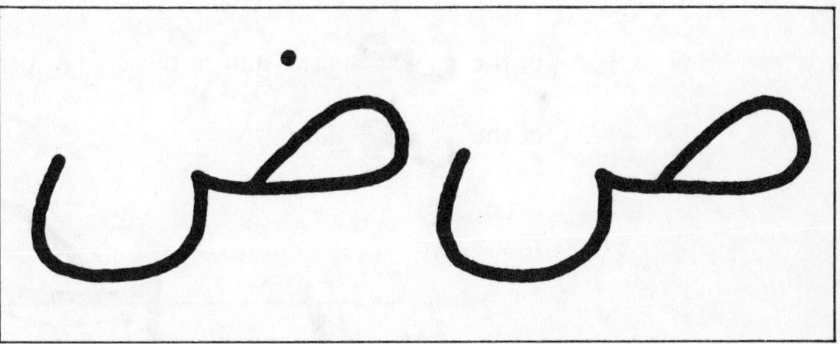

The basic shape shared by the isolated forms of these two letters is: ص

The basic shape alone is *s̲a:d*.

There is no equivalent sound in English. ص *s̲a:d* is an 's' sound, but distinguished in several respects from Arabic س *si:n* and English 's'. In pronouncing س the tip of the tongue is behind the upper teeth, while for ص *s̲a:d* the tip of the tongue moves further back in the mouth to the gum ridge behind the upper teeth. An emphatic quality is achieved by tensing the back of the tongue and at the same time raising it towards the back of the roof of the mouth.

ص *s̲a:d* is transliterated as /s̲/.

The basic shape with one dot above is *d̲a:d*. ض

There is no equivalent sound in English. ض *d̲a:d* is a 'd' sound, but distinguished in several respects from Arabic د *da:l* and English 'd'. In pronouncing د the tip of the tongue touches the upper teeth, while tor ض *d̲a:d* the tip of the tongue moves further back in the mouth to touch the gum ridge behind the upper teeth. An emphatic quality is achieved by tensing the back of the tongue and at the same time raising it towards the back of the roof of the mouth.

ض *d̲a:d* is transliterated as /d̲/.

The Arabs have traditionally claimed that this is the one unique sound which distinguishes their languages from all others. Arab authors have frequently referred to Arabic as 'the language of the ض *d̲a:d*' and to those who speak it as 'pronouncers of the ض *d̲a:d*'.

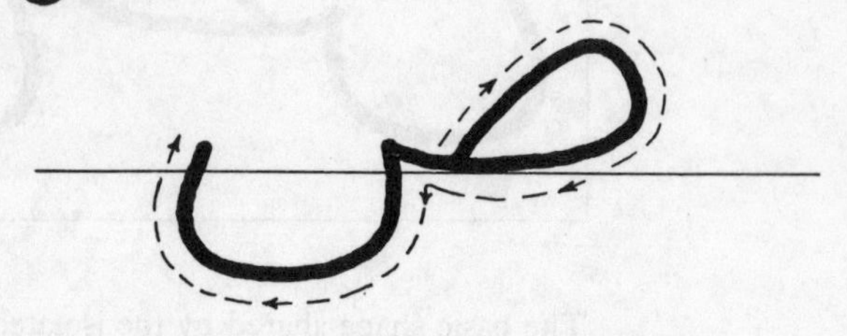

**Isolated form**

**Writing instructions** The ص / ض shape consists of two elements, a body and a tail, and is written in one continuous movement. The body is exactly the same shape as the body of ط / ظ (see writing instructions to the last Unit) and is written first. The tail is the same shape as ن *nu:n* and descends below the line. The dot for ض *d̲a:d* is added after both body and tail have been completed.

**Reading and writing practice** Trace and copy the models below, saying the name of each letter as you write it. Don't worry if you feel that you are unable to produce an exact imitation of the tape models or your teacher's pronunication immediately. These sounds, like those represented by

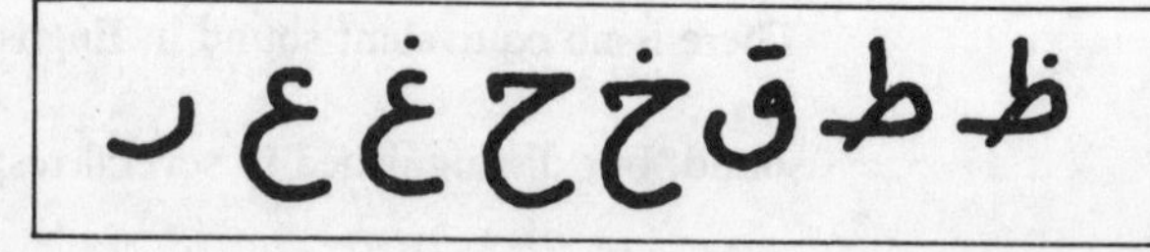


require particular attention, but with practice neither of them is beyond the capacity of a native English speaker.

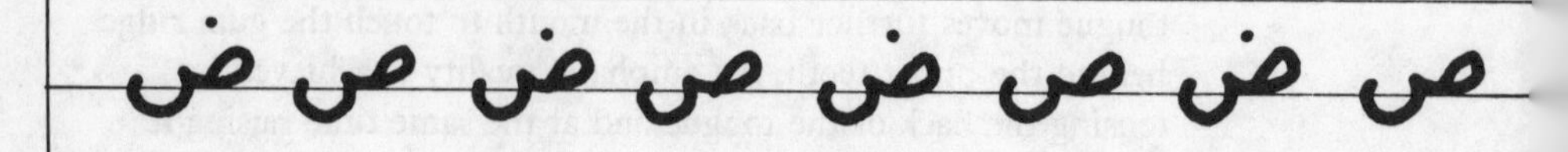

**Proportion guide** Below are all the letters of the Arabic alphabet in the order in which they have been introduced in the book. Copy the models for further writing practice of isolated forms, and say the name of each letter as you write it.

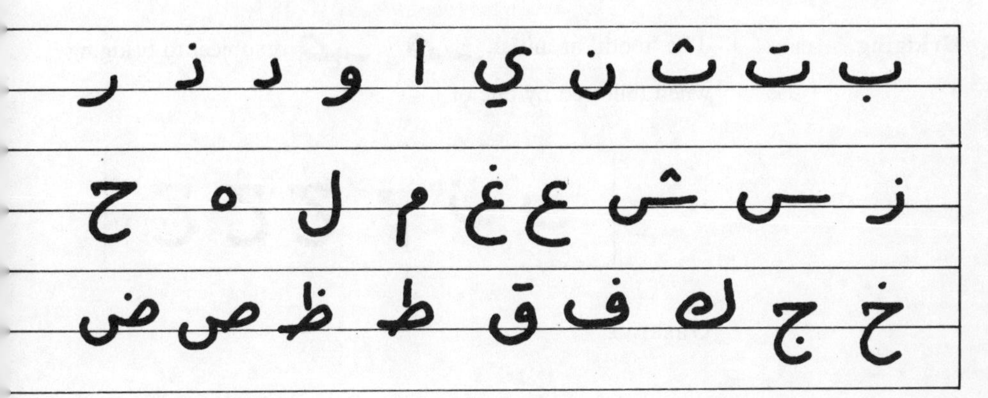


***Initial position***

When these letters occur at the beginning of a word they lose most of their tail and join to the following letter. A vestige of the tail remains in the form of a small 'tooth' which is an integral part of the initial form.

OBSERVE

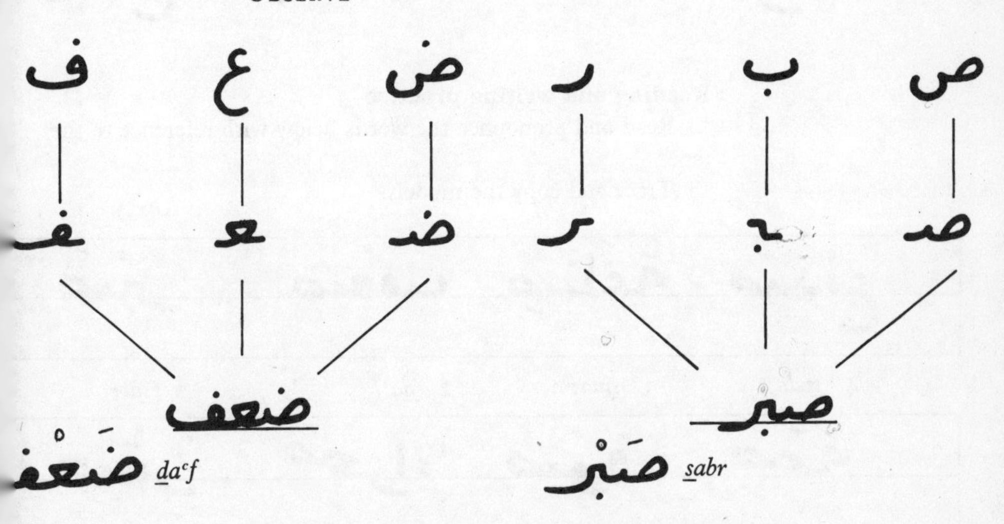


**Writing instructions** Same as for the initial form of ط / ظ, minus the mast, but with the addition of the small tooth, representing the missing tail, in the connecting line from the base stroke to the body to the next letter:

**Bridging** The 'tooth' of initial ضـ / صـ is subject to bridging when followed by one of

| ج ح خ م ز ر |
|---|

OBSERVE

*d̲irs* ضْرس ⟵ ض + ر + س

*s̲ah̲ra:'* صَحْراء ⟵ ص + ح + ر + ا + ء

### Reading and writing practice

Ⓣ ☐ Read and pronounce the words below with reference to the tape.

☐ Trace and copy the models.

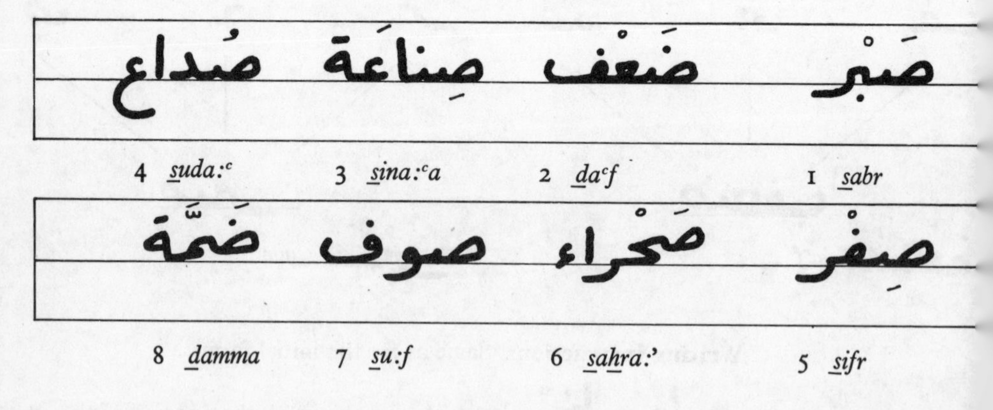

**Points of interest**

3 صِناعة

'trade, craft'. Part of the Arabic phrase:

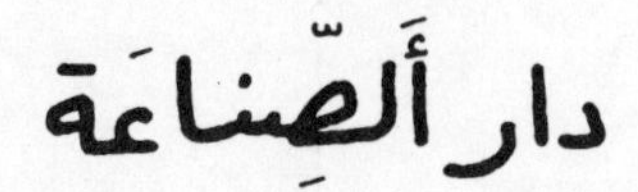

*da:r ’as-sina:*$^c$*a* (literally 'workshop'), from which English 'arsenal' is derived, probably via Spanish 'darsena'.

4 صُداع

' "soda", which in Latin meant headache and in the form "sodanum", "headache remedy", comes ultimately from Arabic *suda*$^c$, splitting pain in the head.' (P. Hitti, *The Arabs: a short history*, page 141)

5 صِفْر

'naught; nothing' from which English 'zero' and 'cipher' are derived.

6 صَحْراء

'desert'. The English name for the largest desert in the world is derived from this Arabic word.

7 صوف

Literally 'wool' – believed to be the word from which 'Sufi', the name applied to the mystics of Islam, is derived.

8 ضَمّة

Name of the short vowel.

**Medial position** When these letters occur in the middle of a word they retain the shape of their initial form but join to both the preceding and following letters.

OBSERVE

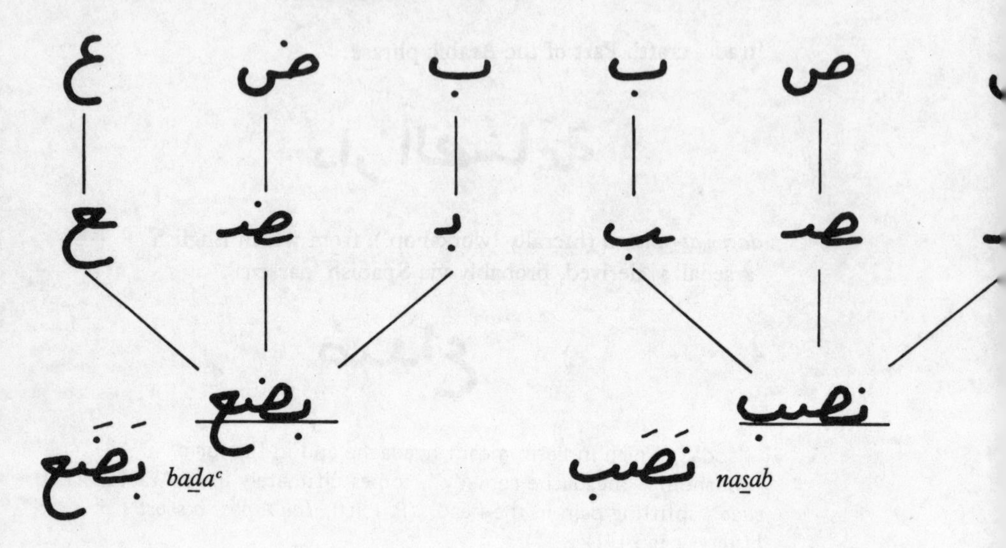


**Writing instructions** Same as for medial ـظـ / ـطـ minus the mast, but with the addition of the characteristic 'tooth' in the connecting line to the next letter.

**Bridging** The tooth of medial ـضـ / ـصـ is subject to bridging when followed by one of

| ج خ ح م ز ر |
|---|

OBSERVE

qasr قَصْر ← ر + ص + ق

When preceded by one of the non-connectors, medial ص sa:d and ض da:d appear in their initial form and join to the preceding letter only.

*wusu:l* وُصول ⟵ و + ص + و + ل

*wudu:h* وُضوح ⟵ و + ض + و + ح

**Reading and writing practice**

Ⓣ □ Read and pronounce the words below with reference to the tape.

□ Trace and copy the models. Don't forget the 'tooth' of medial ص *sa:d* and ض *da:d*.

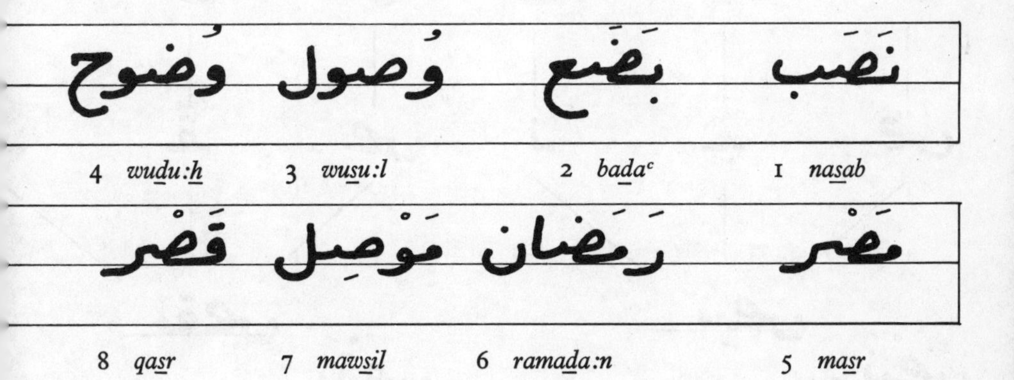


**Points of interest**

5 مَصْر

The Arabic name for 'Egypt'.

6 رَمَضان

The ninth month of the Islamic year, observed by Muslims as a fast during the hours of daylight.

7 مَوْصِل

'Mosul', city in northern Iraq, from which the English 'muslin' is derived.

8 

'palace; castle', from which the name of the historic Spanish building the 'Alcazar' (literally 'the palace') is derived.

**Final position** When these letters occur at the end of a word they retain the shape of their medial form, regaining their tail and joining to the preceding letter.

OBSERVE

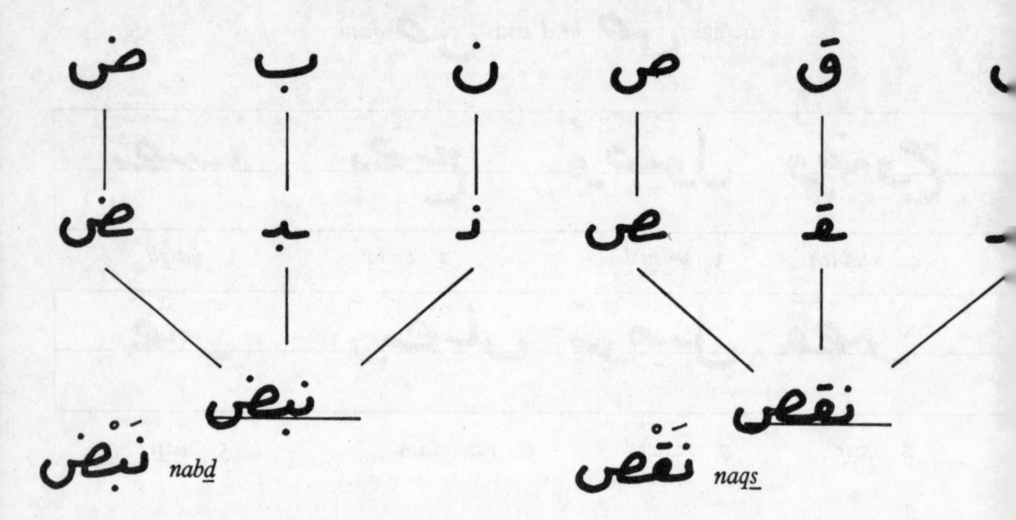

نَبْض *nabd̲*

نَقْص *naqs̲*

**Writing instructions** Same as for medial form, but with the down stroke of the 'tooth' leading into the ں shaped tail, rather than beginning the connecting line into the following letter.

When preceded by one of the non-connectors, final ص *s̲a:d* and ض *d̲a:d* stand alone in their isolated form.

*qurs̲* قُرْص ⟵ ص + ر + ق

*'ard̲* أَرْض ⟵ ض + ر +

## Reading and writing practice

Ⓣ □ Read and pronounce the words below with reference to the tape.

□ Trace and copy the models.

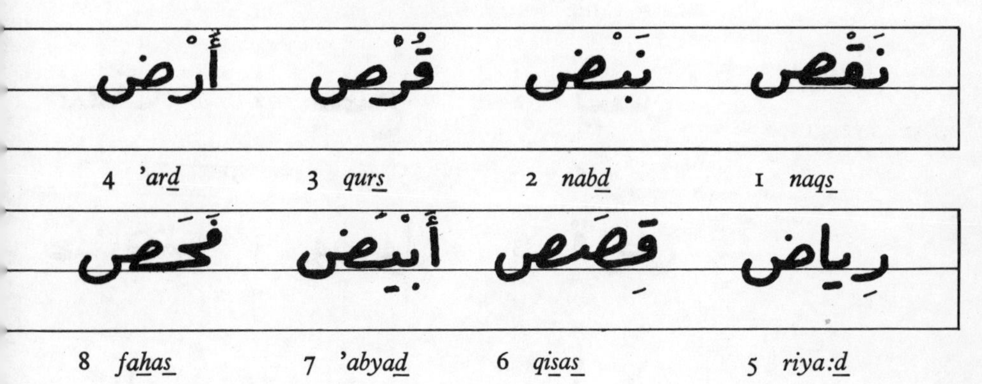


## Points of interest

5 رِياض 'Riyadh', the capital of Saudi Arabia.

'rinted forms
f examples
rom writing
ractice

**For reading and pronunciation practice only**

The major difference between the handwritten and printed forms of the two letters introduced in this Unit is that the medial and final printed forms sit on the horizontal line, whereas in handwriting they join to the preceding letter from below and hover above the line.

OBSERVE

**handwritten** صصص ص

**printed** صصص ص

| Final | | Medial | | Initial |
|---|---|---|---|---|
| تقص | 1 | نصب | 1 | صبر |
| نبض | 2 | بضع | 2 | ضعف |
| قرص | 3 | وصول | 3 | صناعة |
| أرض | 4 | وضوح | 4 | صداع |
| رياض | 5 | مصر | 5 | صفر |
| قصص | 6 | رمضان | 6 | صحراء |
| أبيض | 7 | موصل | 7 | صوف |
| فحص | 8 | قصر | 8 | ضمة |

**Pronunciation drill** Ⓣ

**Contrast** س **and** ص

ض **and** د

| /ḍ/ | /d/ | | /ṣ/ | /s/ | |
|---|---|---|---|---|---|
| ضار | دار | 1 | صاحِب | ساحِب | 1 |
| ضَرَب | دَرَب | 2 | صَبَر | سَبَر | 2 |
| بَيْض | بَيْد | 3 | نَصيب | نَسيب | 3 |
| يَضِب | يَدِب | 4 | نَبْصُر | نَبْسُر | 4 |
| يَضور | يَدور | 5 | بوصَة | بوسَة | 5 |
| مُض | مُد | 6 | يَصْدُر | يَسْدُر | 6 |

## The Arabic Numbers

'The cipher, the so-called Arabic numerals, and the decimal system of notation were all invented by the Indians, but it was the Arabs who brought them into the service of world civilisation and handed them on to Europe, thus making possible not only everyday arithmetic as we know it, but also far-reaching mathematical developments which the Greeks, for all their original genius and intellectual power, had not been able to embark upon without the cipher and the Arabic numerals.' (Edward Atiyah, *The Arabs*, page 52)

| | **handwritten** | **printed** | | |
|---|---|---|---|---|
| 0 | ٠ | ٠ | *ṣifr* | صِفْر |
| 1 | ١ | ١ | *wa:ḫid* | واحِد |
| 2 | ٢ | ٢ | *'ithnayn* | ثْنَين |
| 3 | ٣ | ٣ | *thala:tha* | لاثَة |
| 4 | ٤ | ٤ | *'arbaᶜa* | ربَعة |
| 5 | ٥ | ٥ | *khamsa* | خمْسَة |

| | | | | |
|---|---|---|---|---|
| 6 | ٦ | ١ | *sitta* | سِتَّة |
| 7 | ٧ | ٧ | *sabᶜa* | سَبْعَة |
| 8 | ٨ | ٨ | *thama:niya* | ثَمانِيَة |
| 9 | ٩ | ٩ | *tisᶜa* | تِسْعَة |
| 10 | ١٠ | ١٠ | *ᶜashra* | عَشْرَة |

**Notice the following points:**

1 The Arabic and English symbols for one are virtually identical.

2 The Arabic symbol for five is very similar to English zero, while Arabic zero is simply a dot.

3 The Arabic symbol for six is very similar to English seven.

4 The Arabic and English symbols for nine are virtually identical.

5 Arabic numbers are written from *left to right*, just like ours (look at ten).

Beware of the potentially confusing situations which can arise from the visual similarity between certain Arabic and English numbers:

| e.g. | Arabic | | English |
|---|---|---|---|
| | ١٩٦٥ | = | 1965 |
| | ١٥ | = | 15 |
| | ٦٩ | = | 69 |

Though we have given the pronunciation of only the first ten numbers, you are now of course in a position to write and decipher any Arabic number.
OBSERVE

| | |
|---|---|
| 12 August 1951 | ١٢ أغسطس ١٩٥١ |
| 17 May 1945 | ١٧ مايو ١٩٤٥ |
| 1978 | ١٩٧٨ |
| 1984 | ١٩٨٤ |
| 2001 | ٢٠٠١ |
| 7,152,814 | ٧,١٥٢,٨١٤ |
| 71,010,034 | ٧١,٠١٠,٠٣٤ |

'Diffusion of the Arabic numerals in non-Moslem Europe was incredibly slow. Christian arithmeticians throughout the eleventh, twelfth, and part of the thirteenth centuries persisted in the use of the antiquated Roman numerals and the abacus, or made a compromise and used the new algorisms * together with their old system. It was in Italy that the new symbols were first employed for practical purposes. In 1202 Leonardo Fibonacci of Pisa, who was taught by a Moslem master and had travelled in North Africa, published a work which was the main landmark in the introduction of the Arabic numerals. More than that, it marks the beginning of European mathematics. With the old type of numerals, arithmetical progress along certain lines would have been impossible. The zero and Arabic numerals lie behind the science of calculation as we know it today.' (Philip K. Hitti, *The Arabs: a short history*, pages 139-40.)

*The word 'algorism' itself (a technical term for the Arabic, or decimal, system of numbers) is a corruption of the name of the Arab mathematician أَلْخَوَارَزْمي *'al-khawarazmi*:.

1 2 3 4 5 6 7 8 9 0
١ ٢ ٣ ٤ ٥ ٦ ٧ ٨ ٩ ٠

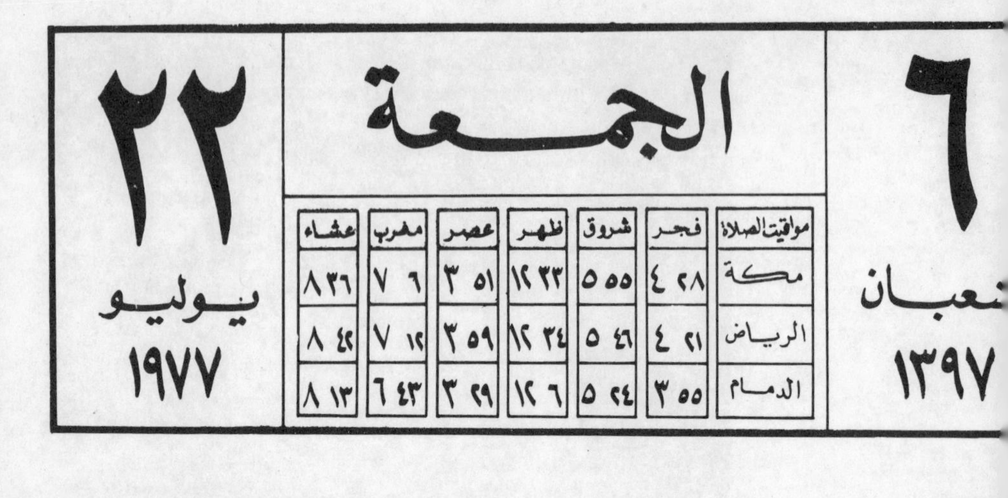

٢٢
يوليو
١٩٧٧

الجمعة

٦
ـعبان
١٣٩٧

| مواقيت الصلاة | فجر | شروق | ظهر | عصر | مغرب | عشاء |
|---|---|---|---|---|---|---|
| مكة | ٤ ٢٨ | ٥ ٥٥ | ١٢ ٣٣ | ٣ ٥١ | ٧ ٦ | ٨ ٣٦ |
| الرياض | ٤ ٢١ | ٥ ٤٦ | ١٢ ٣٤ | ٣ ٥٩ | ٧ ١٢ | ٨ ٤٢ |
| الدمام | ٣ ٥٥ | ٥ ٢٤ | ١٢ ٦ | ٣ ٢٩ | ٦ ٤٣ | ٨ ١٣ |

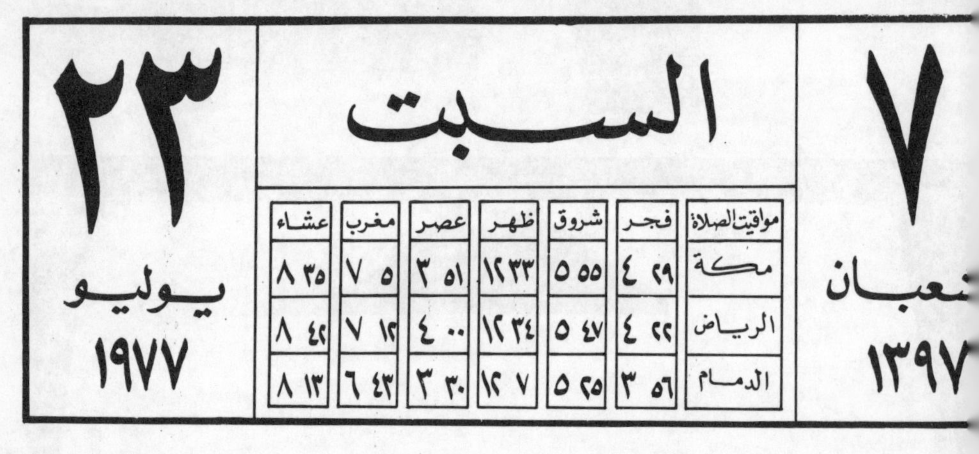

٢٣
يوليو
١٩٧٧

السبت

٧
ـعبان
١٣٩٧

| مواقيت الصلاة | فجر | شروق | ظهر | عصر | مغرب | عشاء |
|---|---|---|---|---|---|---|
| مكة | ٤ ٢٩ | ٥ ٥٥ | ١٢ ٣٣ | ٣ ٥١ | ٧ ٥ | ٨ ٣٥ |
| الرياض | ٤ ٢٢ | ٥ ٤٧ | ١٢ ٣٤ | ٤ ٠٠ | ٧ ١٢ | ٨ ٤٢ |
| الدمام | ٣ ٥٦ | ٥ ٢٥ | ١٢ ٧ | ٣ ٣٠ | ٦ ٤٣ | ٨ ١٣ |

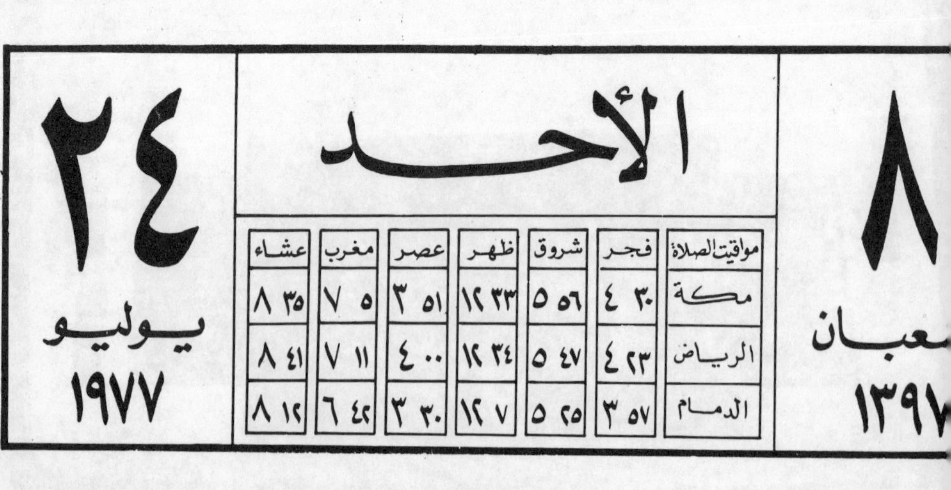

٢٤
يوليو
١٩٧٧

الأحد

٨
ـعبان
١٣٩٧

| مواقيت الصلاة | فجر | شروق | ظهر | عصر | مغرب | عشاء |
|---|---|---|---|---|---|---|
| مكة | ٤ ٣٠ | ٥ ٥٦ | ١٢ ٣٣ | ٣ ٥١ | ٧ ٥ | ٨ ٣٥ |
| الرياض | ٤ ٢٣ | ٥ ٤٧ | ١٢ ٣٤ | ٤ ٠٠ | ٧ ١١ | ٨ ٤١ |
| الدمام | ٣ ٥٧ | ٥ ٢٥ | ١٢ ٧ | ٣ ٣٠ | ٦ ٤٢ | ٨ ١٢ |

*Three days in July 1977 showing the times of the calls to prayer in Makkah, Riyadh and Dammam.*

The Muslim era dates from 16th July, 622 A.D. – the date ascribed to the emigration of the Prophet Muhammad and his followers to Medinah after several years of opposition to his message in his native city of Makkah. It is from this date that the years of the Muslim calendar are reckoned, and in writing they are accordingly followed by an initial هـ *ha:'* – standing for the adjective هِجْرِيَة *hijri:ya*, from هِجْرَة *hijra* 'emigration', and corresponding to the European abbreviation 'A.H.' (anno hegira).

Since the Muslim year has only 354 days (12 lunar months, each of 29½ days), it progressively outstrips the Christian year – most of 1977 A.D., for example, was 1397 A.H. The Muslim calendar is rarely used alone in the Arab world today – newspapers and most official and business documents show the Christian date as well.

**The Muslim Calendar:**

| | | |
|---|---|---|
| 1 | أَلْمُحَرَّم | *'al-muharram* |
| 2 | صَفَر | *safar* |
| 3 | رَبِيع الأَوَّل | *rabi:c'al-'awwal* |
| 4 | رَبِيع الثَّاني | *rabi:c'ath-tha:ni:* |
| 5 | جُمادى الأَوَّل | *juma:da:'al-'awwal* |

| | | |
|---|---|---|
| 6 | جُمَادَى ٱلْآخِرَة | *juma:da: 'al-'a:khira* |
| 7 | رَجَب | *rajab* |
| 8 | شَعْبَان | *sha<sup>c</sup>ba:n* |
| 9 | رَمَضَان | *ramada:n* |
| 10 | شَوَّال | *shawwa:l* |
| 11 | ذُو ٱلْقَعْدَة | *dhu: 'al-qa<sup>c</sup>da* |
| 12 | ذُو ٱلْحِجَّة | *dhu: 'al-hijja* |

Saudi Gazette

Price SR1

No. 600—TUESDAY, April 4, 1978 ● Rabi-al-Thani 26, 1398 A.H.

سعودي جازيت
العدد رقم ٦٠٠
الثلاثاء ٢٦ ربيع
الآخر ١٣٩٨ هـ
الموافق ٤ ابريل
١٩٧٨ م

الثمن : ريال واحد


**alif maqsu:ra** أَلِف مَقْصُورَة

In many Arabic words, the *final* long vowel sound /a:/ is represented not by the usual ا *alif*, but by ى ( ي *ya:'*

without dots), called *alif maqs̲u:ra*. ى *alif maqsu:ra* occurs *only* as the last letter in a word. It is pronounced (and transliterated) exactly like regular ا *alif*.

Observe

| | | | |
|---|---|---|---|
| *maqha:* | مَقْهى | *layla* | لَيْلى |
| *lada:* | لَدى | *najwa:* | نَجْوى |

madda

مَدَّة

If a ء *hamza* 'sitting' on a silent ا *alif* and accompanied by the short vowel *fatḫa* is immediately followed by the long vowel sound /a:/, the *hamza* and *fatḫa* are dropped in writing and the long vowel letter ا *alif* is written, slightly modified, as a short horizontal stroke over the first silent ا *alif*. In other words, *madda* over ا *alif* represents the sound sequence /'a:/

Observe

| | |
|---|---|
| *'a:tha:r* | آثار |
| for | أَاثار |
| *qur'a:n* | قُرْآن |
| for | قُرْأَان |

The second of these examples is the name of the Holy Book of Islam, commonly spelt 'Koran' in English.

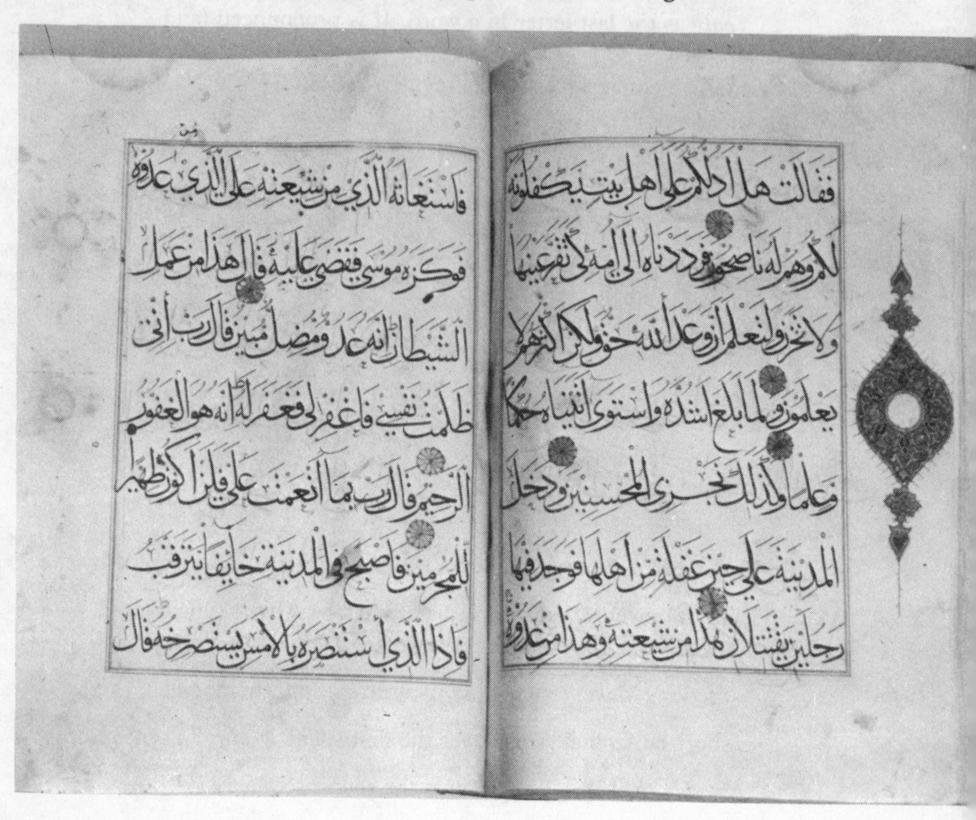

**Dagger alif**

This letter is an archaic form of regular ا *alif* and has survived to the present day in only a very few common words. For pronunciation purposes it is identical to regular ا *alif*, but is written as a shortened ا *alif* above the consonant which precedes it in pronunciation.

Observe

*ha:dha:* هٰذا

*dha:lik* ذٰلِك

A very common use of the *dagger alif* is in the Arabic word for God, the spelling of which has become conventionally established as:

*'alla:h* أَللّٰه

**ariants forms of:**

ن ش ق ض

When these letters occur in their isolated or final forms they are often written with a 'broken' tail and their dot or dots are omitted.

OBSERVE

1 words with final ن *nu:n*

تَبْن تَبْن

يابان يابان

2 words with final ش *shi:n*

نَتَش نَتَش

وَرَش وَرَش

3 words with final ق *qa:f*

حَلْق حَلْق

سوق سوق

4 words with final ض *da:d*

نَبْض نَبْض

أَرْض أَرْض

This variant is a very common feature in handwritten Arabic, and even though you may not choose to use it, you should be able to recognise it.

Decorated archway – Iran

**Letters of the Arabic alphabet in traditional order with transliteration:**

| | | | |
|---|---|---|---|
| *'alif* | الف | /a:/ | ا |
| *ba:'* | باء | /b/ | ب |
| *ta:'* | تاء | /t/ | ت |
| *tha:'* | ثاء | /th/ | ث |
| *ji:m* | جيم | /j/ | ج |
| *ha:'* (h underlined) | حاء | /h/ (h underlined) | ح |
| *kha:'* | خاء | /kh/ | خ |
| *da:l* | دال | /d/ | د |
| *dha:l* | ذال | /dh/ | ذ |
| *ra:'* | راء | /r/ | ر |
| *za:y* | زاي | /z/ | ز |
| *si:n* | سين | /s/ | س |
| *shi:n* | شين | /sh/ | ش |

| | | | |
|---|---|---|---|
| *s̲a:d* | صاد | /s̲/ | ص |
| *d̲a:d* | ضاد | /d̲/ | ض |
| *t̲a:'* | طاء | /t̲/ | ط |
| *d̲h̲a:'* | ظاء | /d̲h̲/ | ظ |
| *ʿayn* | عين | /c/ | ع |
| *ghayn* | غين | /gh/ | غ |
| *fa:'* | فاء | /f/ | ف |
| *qa:f* | قاف | /q/ | ق |
| *ka:f* | كاف | /k/ | ك |
| *la:m* | لام | /l/ | ل |
| *mi:m* | ميم | /m/ | م |
| *nu:n* | نون | /n/ | ن |
| *ha:'* | هاء | /h/ | ه |

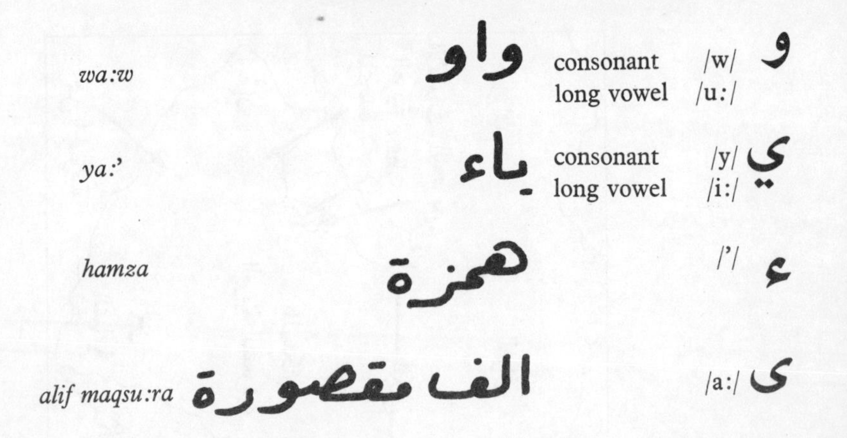

| | | | | |
|---|---|---|---|---|
| *wa:w* | واو | consonant<br>long vowel | /w/<br>/u:/ | و |
| *ya:'* | ياء | consonant<br>long vowel | /y/<br>/i:/ | ي |
| *hamza* | همزة | | /'/ | ء |
| *alif maqsu:ra* | الف مقصورة | | /a:/ | ى |

**The fourteen 'sun letters' are:**

ت ث د ذ ر ز س

ش ص ض ط ظ ل ن

**The fourteen 'moon letters' are:**

ا ب ج ح خ ع غ

ف ق ك م ه و ي

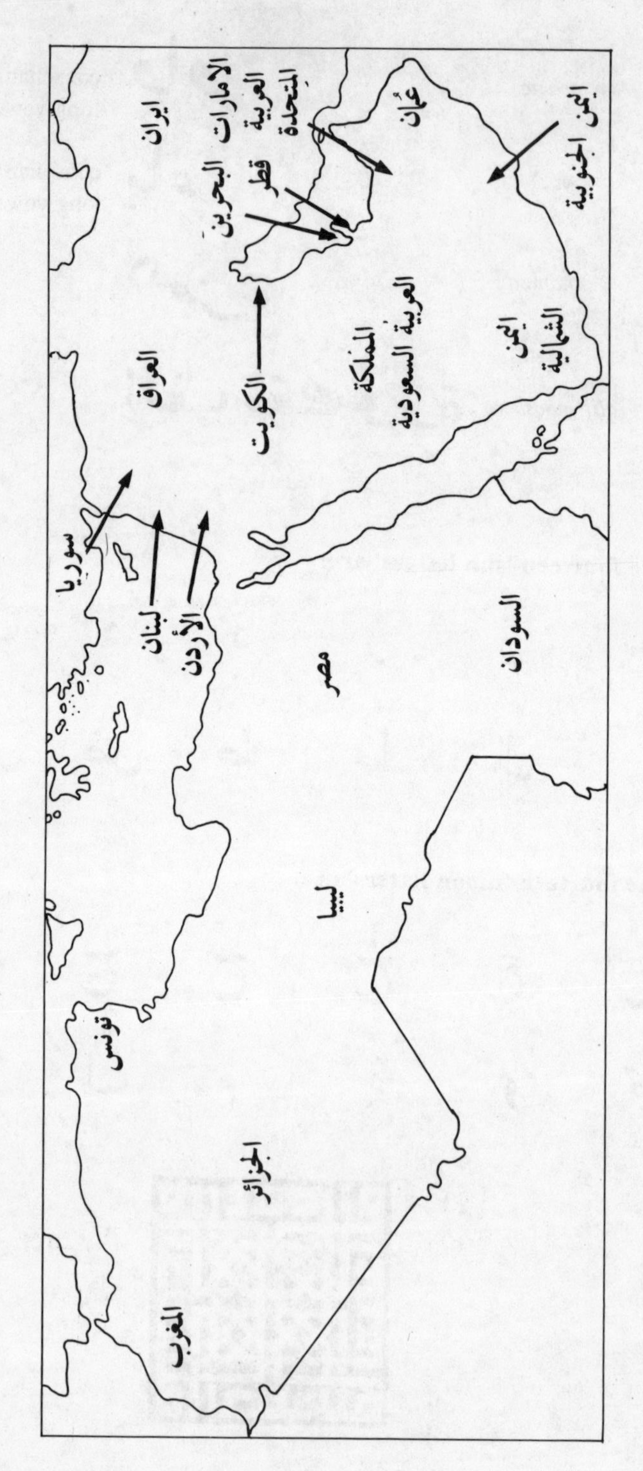


Map of the Arab World

**Key to map** (See also page 19).

**Countries**

Algeria أَلْجَزائِر

Bahrain أَلْبَحْرَين

Egypt مَصْر

Iran ايران

Iraq العراق

Jordan أَلأُرْدُن

Kuwait أَلْكُوَيْت

Lebanon لُبْنان

Libya ليبِيا

Morocco أَلْمَغْرِب

Oman عُمان

Qatar قَطَر

**Countries**

| | | | |
|---|---|---|---|
| Saudi Arabia | أَلسُّعودِيَّة | North Yemen | أَلْيَمَن أَلشِّمالِيَّة |
| Sudan | سودان | South Yemen | أَلْيَمَن أَلْجُنْوبِيَّة |
| Syria | سورِيا | | |
| Tunisia | تونِس | | |

United Arab Emirates أَلْإِمارات أَلْعَرَبِيَّة أَلْمُتَّحِدَة

| | |
|---|---|
| Abu Dhabi | أَبوظَبي |
| Al-Ajman | أَلْعَجمان |
| Dubai | دُبَي |
| Sharja | شارِقَة |
| Umm al-Qaywan | م أَلْقَيْوان |
| Ras al-Khayma | رأس أَلْخَيْمَة |
| Fujairah | فُجَيْرَة |

بسم الله الرحمن الرحيم
إن الصلاة كانت على المؤمنين كتابا موقوتا

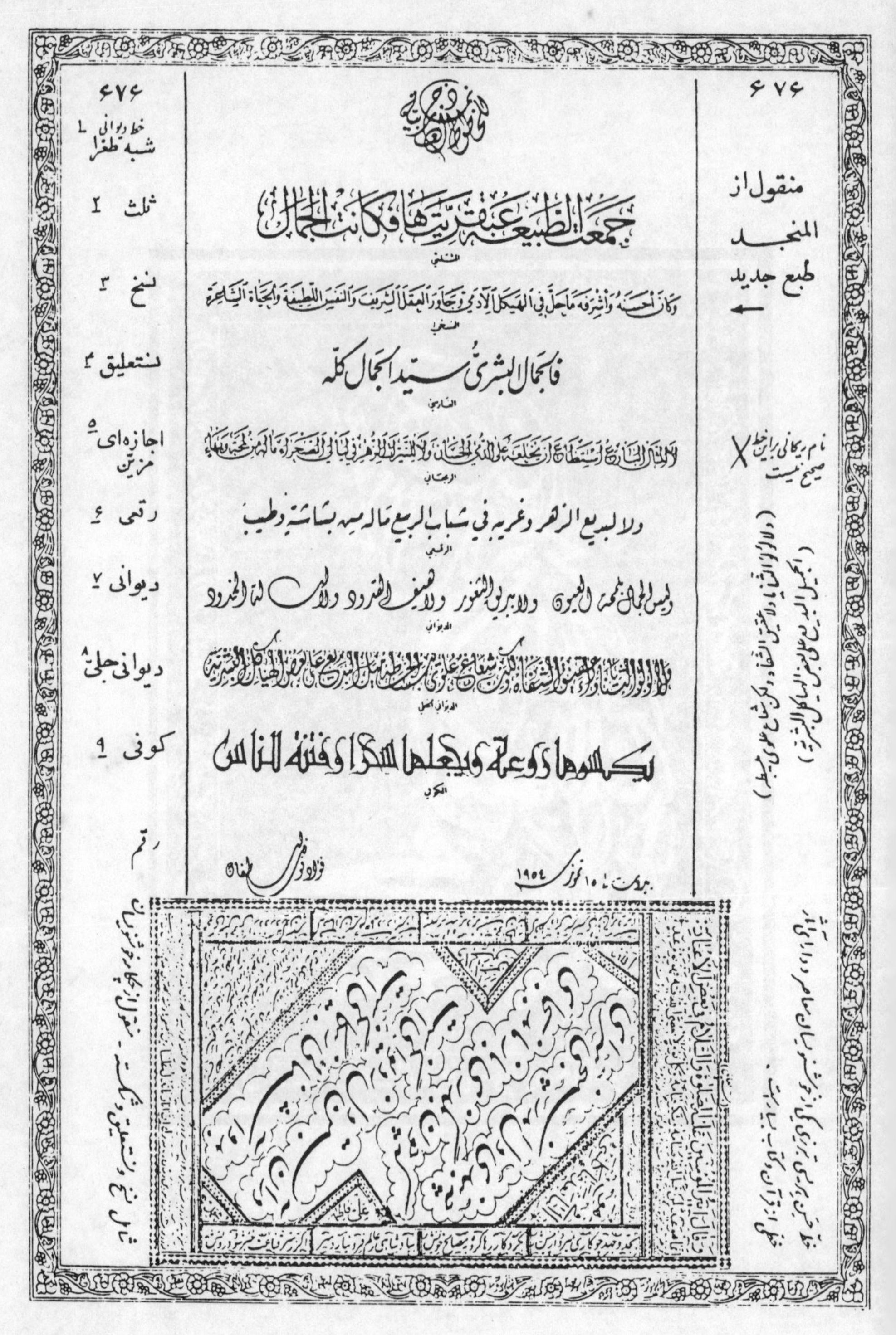


A variety of calligraphic styles

## Calligraphy

'Script is a spiritual art which is manifested through a physical instrument.'
Due to Islam's prohibition of the use of the human and animal form in art, Arabic writing and calligraphy have always been an important means of artistic expression in the Islamic world. As a historical phenomenon Arabic calligraphy dates, in its codified form, from Ibn Muqlah, who lived in the tenth century A.D. (886–940) and its decline coincides with the introduction of the printing press. The calligraphic tradition spans ten centuries of history and a geographical area covering not only the Arabic speaking world, but also many parts of the Muslim world, for both Persian and Urdu are written in the Arabic alphabet, as was Turkish before the introduction of the Latin alphabet under Ataturk in 1928. In the absence of a tradition of representational painting and sculpture, calligraphy developed into a highly sophisticated decorative art form, drawing inspiration from certain words and phrases used in the Qur'an, in much the same way as mediaeval Christian artists drew their inspiration from themes in the Bible. Arabic letters worked into intricate designs have been used to decorate mosques, public buildings, pottery, metal work and manuscripts; and today many public notices and signs are written in a variety of calligraphic styles. Although originally handwritten, these styles have been adapted to type and are used in modern printed material particularly in newspaper and magazine headlines, and in book titles.

Many styles of Arabic script have evolved in the course of history; some have changed their names from country to country or merged with other styles. These are examples of the most common types still in use today:

أَلكوفي *ku:fi:* commonly known as Kufic in the West.

This is the oldest style and was, and still is, used for documents, inscriptions, on public buildings, signs and logos. Its distinguishing feature is its angularity and use of severe straight lines which the Arabic script normally avoids.

الكوفي في الخط الكوفي

أَلنَّسْخي *naskhi:* has been widely used since the tenth

century. It has the familiar smooth rounded appearance of

Arabic writing and was used for books and manuscripts. The most common style of typeset Arabic used in books and newspapers is an adaptation of *naskhi:*,

النسخي في الخط النسخي

أَلثُّلُث *thuluth* is very similar to *naskhi:*, but a little more ornate and decorative. It is often used for headings and titles in books, newspapers and magazines.

الثلث في خط الثلث

أَلديواني *diwa:ni:* is a style that exists in many forms from the simple to the highly ornate. It was used widely by the Ottoman Turks for government documents, records and decrees.

الدّيواني في الخط الدّيواني

أَلرُّقْعَة *ruqᶜa* is the style on which most modern handwriting is based. Before Arabic was printed and the Arabic typewriter designed, this style was used for everyday writing of documents, letters, government papers, etc. The style of handwriting taught in this book is a simplified adaptation of *ruqᶜa.*

الرقعة في خط الرقعة

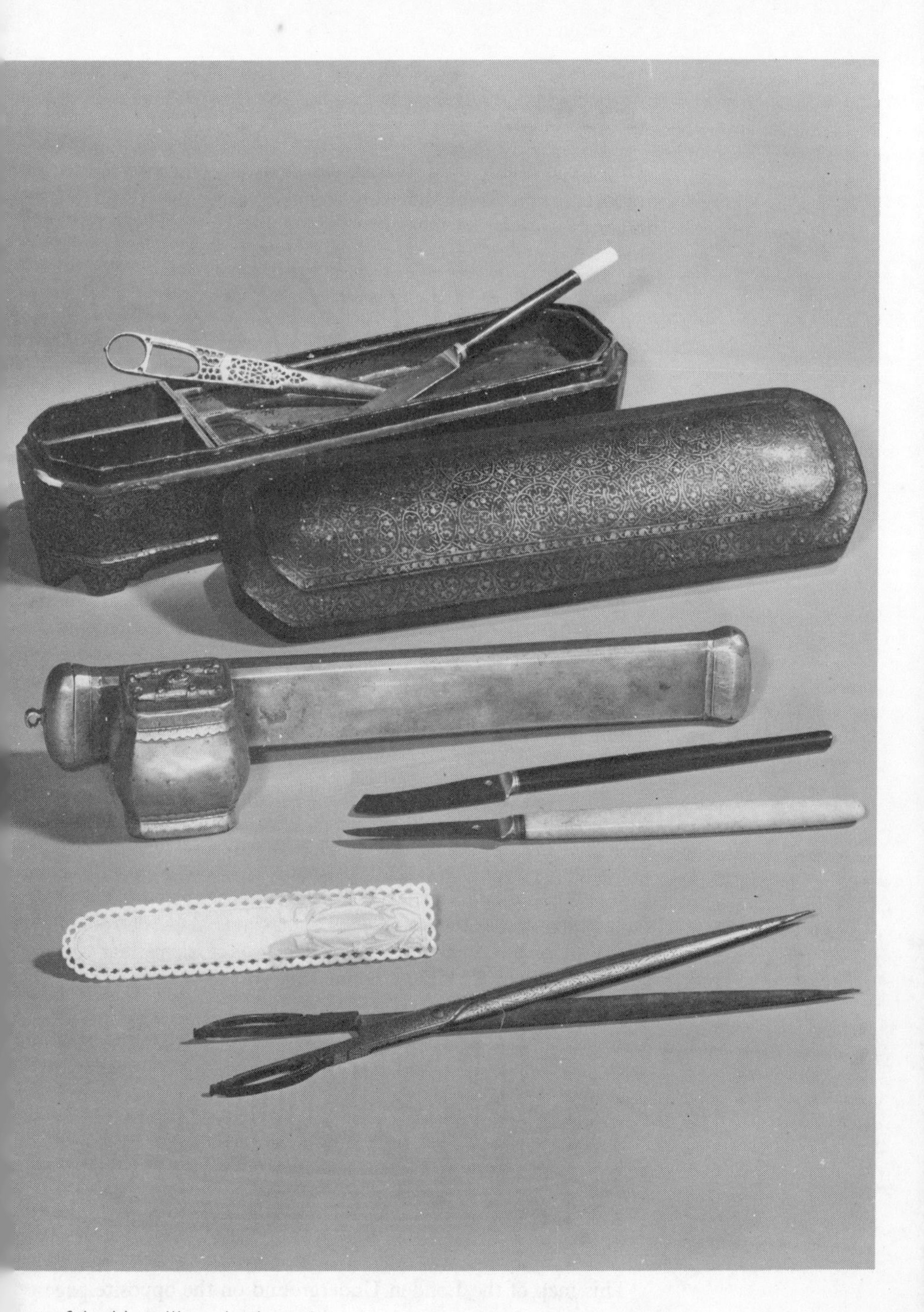

set of Arabic calligrapher's tools

أَلْفارِسي *fa:risi:* often known as أَلنَّسْتَعْليق *nasta*$^c$*li:q*

– most commonly used in Iran and Pakistan – the two most important non-Arabic speaking countries using the Arabic script today.

# الفارسي في الخطّ الفارسي

'In calligraphy, the rhythmic intervals afford rest to the eye as it runs over the text, providing a subtle pause between the forward movement of the line, a kinetic design emphasised by several elements: alteration of the characters' vertical sections; juxtapositior of unequal spaces; groupings of words in sequence or in insertion so as to create, outside the bounds of their assigned space, assymetry and rhythmic breaks in the reading. Other formative elements shar in the process, including: elongation and cursive linkings above and below their axies; serpentine lines between certain letters; cursives containing the next word within their decorative flourishes; stately and delicate positioning of letters so as to establish a subordinate relation in form and meaning; and finally, the spiral. Add to these a distribution of the major masses of the text: down strokes and up strokes, open spaces, diacritical signs, vowel accents, floral and geometric motifs; and there results a cadence of arabesques which impresses itself upon the space/time continuum, by a process of artistic selection within the hand itself of the calligrapher and in the nerve ends of his fingers.' (Abdelkebir Khatibi; Mohammad Sijelmassi, *The splendour of Islamic Calligraphy*, page 84 (Thames & Hudson, London 1976))

This map of the London Underground on the opposite page with the names of the stations written in Arabic will give you an idea of how the Arabic alphabet can be used to write English. Try to work out the names from the Arabic before checking with the English version.

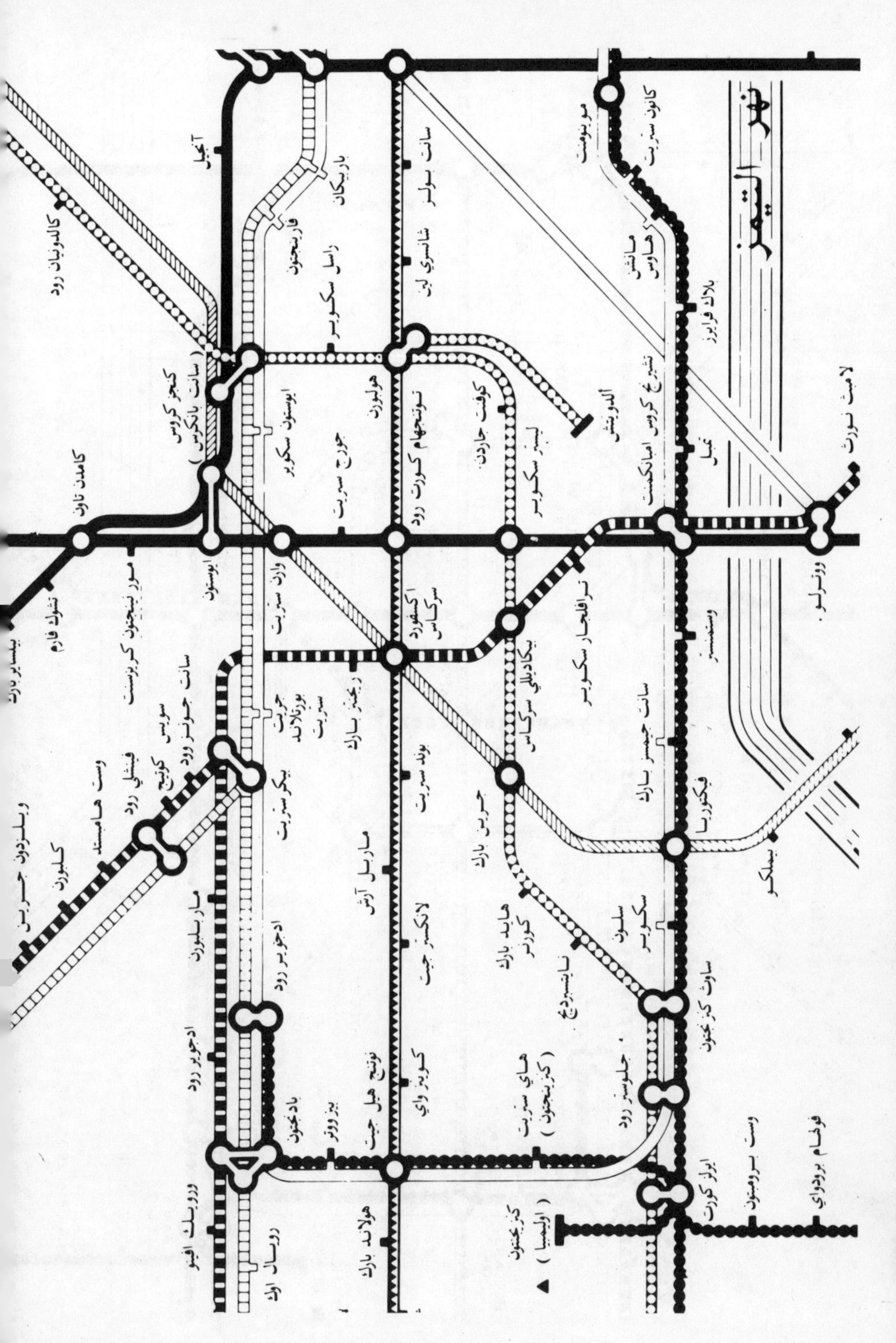

ondon underground map in Arabic

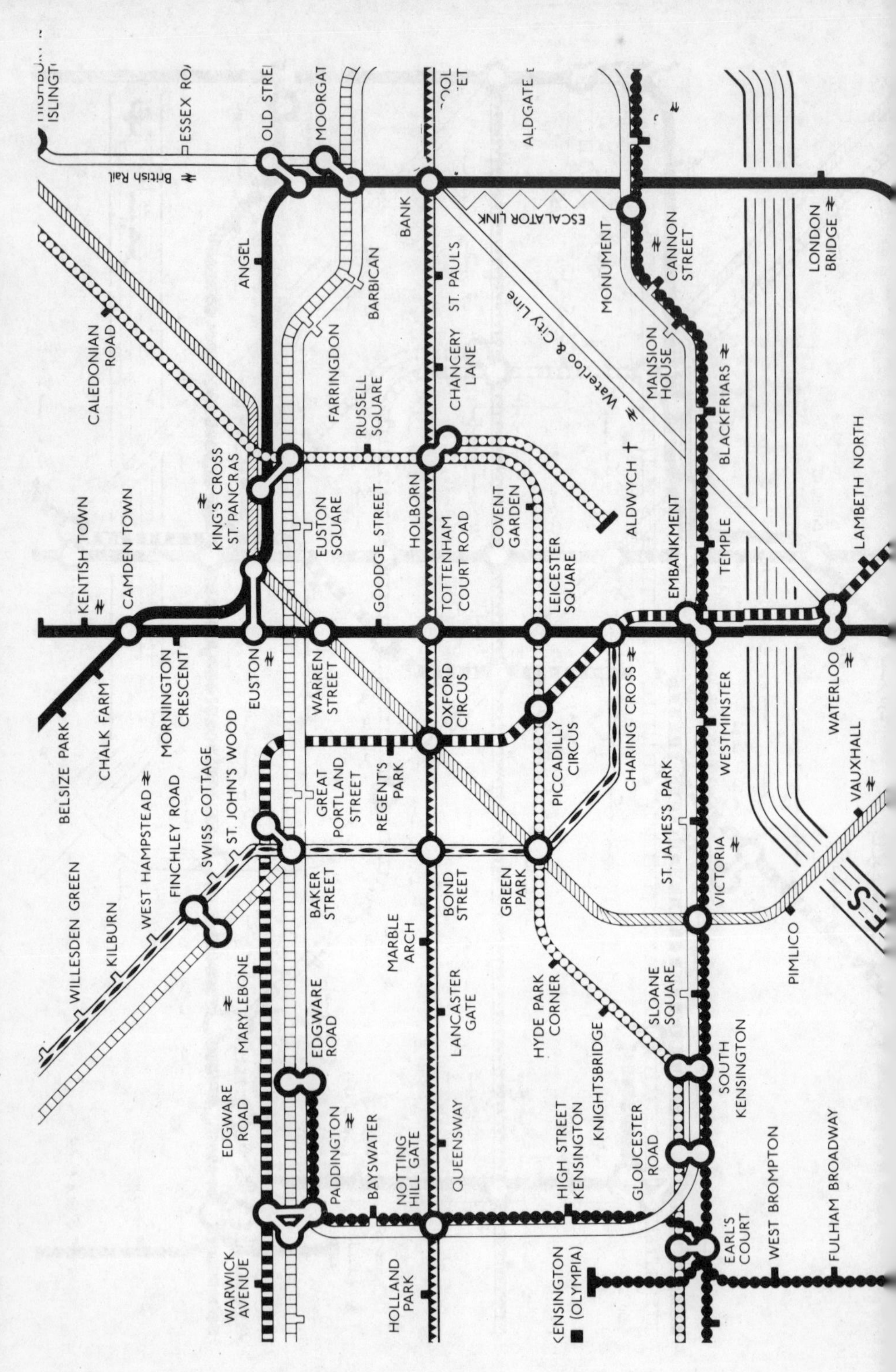


London underground map in English

**Writing foreign sounds in Arabic**

Having learned to write the Arabic alphabet, there is no reason why you should not use it to write English, or any other language; an alphabet is not the exclusive property of any one language. To get used to using the Arabic alphabet, keep a diary or journal, transliterating English into Arabic letters.

There are certain letters you will not need to use, those representing sounds that do not exist in English:

| ح خ ع غ ص ض ط ظ ق |
|---|

Likewise there are sounds in English which do not exist in Arabic. 'ch' as in '*ch*ase'; 'p' as in '*p*ot'; 'v' as in '*v*enus'. To accommodate non-Arabic sounds in borrowed words, certain letter shapes have been adapted (by the addition of dots) to represent them:

'ch' can be represented by a ح shape with three dots

/ ∴ / *below* چ .

or by the combination تش

e.g. الدويچ

Aldwi*ch* الدويتش

'p' can be represented by a ب shape with three dots

/ ∴ / *below* پ although a ب *ba:'* is often

substituted for 'p' in words adopted from other languages.
e.g.

هولاند پارك

Holland *P*ark

هولاند بارك

'v' can be represented by the *fa:'* shape ف with three dots
/ ∴ / *above* ڤ although the letter ف *fa:'* itself is

often substituted for 'v' in words adopted from other languages. e.g.

ڤيكتوريا

*V*ictoria

فيكتوريا

**Regional variations in pronunciation**

The pronunciation which has been given throughout this book is one which is intelligible to most native speakers in the Arab world. The most common regional pronunciation variants are as follows:

ج sometimes pronounced like the 'g' in '*g*ame' (notably in Egypt); sometimes like the 'y' in '*y*oung' (notably in the Gulf); sometimes like the 's' in 'vi*s*ion' (Lebanon and Syria).

ذ sometimes like the 'd' in '*d*eep', and sometimes like the 'z' in '*z*ip'. Both of these variants occur very widely.

ث sometimes like the 't' in '*t*ongue'. This variant occurs primarily in Egypt, Lebanon and Syria, but also in other areas.

ض sometimes 'z', and sometimes 'th' as in '*th*is', Despite the epithet 'language of the ض ' which is applied to Arabic, this is one of the least consistently pronounced letters of the alphabet, and both of these variants occur widely.

ظ sometimes 'z', particularly in Egypt. In many other areas it is pronounced like ذ

ق sometimes 'g' (in Iraq and much of the Peninsula), and sometimes glottal stop (Lower Egypt, Syria, Lebanon and parts of Jordan).

ك sometimes like the 'ch' in '*ch*ase' (in parts of Iraq and the Gulf).

SANYO سانيو
ROLEX
رولكس
برتقال
كروش
ياشيكا
الخطوط الجوية الكويتية
GULF AIR
كوداك
السعودية
National
ناشيونال
كاميرا
كوداك
"انستانت"
SA. PRIV.
118734
خصوصي السعودية
١١٨٧٣٤
ستيريو هاي فيداليتي

# Bibliography

The following is a very brief list of titles which will give you a starting point for further study in areas touching on this book.

**1 Alphabets and writing**

Anthony Burgess: *Language Made Plain*, Fontana, 1975.

David Diringer: *The Alphabet: a key to the history of mankind*, London 1945.

*Writing*, London, 1962.

G. R. Driver: *Semitic writing from pictograph to alphabet*, London 1948.

I. J. Gelb: *A study of writing*, The University of Chicago Press, 1952.

Cyrus H. Gordon: *Forgotten Scripts*, Penguin, 1971.

Hermann Zapf: *About alphabets: some marginal notes on type design*, M.I.T. Press, Cambridge, Mass., 1970.

**2 Arabic writing and calligraphy**

Abdelkebir Khatibi and Mohammed Sijelmassi: *The splendour of Islamic Calligraphy*, Thames and Hudson, London 1976.

T. F. Mitchell: *Writing Arabic – a practical introduction to the Ruq'ah script*, Oxford University Press, 1953.

Y. H. Safadi: *Islamic Calligraphy*, Thames and Hudson, London 1978.

**3 Arab history and culture**

Sir T. W. Arnold and A. Guillaume: *The legacy of Islam*, Oxford, 1931.

Edward Atiyah: *The Arabs*, Penguin, 1958.

Philip K. Hitti: *The Arabs : a short history*, Macmillan, 1968.

Bernard Lewis: *The Arabs in history*, Hutchinson University Library, 1970.

**4 The Arabic language**

Mary Catherine Bateson: *Arabic language handbook*, Centre for Applied Linguistics, Washington, 1967.

A. F. L. Beeston: *The Arabic language today*, Hutchinson University Press, 1970.

Anwar G. Chejne: *The Arabic Language – its role in history* , University of Minnesota Press, 1969.

David Cowan: *Modern literary Arabic*, Cambridge University Press, 1968.

J. Milton Cowan (Ed.): *A dictionary of modern literary Arabic*, Wiesbaden, 1971.
N. S. Doniach: *The Oxford English-Arabic dictionary of current usage*, Oxford University Press, 1972.
J. A. Haywood and H. M. Nahmad: *A new Arabic grammar of the written language*, Lund Humphries, London 1976.
*Key to a new Arabic grammar*, Lund Humphries, London, 1976.
Ernest McCarus and Raji Rammuny: *A programmed course in modern literary Arabic phonology and script*, University of Michigan Centre for Research on Language and language Behavior, 1974.